THEMATIC PREACHING

AN INTRODUCTION

THEMATIC PREACHING

AN INTRODUCTION

JANE RZEPKA

KEN SAWYER

Chalice Press®

St. Louis, Missouri

Cover art: © Artville
Cover and interior design: Elizabeth Wright
Art direction: Elizabeth Wright

This book is printed on acid-free, recycled paper.

Visit Chalice Press on the World Wide Web at
www.chalicepress.com

10 9 8 7 6 5 4 3 2 1   01 02 03 04 05 06

Library of Congress Cataloging–in–Publication Data

Rzepka, Jane Ranney, 1950-
    Thematic preaching : an introduction / Jane Rzepka and Ken Sawyer.
        p.   cm.
    Includes bibliographical references.
    ISBN 0-8272-3653-0
    1. Topical Preaching.   I. Sawyer, Kenneth W.   II. Title.
BV4235.T65 R94   2001
251–dc21   00-008999

Printed in the United States of America

CONTENTS

ACKNOWLEDGMENTS

The authors are deeply grateful to all those who helped create this book. Among our advisers, readers, and researchers were Rita Anderson, Cindy Battis, Mark Belletini, John Beuhrens, Ellen Brandenburg, Pat Carol, Laura Cavicchio, Helena Chapin, Rebecca Cohen, Katie Lee Crane, Calvin Dame, Celeste DeRoche, Marta Flanagan, Ann Flowers, Roger Fritts, Geron Gadd, Laura Gates, Gail Geisenhainer, Pamela Gore, Mary Henderson, Liz Hiser, Rebecca Howard, Sandy Hoyt, Peter Hughes, Yielbonzie Charles Johnson, Noreen Kimball, Ruth MacDonald, Judith Mannheim, Anne Mark, Chris May, Jerry Mitchell, Makanah Morriss, John Nichols, Phyllis O'Connell, Eugene Pickett, Peter Raible, Maggie and Rick Rebmann, Kimi Riegel, Dudley Rose, Chuck Rzepka, Kathy Schmitz, Hillary Smith, Margaret Studier, Diane Teichert, Norma Veridan, Leslie Westbrook, Sally White, Jon Winder, Alison Zetterquist, Robin Zucker, and some of our dearest, most helpful friends whom we have inexcusably forgotten to mention.

Thanks go as well to those who have allowed us to use their writing; to our spouses and families for their support and forbearance; to the congregations we served while we were writing this book, the Unitarian Universalist Church of Reading, Massachusetts, and the First Parish in Wayland, Massachusetts; to the students in our classes and the participants in our workshops, who have taught us so much; and to the Theological Grants Panel of the Unitarian Universalist Association, which funded the book's development.

INTRODUCTION
"Preaching on Blue Ducks"

It is Sunday morning and there they are again, members of a congregation, people who could be home reading the paper or getting the house or yard in order. But instead they've come to a worship service.

After the service, several ask for copies of the sermon to save or to send to a relative or friend. One says, "You were speaking straight to the needs of my heart this morning." Another says, "I've decided to change jobs because of something you said in a sermon last year; I've been thinking about it ever since."

A colleague of ours writes, "Last summer I was speaking to a friend I had not seen for several years. She said, 'I will always remember the sermon you gave on death' (I had forgotten)—and she proceeded to quote an entire paragraph from memory. It is a common occurrence with the best and worst of preachers."[1] Over and over, the preacher is reminded just how much preaching can matter.

Of course, there are other reasons why people attend worship. They come for the music, the ritual, and the company. They come to socialize, to campaign, and to accompany their families. They come to mull over matters they bring along with them, matters from which no sermon will distract them. They come to have one hour protected from phone calls and demands. But for many people, the most important part of Sunday morning is the sermon. Some will say that it is the most important part of their whole week.

1

In some circles, it has been popular to argue that congregants should feel otherwise, that they should be less focused on the pulpit and the sermon. And many congregants are. Some Sundays, the preacher may also be more focused on other aspects of the gathering than the sermon—the children's message, a special ritual, an overall feeling of celebration or sadness, or the artistry of dance, music, or theater.

But many people attend worship services precisely because of the power of an old, persistent form of art and faith combined: the sermon. And almost all who attend may profit from that power if it is used well. The congregation gives that power to the preacher to use, with hopes of being moved, informed, vitalized, comforted, challenged, grounded, connected, and even transformed.

This book is an attempt to help preachers achieve some of those worthy aims. It grows out of the years that we have been teaching preaching to students at Harvard Divinity School, Meadville/Lombard Theological School, and elsewhere and leading workshops in preaching for settled ministers and laypeople. It grows out of our experience of listening to hundreds and hundreds of sermons and hearing them critiqued. And it grows out of our experience in parish ministry, which between the two of us now totals almost a half century.

We have learned some lessons from our classroom experiences. One is that theological-school students and settled ministers alike tend to care about preaching these days and to respect its possibilities.

This has not always been the case. Not that long ago, preaching was widely regarded as an antiquated practice, especially in some liberal traditions. Writing in 1965, John T. Stewart noted, "Few general practitioners are left who find their chief satisfaction in the pulpit…Members of the younger generation of pastors with churches do not really enjoy preaching; they kiss it off as a quaint chore."[2]

But only seventeen years later, the eminent professor of preaching Fred Craddock[3] said that preaching had become "much stronger. The increased expectation of the congregation is finding a response…Appreciation for preaching has demonstrably increased and ministers are responding to that challenge."[4] That situation continues.

A second lesson has been that people can in fact learn to preach better. There is a degree to which the ability to preach well is a gift. But even for those lucky souls who are thus favored, the gift must be opened—the talents discovered and developed. Meanwhile, those who may not have the same measure of natural talent—the mellifluous voice, the confident manner, the quick humor, the verbal facility, and all the rest—can still become first-rate preachers.

Study, reflection, and dedication help, and we hope this book will contribute to that effort. In addition, students and settled ministers alike can benefit from course work, workshops, and retreats on preaching and from practice, especially when accompanied by criticism and encouragement.

Finally, one of the greatest lessons we have learned from listening to and discussing so many sermons is how very many ways there are for sermons and preachers to be good, even terrific. This has been true whether we were listening to colleagues, theological-school students, or laypeople.

Some were flamboyant, some reserved in their manner. Some worked our neurons hard, others our tear ducts. They preached from notes or outlines, full manuscripts, or nothing at all. They gestured minimally or much, quoted liberally or little, and were prophetically public or poignantly personal. They used lots of alliteration, and assonance and allusion too; or they didn't, and they just spoke plainly.

In most ways one could imagine, these preachers and their sermons were successful in their own particular ways. Just so, the goal of this book is not to urge conformity to one model of preaching, even as we may offer our own outlooks along the way. The goal is not acquiescence, but encouragement of every reader to find his or her own most effective preaching style.

We write as two ministers who serve local congregations, and as two religious liberals. It will show. For instance, as settled parish ministers, when we consider various kinds and styles of sermons in the second of the book's three sections, it will be from the perspective that preaching is an integral part of ministering to a congregation, continuous with other pastoral functions. We think this is true for guest preachers too.

As religious liberals (as Unitarian Universalists, to be precise) we are part of a faith tradition in which references to God, Jesus, and biblical passages are usually perfectly welcome if they serve to make or illustrate the points of a sermon—but they are not required. What is required—or at least hoped for, and ardently sought by the preacher—is a sermon that will touch and even move the hearts and minds and souls of those in the congregation.

For us, the theme of the sermon is not determined by any particular text, but by the particular needs of a particular congregation at a particular time being addressed by a particular preacher. What matters is the ministry of the preacher to the congregation on that morning. Just as Jesus noted that the religious institution of the Sabbath was made for people, not the other way around (Mk. 2:27), sermons exist to serve the religious needs of those in the pews. They must address the themes that arise, not so much out of any textual passage or schedule, but out of human lives.

There are many other books about preaching in print, some of them quite fine. But nearly all of them assume that the preacher is addressing a "textual community,"[5] and therefore proceeding from a biblical text or set of texts, and that "preaching's purpose is the proclamation of the Word of God."[6] At the very least, they assume that a sermon will necessarily express a basically biblical and Christian outlook.

We make different assumptions. We think that preaching is an opportunity for ministering that the members of a congregation offer to the preacher. We believe the preacher is as free as the congregation will allow to draw on a rich range of sources for inspiration, information, and advice—including the experience of the preacher's own life and that of the congregation. In this book, sections one ("The Art and Craft of Preaching") and two ("Preaching as Ministry") treat the "how" and "why" of sermon preparation from this point of view.

Similarly, section three ("Issues in Preaching"), our section about personal quandaries such as "authority" and "authenticity," treats these topics from the standpoint of preachers as human beings, wholly responsible for the messages they proclaim on Sunday morning. Such men and women, in all humility, cannot fall back on claims of knowing the word of God or possessing authoritative scripture. They must preach on a certain kind of "blue ducks."

It was Martin Luther who introduced the image of blue ducks, as Bernard Lang recalls.

> Luther knew…that many ministers were not talented at speaking in public or had simply never received an adequate training…If every minister produces his [or her] own sermons, "the final result will be that everyone preaches his [or her] own whims and instead of the gospel and its exposition we shall again have sermons on blue ducks." So Luther himself supplied several books of sermons that could be read to the congregation.[7]

The authors of this book sympathize with Luther's concern about ministers preaching on matters of merely personal whim; but we take the side of a sermon on blue ducks, as opposed to one drawn from the gospels, if the former might better minister to the cares, concerns, hopes, and dreams of the people in the pews.

The contrast between our attitude and that of most textbooks on preaching was one inspiration for this book's creation. In searching for a textbook to assign our students, we have looked at scores of books that deal with a wide range of preaching issues. A singularly theistic, christocentric, and Bible-based perspective prevails. Asked about biblical preaching, the

Reverend Richard Jackson, retired minister of a Baptist church, said, "I don't think any other form of preaching is legitimate."[8] R. T. Kendall said, "Preaching must be expository...Expository preaching is simply making clear the meaning of the text and showing its relevance and application for the lives we live."[9] Karl Barth wrote, "Preaching must be exposition of holy scripture."[10] Further examples abound.

While we know that the Bible will remain a special, even authoritative, source of such wisdom for many of our readers, our goal is more general: to help preachers from a variety of theological traditions find the words and style to make their preaching an important part of their congregations' worship experience. In our classes, such advice has been gratefully received by Catholics, Jews, and liberal Protestants of many denominations, as well as by Unitarian Universalists and some who weren't sure yet just where their convictions lay.

We hope this book may prove of equally broad use, and that preachers of many outlooks will be creative and generous in interpreting our words to fit their own needs (just as religious liberals have long done with the abundance of normative textbooks).

For whatever the intent of a sermon or its theological grounding, preachers share similar goals: to put across meaning and emotion; to use the time well to make a difference in the lives of the congregants, their institution, and the world; and to create preaching that matters.

SECTION ONE

THE ART AND CRAFT OF PREACHING

> There is a special place for sermons in the midst of life's babble
> that is not filled by other forms of communication, a place for
> that unique discourse which is both thoughtful and emotional,
> practiced within the context of worship, [relating] preacher and
> people to shared religious traditions, faiths, and meanings, that
> all might enlarge their understanding, experience broader
> sympathies, awaken slumbering hopes, explore new cosmic
> expanses, change their lives, and be moved to redemptive action.[1]
>
> Jack Mendelsohn

That might seem an intimidating assignment to a ministry student. Indeed, those who have tried for many years to craft effective sermons generally remain impressed by the difficulty as much as by the potential. But over time, some insights prove helpful. Preachers come to a better sense of what a sermon can hope to be, and how to achieve that goal. They come to know their own most successful styles of preparation and delivery. They learn how to garner ideas and illustrations for sermons, how to overcome their debilitating tendencies, and how to find a sermon topic and give it a message, form, and flair. They develop the craft of creating an eventful, meaningful, often enjoyable, sometimes transformative worship experience for the congregation to which they minister.

There are larger understandings involved, which we will consider in subsequent sections, but there are immediate concerns that can be every bit as significant. What is there to talk about? When should a preacher indicate what the point of the sermon might be? How much can one use humor, even irony? How loud a tie can one wear, or how long can earrings be?

Like a potter, politician, or poet, the preacher must ask, What am I up to? And how can that best be done?

1

WHAT MATTERS IN A SERMON?

Have you ever heard a sermon or a public address of some other sort that moved you? Do you remember a time when, while sitting in the pews of a well-established church or the folding chairs of a start-up congregation or lecture hall, you felt your eyes fill with tears, or you resolved to take action, or you learned something new and exciting, or you wanted to jump for joy? Maybe you felt overwhelmed by a sense of mystical belonging or inspired to let your love flow more deeply. Maybe you laughed out loud. Maybe you felt utterly absolved.

Did your history teacher in college have that knack? the eulogizer at your cousin's funeral? the union organizer? the lay leader of the Easter sunrise service? the minister of an ordinary church on an ordinary Sunday when everything fell together for you in an extraordinary way?

What was your experience? Why did the words work so well?

To be sure, at least at first, many people can't recall having heard an effective sermon or public address—ever. Deep down, they agree with unappealing definitions of *preaching*, such as "to exhort in an officious or tiresome manner," or they think that a *sermon* is "a lecture on one's conduct or duty; a homily; hence, an annoying harangue."[1] Even *Webster's Dictionary* defines *preach* as "to give moral or religious advice, especially in a tiresome manner" and *sermon* as "any lecture or serious talk on behavior, responsibility, etc., especially a long, tedious, annoying one."[2]

A few people have been alienated by overly restrictive understandings of the role of preaching—Francis de Sales', for example: "To preach is the publication and declaration of God's will, made to men by one lawfully

9

commissioned to that task, to the end of instructing and moving them to serve his divine Majesty in this world so as to be saved in the next."[3] Nonetheless, once these limited interpretations of preaching are removed, most people are able both to remember a meaningful sermon or speech and to generate a list of critical elements that contributed to the address's success.

We ask the following questions of our preaching students on the first day of class: (1) Can you recall a sermon or public address that moved you? (2) What did the speaker do or say? (3) What qualities did he or she exhibit? (4) What made the address effective?

Their list of responses is long and the items varied; some of them refer to the words themselves and others to the preacher's persona, delivery, or spirit:

passion	surprise
congregational participation	facial expressions
hope	empowerment
caring	poetry
artistic structure	cadence
accessibility	evident preparation
grounding	congruence
the message mirrors reality	recognizable truth
a reasoned foundation	humor
an involved sharing	validation
wit and timing	potential for transformation
earnestness	confidence
a wide web of example and metaphor	power
imagery	presence
conviction	deeply felt emotion
compelling use of language	personal references
value to the soul	authenticity
personal challenge to act	the use of story

Each year, with some small variation, our students tell us that this is the list of what makes sermons work. These are the aspects of sermonizing that we preachers aspire to when we step into the pulpit every week. These are the reasons why the members of our congregations listen. And these are some of the subjects we'll be discussing in this book.

Our list reflects the fact that good sermons incorporate both words and spirit; it shows that preaching "has in it two essential elements, truth and personality," as the great nineteenth-century Episcopal bishop, Phillips Brooks, put it.[4] "The real power of your oratory must be your own intelligent delight in what you are doing…You have enthusiasm which is the breath of life."[5]

One may be quick to notice other aspects of effective preaching, critical elements that we did not invite our students to catalog. For one thing, the context matters: Where are we? in a rented high school auditorium? a sweet, small chapel in the woods? corporate headquarters, rented on Sundays? outdoors near the grave site? the huge modern cathedral right next to the freeway? the meditation room in the local hospital? Some settings are so lovely, inspiring, grand, or peaceful that our words gain impact when we but acknowledge and build upon the spiritual qualities of the environment. Other places work against us, what with the fire engines driving by, the dreary portrait of the founder front and center, the radiators clanging, and the ceiling oppressively low.

These days, in the age of large-screen monitors in overflow areas, local cable TV, videos, radio, and the Web, our congregations may participate in our worship services from a variety of locations. It's helpful to keep this fact in mind while writing, as the Reverend Monsignor Kenneth Velo did so effectively in this funeral homily:

> Whether you are in the first pew or the thirtieth pew of this great cathedral, whether you are participating through the public-address system or seated in the auditorium, whether you are listening on the radio as you travel the Dan Ryan Expressway or sitting in a kitchen in Roger's Park, whether you are watching television coverage of this funeral service in a nursing home in Waukegan, a living room in Calumet City, or a classroom on Chicago's West Side, today, this day, you are all dignitaries, for God has touched you through the life of Cardinal Bernardin.[6]

When preparing a sermon, imagine the listener's environment and locate your writing.

Other contextual elements that contribute to the effectiveness of a sermon extend beyond the immediate physical location; for example, the morning's national and international headlines, the hot topics of conversation in town, the local economy, the movie or TV show everybody's seeing, the latest craze at the mall, unusual weather, and big sports news. What is in the background of people's minds when they walk in the door? Why not find a way to mention in your sermon the ice storm just past, or the fact that it's ninety degrees where we're sitting, or how nice the Gay Men's Chorus holiday caroling was in town, or the toy that every eight-year-old is obsessed with this summer and the frenzied sale that went on down the street.

And who are the people? Are two-thirds of your congregation transplanted from the South? Include a reference to grits in your sermon. Have the people of your religious community been gathering for two hundred years? Use that fact, talk about the strong beams and rippled windows. Does the congregation have a self-image as a gregarious church, especially welcoming to newcomers? Note that. Make them proud. Sermons work better when the preacher is aware of the piece of the world we live in together.

Understandably, ministers are often tempted to articulate the day-to-day perspective of life as a minister. We have all read newsletter columns and heard sermons that begin, "Last Monday afternoon, I was sitting in my study looking out the window at the squirrels" or some such. Admittedly, your authors themselves have written similar lines. However, if most parishioners are working down at the plant at 3:00 in the afternoon, or have young children just waking up from naps, or live in housing complexes inhospitable to squirrels, the minister's life is not easy to relate to. Writing about authors who chronicle their own professional lives, Carol Shields maintains:

> It's tiresome to read, an offense to those outside the club, a public stroking of our own professional plumage...We know perfectly well we ought to be writing about bus drivers and dentists and people who manufacture knife sharpeners. These individuals have valid lives, after all, and built-in narratives that may be every bit as meaningful as that of the misunderstood novelist suffering in his Brooklyn basement...We should buckle down and produce fictions that center on dedicated manicurists or those folks who design the drainage beds for interstate highways or make canoes out of natural materials. A certain amount of research would be required, naturally—some personal interviews, or else serious grind sessions in the public library. Only think how the range...would widen out.[7]

Furthermore, when considering what makes sermons work, one must not underestimate the importance of the internal life of the listeners: their moods and states of mind, their general receptivity. The sermon that changes the life of any one parishioner on a Sunday in May may not work at all for that same person the next November, after his or her mom died or the car's engine seized. The sermon "Autumn: A Time for Joy," for example, might be rethought and expanded to include those in a less-than-joyous frame of mind.

Finally, our readers may well wonder about the importance of the actual *content* of the sermon. Clergy struggle to create sermons that have coherent messages. Where is that effort reflected on our list?

When asked to recall the aspects of preaching that made sermons effective, students do not usually mention the sermon's point! In fact, they often claim that although the sermon was somehow memorable and transformative, they no longer have any idea what the specific subject was. But still they remember that as a result of that sermon, on that particular Sunday morning they decided to stay in their marriage; or that because the preacher created such a compelling atmosphere of love and acceptance, they felt more at home in the universe from that day forward; or that because the minister talked about trouble in—well, who can remember where anymore—so vividly, they committed their vacation savings to a local charity, and have continued that practice for years.

The listener brings a world of personal history, attitude, emotion, knowledge, and spirituality to every worship service. That the sermon reaches into the lives of the listeners, that, as Jesus put it, they "may have life, and have it abundantly" (Jn. 10:10) by means of the sermon, is in large part due to the qualities they themselves bring to it. Professor Lucy Atkinson Rose describes it this way: "According to transformational understandings of preaching, whatever else a sermon does, its primary purpose is to facilitate an experience, an event, a meeting, or a happening, for the worshipers."[8] While the precise content is important in that it may trigger transformation in the congregant, the sermon's intellectual point is only part of the picture.

When asked about examples of effective preaching, many cite the Reverend Dr. Martin Luther King's "I Have a Dream" address, even if they are too young to have experienced it firsthand. In his speech, Dr. King makes exemplary use of nearly every item on our students' lists. Coupled with the power of his location in front of the Lincoln Memorial, the size and energy of the crowd, the larger context of the civil rights movement, and his general knowledge of his listeners' circumstances, King's preaching style was remarkable. His passionate call to action included personal references ("my four little children," etc.), familiar references (from the Bible, the Gettysburg Address, the Declaration of Independence, well-known spirituals, etc.), accessible metaphors ("bad check," "warm threshold which leads into the palace of justice," etc.), literary devices (alliteration, assonance, anaphora, epistrophe, echo, repetition), and, particularly during the second half of the speech, a congruent delivery style (which was, for him, impassioned, slow, pounding, determined). He read the crowd well, his timing was sensitive, and he offered an earnest empathy and sense of hope. King was prepared (manuscript plus memorized "set pieces"), emotionally present, and what he said was true.

None of us will ever be Martin Luther King, Jr., exactly, but we may be excellent preachers in our own ways. The study of preaching technique can only help, and attention to long lists of stellar sermon qualities is all to the good. Whatever we can do to help make a sermon matter is well worth our time.

However, in our opinion, outstanding preaching requires more than technique. A good sermon begins, as we shall see, with the people in the pews.

2

PREACHING TO REAL PEOPLE

I am an African American preaching to an Asian in Winnipeg. Or I am the preacher and I am gay; the listener is straight. I, a working-class minister from Chicago, am preaching to a wealthy parishioner from San Francisco, by way of Barcelona. I am a woman, sixty years of age, and in the second pew sit four young men in the youth group. I am a pastor who has always been employed, and members of my congregation are losing their jobs.

And that's not all. According to Fred Craddock, there are also

> those still listening for an authoritative voice to relieve them of the responsibility for their own faith, those weary of the old jargon who are turning to poets and tellers of stories for a fresh word, those who are still on the porch of the church and nervous about coming inside, those who have been there since day one but who can no longer remember why, and those who reverence Scripture and things sacred but who fear investigations. Some are accustomed to being listened to; others, long silent, are surprised and empowered by the sound of their own voices.[1]

Expectations of the preacher vary. Some parishioners hold the model of their childhood minister close to their hearts; that is how you, their current minister, should look, sound, and behave. Others have come to your church precisely to find a new version of ministry, and similarities to "the old style" count against you. Some members of the congregation are tired of authoritarian ministers; others want, finally, to encounter a professional preacher's presence, after too many years of hearing empowered lay voices. Some come to church to find connection and community, while others seek a quiet time for reflection without the burden of interpersonal interaction.

A sixteenth-century survey of what people wanted in sermons found that:

> Some would have long texts:
>> some short texts...
>
> Some would have it polished by Rhetoric:
>> some call it persuasibleness of words.
>
> Some love study and learning in Sermons:
>> some allow only a sudden motion of the spirit.
>
> Some would have all said by heart:
>> some would have recourse made often to the book.
>
> Some love gestures:
>> some no gestures.
>
> Some love long Sermons:
>> some short Sermons.
>
> Some are coy, and can brook no Sermons at all.[2]

As a preacher, your assignment is to serve the people in the pews, who-ever they are, wherever they have come from, whatever their pain and joy. And that, of course, is impossible.

In the face of this predicament, some preachers aim for the "univer-sals." Everyone, after all, faces death, encounters difficulties, achieves small triumphs, lives with a childhood, develops a view of life. Ministers can speak from their own small place within the universal human condition, as long as they acknowledge that they are speaking from the perspective of a single human being.

Other ministers try to preach not to the universal aspects of life but to the particulars of their parishioners' lives and worlds: the factory that closed and the resulting despair; the high school prom that got out of hand and the standards we try to maintain for our children here in St. Louis; the Native American story of how the river behind the meetinghouse rose to meet the sacred mountain.

Why not keep both the universal and the particular in mind? Leonora Tubbs Tisdale writes, "Cultural anthropologists tell us that people are, in certain respects: (1) *like all others* (sharing certain universals with the whole human race); (2) *like no others* (having distinctive traits that mark them as individuals); and (3) *like some others* (sharing cultural traits with a particu-lar group of people)."[3] In sermons, preachers need to acknowledge all of these truths.

Throughout the history of preaching, teachers have emphasized preaching to particular people:

- "It...makes a great difference," wrote Augustine in the fifth century, "...whether there are few or many; whether learned or unlearned, or a mixed audience made up of both classes; whether they are townsfolk or countryfolk, or both together; or a gathering in which all sorts and conditions of [humanity] are represented. For it cannot fail to be the case that different persons should affect in different ways."[4]

- In the thirteenth century, Alan of Lille, who wrote a pioneering preaching handbook (*Ars Praedicandi*), included a preaching series for different kinds of audiences—widows, virgins, and princes.[5]

- In the contemporary literature, J. Alfred Smith quotes Henry H. Mitchell's two hermenuetical principles: that "one must preach in the language and culture of the hearers," and that the "message must speak to the needs or life situation of the listeners."[6]

- Finally, throughout her book, Leonora Tubbs Tisdale advocates preaching in a cultural context, "indigenizing," and exegeting a congregation.[7]

In spite of these directives, in some circles parishioners continue to complain that they do not feel acknowledged in sermons, that the ministers preach from within their own contexts and experiences to the exclusion of individual listeners. Preachers speak neither to the particular congregation nor out of universal human experience. Whether the minister is simply "old school" and locked into his or her own perspective, unwilling or unable to imagine the world in any other way, or the minister is of the more contemporary school that encourages wholehearted preaching exclusively from one's own experience, the effect is the same: The sermon is inaccessible to the church member.

The point occurs again and again throughout this book: The authors believe that the fundamental key to good preaching is that, overall, ministers pay attention and relate to their listeners.

Current thinking in the field of homiletics suggests that the people in the pews want to feel "connected" in church: connected to one another, connected to what for them is holy, and, most important for the purposes of our discussion, connected to the preacher and the preacher's sermon.

Indeed, in the history of preaching instruction, the message is constant. The people in the pews are the ones who matter in preaching; relate to them, know them. Advice is abundant:

- From the seventeenth century: "It is more essential to study people than books."[8]

- From the nineteenth century: "Be the amazed listener who sits and hears what the other finds the more delight in telling you because you listen with amazement...If you are capable of it, present the aesthetic with all its fascinating magic, enthrall if possible the others, present it with the sort of passion which exactly suits them, merrily for the merry, in a minor key for the melancholy, wittily for the witty, &c."[9]

- From the 1920s: "Preachers cannot think enough about the people to whom they are preaching."[10]

- From the 1990s: "The preacher must be more relational if communication is really to take place...I think the relational aspect is now the most pressing issue in the communication of the sermon."[11]

- "Whatever style of sermon I preach, it must first ask the question: What are the listener's needs?...As I prepare messages, I think of the guy in the pew. I keep a photograph of the church filled with people before me as I prepare."[12]

- "Preachers can speak in monologue, and yet the sermon can have the quality of a conversation in which the congregation actively participates. Given the postmodern emphases on community and mutuality, this quality is important."[13]

Even though preaching instruction has long encouraged ministers to relate to members of their congregations "person-to-person," laity often comment on the lack of connection they feel to preachers and their sermons. In some traditions and among some personalities, the minister, though relating to parishioners regularly, assumes a role that seems pompous, aloof, or superior—and therefore distancing—to the people in the pews. When the preacher sees herself or himself as a partner among equals, a fellow member of a religious community who is searching for an appropriate spiritual life along with everybody else, perceptions of the distance between pulpit and pew diminish.

Ministers who serve in denominations where the clergy are not set apart will recognize Lucy Atkinson Rose's description of sermons born out of relatedness:

Although *one* may do the speaking, the preacher is never isolated or alone. The one speaks the language of the community of faith in its historical and global configurations. The one speaks with, among, and sometimes on behalf of them because she or he has already in countless prior conversations been speaking with, among, and sometimes on behalf of others. The one speaks of personal experiences, interpretative possibilities, and convictions, using words that invite the personal experiences, interpretations, and convictions of all the worshipers as participants in the ongoing, communal conversations.[14]

In some religious traditions, the preacher knows the answers and the laity do not. At least this is an image that some in the field of contemporary homiletics are still trying to fight. In our experience, this battle has long since been won:

- In the mid-1800s, the great Unitarian minister Theodore Parker wrote: "I had an intense delight in writing and preaching; but I was a learner quite as much as a teacher, and was feeling my way forward and upward with one hand, while I tried to lead with the other...The simple life of the farmers, weavers, mechanics about me, of its own accord, turned into a sort of poetry, and re-appeared in the sermons, as the green woods, not far off, looked in at the windows of the meeting-house. I think I preached only what I had experienced in my own inward consciousness, which widened and grew richer as I came into practical contact with living people, turned time into life."[15]

- More recently, an Episcopal clergyman, Eldred Johnston, suggested, "Take away the pulpit, the pews, the choir. Move to a kitchen table with you on one side and a couple of your friends on the other. Notice how things change: the volume of your voice and the frequency of your gestures decrease. Your theology becomes more modest—less confident. Notice your increased concern for the response of your listeners—and perhaps even a *request for their help* in this vital quest."[16]

- In describing Fred Craddock's approach, Charles Campbell tells us that "the preacher doesn't simply deposit conclusions in the hearers' minds but enables the congregation to participate actively in the movement and meaning of the sermon. Inductive movement encourages listeners to think their own thoughts, feel their own feelings, draw their own conclusions, and make their own decisions, with the result that they take a measure of responsibility for the message. Preaching becomes the shared activity of preacher and congregation."[17]

- Lucy Atkinson Rose believes that preaching should be "non-hierarchical, heuristic, and communal...rooted in a relationship of connectedness and mutuality between the preacher and the worshipers."[18]

- Finally, from a Unitarian Universalist (UU) perspective, Judith Meyer remarks, "Preaching is not…a unilateral interpretation of any reality—the word of God, the exegesis of Hebrew or Christian scripture, or any other text for that matter. UU preaching does not derive its authority from these sources, but is a resource for the members of a congregation to use as each listener struggles to apply the spoken word to the experience of being alive. If preaching is to respect the individual worth and dignity of each person, it must speak out of an awareness of who the congregation is, and out of a sensitivity to the fact that on any given occasion, each member is coming to grips with life in some unique and potentially transforming way."[19]

Our own view is that, one way or another, the voices of the people in the pews must be heard. We were raised that way. Others, we know, will disagree either because local or denominational custom demands it or, on the contrary, because lay participation is in fact the custom, and it hasn't worked very well.

George W. Swank tells us that in the first several centuries B.C.E., Jewish sermons were participatory, marked by questions, laughter, rude comments, and other interruptions.[20] Dietrich Bonhoeffer says that in earliest Christianity, an elder of the congregation read a text and then addressed a short message to the congregation.[21] Precedent suggests that we involve others in the worship service.

But this is not to say that ministers should abandon the pulpit! Even if only the preacher actually speaks, members of the congregation need to hear that their perspectives are being voiced.

Perhaps you, the minister, have announced a topic well in advance and invited parishioners to an open meeting to talk about their views. Maybe you have asked them to contribute poetry or art and the like; thus, they participate directly or indirectly in the Sunday morning service. Perhaps you have involved musicians from the congregation, or a class of Sunday school children. It could be that at the last minute you called four or five church members to hear what they had to say. Maybe the theme of the morning was suggested, at your invitation, by a parishioner. Perhaps a "worship committee," carefully trained, is occasionally or regularly responsible for aspects of worship in the church you serve.[22]

It may be that your style is more collaborative in nature, and you always work with a group of laity to create the morning worship service. Or perhaps your obvious openness and approachability is enough to encourage even the quietest in your congregation and those who feel most marginalized to offer input and feel confident that they will be represented whether they actually approach you or not.

In many congregations, particularly in some African American churches, it is the custom of parishioners to shout or murmur brief verbal responses during the sermon. Other churches, in the Hispanic Protestant tradition, include "testimonios," the witness of the believers. Still other congregations designate a part of the service, or a time just following, for extended questions, comments, and critique.

All of that said, in most congregations it is you, the paid staff member in charge of worship, whose job it is to ensure that, come Sunday morning, effective worship is at hand. In fact, some congregations are no longer hungry for literal lay participation, but prefer instead sensitive, relational, professional preaching.

The point is, whatever your style and the tradition you serve, it's the people who are important: the people and their religious lives. If you can love them enough to know them, and if your sermons show it to be true, then you are a long way toward successful preaching.

3

WHENCE IDEAS?
Topics and Materials "At Everybody's Hand"

Prayerful study, alert eyes, sensitive ears, and a compassionate heart are ingredients that form the personality of the preacher.

J. Alfred Smith[1]

What is there to talk about? What is there to say?

These are common questions among theological school students as they imagine not just their first pulpit appearances, but hundreds more stretching decades into the future. For many preachers, these are questions that never go away for good.

True, there are seasons when the Sundays can't come fast enough, one has so many sermons in mind. Some preachers are inclined to Søren Kierkegaard's complaint that,

> Since I became an author I have never for a single day had the experience I hear others complain of, namely, a lack of thoughts or their failure to present themselves. If that were to happen to me, it would rather be an occasion for joy, that finally I had obtained a day that was really free. But many a time I have had the experience of being overwhelmed with riches.[2]

Preachers in that dilemma must be content with the thought that other Sundays lie ahead (and perhaps the humble admission that not all their thoughts are as rich as they may seem). But for most preachers, the moments return of wondering if they have anything left to say. "I have discovered barren periods in my preaching," said the Baptist preacher Gardner C. Taylor. "I guess everybody does."[3]

Having had such moments before, these preachers may have the good fortune to know some valuable truths. First, they know that such times may offer insight into the important depths of human experience. Speaking of "dry seasons" in the pulpit, the evangelical preacher Chuck Swindoll says that such "difficult times are where we sharpen our sights for people in the real world who often live in those dry seasons."[4]

Second, they know that such slack times may only be the spirit's fallow season, when some new outlook, some new burst of energy, some more fervent faith is gathering strength. Taylor says,

> I tell my students they ought to be open to things after periods of barrenness. I saw a documentary on Miles Davis, the trumpeter, and he was saying that for five years he lost the sound of his music…Then Davis started producing a new sound—they call it "cool jazz"…I get great lessons from this. Something inside Davis curled up and changed and there was this emptiness, but then a new thing came.[5]

Taylor relates the experience to his own barren periods in the pulpit. "My wife calls them my preaching plateaus." Partners and friends can be so carefully kind. "I go through them. I have discovered that each plateau is a kind of prepatory period—if we allow it to be—for a new burst of energy and insight."[6]

Preachers who have been through uncreative times also know that just as such moments come, often without warning, so too they usually pass. Often their going is as mysterious as their arrival, but there are strategies that assist in their departure and guard against, if not prevent, their return. The preacher seeking sources of resilience may profitably turn to reading, reflection, family activities, prayer, fun, popular culture, and other rewarding aspects of personal life—or professional engagement.

From our perspective, usually the best source of fresh energy and ideas is reengagement with parishioners, their ideas and interests, their worries and struggles, their questions and hopes. "Cast off the haunting incubus of the notion of great sermons," wrote Phillips Brooks. "Care not for your sermon, but for your truth, and for your people; and subjects will spring up on every side of you, and the chances to preach upon them will be all too few."[7]

When preachers are stuck for a topic or unable to develop one, we recommend that they attend to pastoral tasks—visiting parishioners in the hospital, dropping in for some friendly time with the volunteers who collate the church newsletter, listening to the thoughts of a new Sunday school teacher or the folks preparing dinners for the homeless, calling someone recently divorced or bereaved, writing a letter of recommendation or protest, or any of the involvements that constitute a ministry. Remind yourself of the audience: who they are, and what they care about.

Finally, most preachers know that as the "dry seasons" pass, they will begin to return to a world that teems with ideas for topics, titles, illustrations, stories, humor, and insight; and the ability to notice and remember that world and its offerings is as crucial a preaching skill as any.

One could write a whole book just on the importance of noticing, of observing with what has been called a "sermonic eye," the knack of knowing how a scene, song, encounter, ad, thought, movie, poem, fact, emotion, gaffe, trip, game, or whatever could be used on a Sunday morning.

Of course the term *sermonic eye,* as much as we like it, is biased toward visual imagery, but we mean it more broadly. It includes sights, sounds, smells, snippets of overheard dialogue, systematic theologies, news reports, denominational debates, domestic discussions, traffic patterns, legislative agendas, and daily cartoons. Bishop E. E. Cleveland once said, "I can get a sermon out of anything."[8]

For years we have asked our students of preaching to keep a journal for at least a day of all the things they notice that might some day become part of a sermon of theirs, having urged them to be omnivorous in their observation. Skeptical as some students are at first, the lists they compile are almost always extensive, exciting, and creatively observant.

The lists include sources that one might expect: the news, books about religion, scripture, professional journals, conferences, family life, and course work. Every one of these can be important to preachers throughout their careers.

Preachers must know what current events weigh on the minds of their parishioners. The journalist-turned-pundit Michael Kinsley regretted that reading the paper had become an assignment, as was clear when he saw the headline, "CIA CHIEF ORDERS INVESTIGATION OF STATEMENTS IN IRAQ BANK CASE." He wrote, "That headline contains at least three words—'C.I.A.,' 'investigation,' and 'bank'—that together carry the powerful subliminal message 'Do not read this article. Life is too short.' But for the pundit there is no escape."[9]

The preacher may have a little more freedom than that, but for one who would minister to those who know and care about such matters (and some truly do), or about crop failures, zoning changes, shop closings, foreign relations, drugs at the local high school, or anything else that the paper might tell, paying attention is part of the job.

But the news is a small fraction of the study expected of a preacher. Most ministers will be expected to remain in fresh contact with the Bible—and for lectionary preachers, that means Sunday's selections in particular.[10] And all preachers will profit from the ideas and illustrations for their sermons to be found through regular reading, whether in books, magazines, and journals, or on the Internet.

Long ago, Phillips Brooks urged the need for hard study "in its broadest sense, the study of truth, of history, of philosophy; for no [one] can have a richly stored mind without its influencing the style in which he [or she] writes and speaks, making it at once thoroughly his [or her] own, and yet giving it variety and saving it from monotony."[11]

Although many ministers find the time hard to come by, it is equally hard to overestimate the importance of reading and research in the preacher's life. Asked how much study was adequate for the preaching task, Fred Craddock said, "It seems to me that if the minister gives two hours for study every morning, he can do it, she can do it. This leaves the evening and other leisure hours for other kinds of reading. In the morning period, I mean just the hard study—not a lot of fun, but the necessary heart of it."[12]

Likewise, Frank Harrington said,

> In preparing a sermon, I read widely and constantly. I read at least three books a week. I'll read biographies, best-sellers, both fiction and non-fiction—I read all of that. I read the books I know other people read. I read widely, and I think reading is mandatory for the minister.
>
> If a congregation were to ask me if there is one essential thing they ought to do for a minister, I would certainly put high on that list: Be sure the minister has enough financial resources to buy books, and help him [or her] to find the time to read them. I carry a stack of books with me wherever I go.[13]

Most preachers also turn to journals, magazines, newspapers, and other more ephemeral reading matter besides books. When we have asked pastors of a variety of backgrounds to name the sources of stimulation for their sermons, repeatedly mentioned have been *Christian Century, Parabola, The New York Times* (especially *The Sunday Times Book Review*), *National Geographic, The New Yorker, Harper's Monthly, The Wall Street Journal, Christianity and Crisis, Scientific American,* and *Psychology Today.*

But even observations of the most attentive, inclusive, and perceptive sort from any source will not serve the preacher well unless they are "remembered"—a word we put in quotation marks because few people can remember even important observations without help. "To remember" means, for most of us, "to record and somehow to save in a way that we can retrieve." For as Ronald Allen observes, "The pastor who does not have some means of preserving good quality material lives week by week, from hand to mouth."[14]

Take Fred Craddock, for example. He was once asked about his "great ability to draw material" from past reading, his "cognitions," his "seasoned thoughts." He replied with embarrassment that he had no secret—but then revealed just the sort of practical system that preachers employ:

> I have a notebook in which I scribble things I come across—
> journalistic pieces, news items, commentary materials, or just in-
> formational items…Then, in addition, I have a journal that is the
> germinal reflection on what I have read, with whom I have talked,
> and what I have done. It is almost like a diary, but this journal is
> the medium for many items, otherwise merely informational, which
> eventually will find themselves in a sermon.[15]

Ronald Allen himself has a drawer in which he stores materials.

Many ministers who preach regularly have devised filing systems with folders or manila envelopes to collect others' observations and their own. Some use computer files. Others are relying on the Internet as an instant source of information, inspiration, and insight. No doubt as you read these words, still newer techniques have arrived, beyond predicting.

But as important as any other source of insight and inspiration for sermon subjects, messages, and illustrations are the ruminations of pastors' own souls. This book strongly emphasizes the importance of contact with parishioners in deciding what to preach about. But worship services are an ongoing dialectic or conversation between pastors and congregations, and a good part of the input involves the spiritual struggles of the preachers themselves. In that sense, the task of the pastor is akin to "the task of the poet," which Ibsen said was "to make clear to himself [or herself], and thereby to others, the temporal and eternal questions which are astir in the age and community to which he [or she] belongs."[16]

Among other inputs, there is a place for courses, in person or online, that might inspire the preacher with topics, stories, and examples—even the very courses to which one might have objected in seminary. To succeed in ministry, stretching, growing, is a must. There are ministers who always include time for a course and a study group every semester.

Others take advantage of the schedule of conferences and workshops available locally, regionally, or continentally, often with denominational support. With skill and sensitivity, many messages heard there can be brought home to local congregations to their benefit and gratitude.

And then there are all the other, less-established places where a preacher might find inspiration. To take but a few of the responses in the journals kept by the members of just one year's preaching class, sermon ideas came from a soap label in the shower, poems by Robert Frost and Emily Dickinson, the sight of the backs of buildings from a train (provoking thoughts of the richness of life of which we're rarely aware), song lyrics on the radio, complaints heard more than once regarding rain, or something as quirky as a sign in a church parking lot with the ambiguous message "Reserved Minister."

Indulge your old interests, explore new ones, drink from the springs of culture in the area where you and your parishioners live, at least mentally: the library, politics in Washington, the fuss over the funky new sculpture in the town park, the symphony orchestra not far away, Comedy Central on cable TV, Civil War history, minor league baseball, high school drama, Michael Jackson, stock car racing, hometown radio, the latest movie with Vanessa Redgrave or Tom Cruise or a classic with Hepburn and Bogart, National Public Radio, the Daughters of the American Revolution, the Spice Girls.

Introduce such references carefully. A lot of people are so busy with their own lives that most cultural references (old or new) need to be established, without the preacher's looking inane to the dozen or so people in the pews who know the actual birth dates of the Spice Girls or of Bogart and Hepburn.

These paragraphs themselves illustrate the problem: By the time this book is in print, references to Comedy Central or the Spice Girls may have become obscurely quaint and even fewer readers will remember the movie stars of the past. The dwindling of a common cultural corps of characters would seem to be a challenging but inescapable fact of modern North American life.

As Kurt Vonnegut wrote,

> When I started out as a writer, I could refer to events and personalities in the past, even the distant past, with a reasonable expectation that a fair number of readers would respond with some emotion, whether positive or negative, when I mentioned them.
>
> Case in point: The murder of the greatest President this country will ever have, Abraham Lincoln, by the twenty-six-year-old ham

actor John Wilkes Booth…Who is there under the age of sixty, and not in a History Department, to give a damn?[17]

But done well, introduced with just enough information to leave no one behind or patronized, such references can both reward and inform, bringing people to understand deeper, richer points than would have been possible without illustrations from perceptive, artistic souls at work in media other than the sermon.

Occasionally, one will hear a preacher bemoaning the fact that she or he cannot attend a play or go to the beach without seeing how some part of the experience might be used in a sermon. But the situation is not altogether bemoanable. In ways it is a blessing. Preachers have the great good fortune to do their best work by being most alive, most observant, most aware of how their everyday experiences contain knowledge and insight, tragedy and amusement, that can be shared.

Everyone's experiences are like that. The playwright George Bernard Shaw once noted that "all my audacious originalities are simply liftings from stores of evidence that lie at everybody's hand."[18] The preaching minister is one of the lucky few who get paid to stay awake to such evidence and its enjoyment, depth, and wisdom. As Henry James said, "An artist is someone on whom nothing is lost," and the sermon is a central part of the art of most ministries.

4

FINALLY CHOOSING
THIS WEEK'S THEME

For all the input a preacher may gather, eventually she or he is left to decide what to preach on. Even the most observant soul, with the longest daily list of material fit for the pulpit, may quail at the impending deadline of the church newsletter in which the preacher declares the topic(s) ahead— or failing that deadline, the one for Sunday's printed order of service. Of course, no divine or federal law requires that sermon topics be announced in advance, and you may choose not to do so. One minister wrote, "I see no good reason for it. I want them to come to a service of worship so that they can be part of a vital religious community, only one part of which is the business of listening to a sermon."[1] But eventually, a preacher has to decide, What am I going to talk about on Sunday, and what am I going to say?

Lectionary preachers have particular texts to suggest appropriate themes, but they must still see the possibilities and select. At the other extreme are preachers whose traditions give them the freeing, intimidating chance to start most Mondays with a clean slate, their options for Sunday essentially open. In either case, choices have to be made.

Anyone newly facing the prospect of making such choices for a year's worth of Sundays may find some comfort in the fact that a fair number of assignments are decided in advance, at least in the broad sense. On the Sunday before Christmas, most ministers will be preaching either about some aspect of that holiday or about the several religious holidays that occur at that time. Many congregations devote the first Sunday every fall to a sort of ingathering or reunion.

Depending on one's tradition, the list might include such regular occasions as the bishop's visit, the fund-raising kickoff, a celebration of volunteers, a focus on the religious education program, special attention to music, bring-a-friend Sunday, Thanksgiving Sunday, Mothers' Day, the Jewish High Holy Days, the solstices, the spring holidays, and a service when parishioners ask questions of the minister(s).

Phillips Brooks once rejoiced "to see in many churches outside our own, that to which we owe so much as a help to the orderliness of preaching, the observance of a church year with its commemorative festivals, growing so largely common."[2] Today, many congregations are thinking creatively about what those commemorative festivals might be. In planning sermons for the year, such events provide an orderliness that many welcome.

There are other ways of building in order. Some preachers find it helps to structure part of the year as a series of sermons of a similar type, perhaps a month on social action themes, or a series on the basic tenets of one's faith tradition. The Presbyterian minister John A. Huffman, Jr., said, "I am probably half of the time in series, maybe a little bit more than that."[3] Of course, not all congregations would welcome the eighteen sermons on Joshua that Huffman reports he gave or the twenty-three on Jonah that R. T. Kendall once delivered.[4] One preacher spent eight years in Hebrews.[5] This seems excessive to the authors, who rarely string together more than a few sermons on one topic before it seems time for a change of pace.

In fact, we both try to discipline ourselves to give a wide variety of sermons, so that in some regular way it comes time again for each type of sermon described in section two. Others make a similar effort to vary their types of sermons (personal growth, theology, social action, etc.) or theological topics (God, human nature, church community, evil, etc.). The diversity itself becomes a sort of order, one that stretches the preacher in positive ways.

A colleague of ours, Mary Louise Schmalz, told her congregation, "In choosing sermons for a church year, my goal is to have a sense of balance. It is important for me to address several wide areas: denominational history, social action, science, world religions, ethics, general psychology, literature and current events." In addition, "I reserve a couple of Sundays to address internal church issues," leaving her three or four Sundays a year to "choose a topic that I particularly want to talk about and feel is especially important, or a particular theme that someone has asked me to please address in church." She concludes that "by adhering to an objective 'schedule,' I protect you from hearing about my personal agenda week after week. I also stretch and grow as I think about new areas that I wouldn't ordinarily search out."[6]

The Unitarian Universalist minister Judith Walker-Riggs, working from ideas by Harry Lismer Short, developed this outlook into three Intentional Preaching Plans, "models that could help a preacher intentionally plan for balance and variety, the better to reach the variety of people participating." After all, "It is unlikely that all 'types' of people will be best satisfied with one 'type' of sermon/service." Her list of "content structures" includes biographical, historical, topical, idea debate, inspirational/devotional, autobiographical/confessional, shared preaching, "and so on." (Her other plans include varying the artistic structure and the sensory images.)[7]

Others try different balances. Another colleague, Patrick O'Neill, writes that he

> categorizes all sermons based on temperature: sermons are either hot, warm, cool, or cold depending on these variables—(a) subject matter, (b) the style in which they are written, (c) the passion with which they are invested, and (d) the weight the congregation gives them…The desired goal of O'Neill's Theory of Sermonic Temperature is balance over the course of the church year. That does not mean lukewarm. It means the right temperature for the right time.[8]

By now we may have set before the preacher a daunting task: To know the congregation, the world's events, the religious heritage, and his or her own soul so well that just the right topic will appear. Of course, that's more than will often be fully achieved, even for the most observant preacher with the most abundant set of files.

But in addition to all our listening, gathering, research, and pondering, critical as each one is, there are more mysterious, powerful, creative forces that also serve the preacher's needs, that come forth in times of reflection, in prayer or meditation, or just out of the blue.

The composer Anton Bruckner was once reportedly asked, "Master, how, when, where did you think of the divine motif of your Ninth Symphony?" "Well, it was like this," Bruckner replied. "I walked up the Kahlenberg, and when it got hot and I got hungry, I sat down by a little brook and unpacked my Swiss cheese. And just as I opened the greasy paper, that darn tune popped into my head!"[9]

We're not sure we believe this story, but we like it very much because it reflects important aspects of the creative process. The tune did not pop into just *anyone's* head, but into Bruckner's, into the head of someone whose conscious thoughts were much involved with composition and who had training and experience in the field. But it came up unbidden.

Similarly, ideas for a topic, an organization, an illustration, or a title can occur to us upon waking, driving along, or waiting in the checkout line, just as often as they do as we sit at our desks, diligently pondering. Whatever the circumstance, clearly record your ideas as they arrive. The subconscious speaks so eloquently that we can imagine our conscious brains will remember the thought till the end of time. This is not true. Unless we are careful, we are left with only an unintelligible scrawl or a haunting sense of the earlier insight.

Interior sources of inspiration continue throughout the creative process. The novelist Don DeLillo wrote,

> I think my work comes out of the culture of the world around me. I think that's where my language comes from. That's where my themes come from…But the work itself, you know—sentence by sentence, page by page—it's much too intimate, much too private, to come from anywhere but deep within the writer himself [or herself]. It comes out of all the time a writer wastes. We stand around, look out the window, walk down the hall, come back to the page, and, in those intervals, something subterranean is forming, a literal dream that comes out of daydreaming. It's too deep to be attributed to clear sources.[10]

The process of finding ideas and illustrations and turning them into topics and text can be mysterious, exhilarating, and hard, even exhausting. But it is time well spent, finding the right theme, of the right size, for that Sunday, one that stirs your own interest and offers the hope of stirring such interest in the congregation.

If your congregation is used to twenty-minute sermons, it helps to have a twenty-minute-sized theme, a message that can be well developed in about that amount of time, given the ideas, stories, dramatic development, and whatever else you plan to feature. Among the fine topics you've thought of, some just aren't ready yet. Among the best sermons you may ever give, some will have waited for many years to grow to sermon size, in weight as well as length. And some sermon ideas just never do grow big enough. These make better newsletter columns than sermons.

But among new preachers, the more typical problem is a sermon that tries to do more than can be accomplished (sometimes satirized with titles like "Time," or "My Faith Journey," or "A Religion for Our Time: [insert your own faith tradition].") Even experienced preachers need to keep an eye on their burgeoning folders of sermon topics, before the contents and their possibilities overwhelm the original intent.

There are a number of routes by which preachers arrive at their sermon topics. One is suggested by the novelist Barbara Kingsolver: "I always begin with a question I can't answer. Then I climb in and write my way to an answer."[11] In a similar vein, Bruce Marshall writes, "My starting point is a question or issue that catches my attention. If I find myself bothered or wondering about something, that's a good topic."[12]

Probably nothing is more important to the success of a sermon than the preacher's own interest in the topic, her or his enthusiasm for or devotion to the message—and the preacher's ability to share that passion, to make it part of the community's own faith journey. Indeed, for the sensitive preacher, the interest may have come initially out of the congregation itself. But even if it is a fascination of one's own, the skill is in pursuing it in ways that the congregation can follow and profit from too.

The program director of a classical music station was once asked what would happen if he were to program music just according to his own tastes. "It would be a train wreck," he said. "Nobody would listen."[13] Yet the preacher's enthusiasms, elicited in part in response to the congregation's own, are topics that people do want to hear about.

Students for the ministry commonly ask, "Whose issues am I to preach on, theirs or my own?" It is one of the hardest questions to answer. On the one hand, as religious leaders we sympathize with people who say, "We don't go to church because they're giving answers to questions we're not even asking."[14] We want to be intimately attuned to the questions that do matter to those in the pews. On the other hand, most of us know the experience reported by the journalist Donald M. Murray, who wrote, "I am most content when I am by myself reflecting on the life I have lived minutes or decades before. I am an observer, a keeper of the score, a writer who doesn't know what life means, and so I make up a meaning and readers, surprisingly, say, 'Yes, that's what it's like.'"[15]

In bringing our observations, interactions, study, reflection, inspiration, and hard work to the task of selecting sermon topics, we must address issues that are ours and congregants' alike, issues that, if we present them well, they will care about. That is why they come, and why they have employed us. Consequently, "We must be constantly digging and grappling with the central questions, because that's what causes us to grow. In our growth, we can help our people grow."[16]

5

TRUSTING INSTANT INSPIRATION, WORDS ON PAPER, OR WHAT?

There is much to be said for and against preaching extemporaneously, as words come to mind in the immediacy of the interaction with a congregation. Two old, true stories suggest the different attitudes, beginning with Nathaniel Stacy's account of his first sermon:

> One Sunday morning [in 1802]…Mr. Ballou [a distinguished Universalist minister, under whose guidance Stacy was preparing for the ministry] was seized with a violent pain in the head, and came to me with his hand on his forehead, saying, very mournfully, "Brother Stacy, you must preach today; for I am in such violent pain, I can not…"
>
> Seeing that he looked quite serious, I replied, "Why…if you had any idea of setting me to preach today, you should have informed me before we left home. I have some manuscripts which I could have taken for assistance; but I have not a scroll of writing with me. I can not attempt to go into the desk today." "I am glad," he said, "you have no writing with you; it would only be a trouble to you. You must learn to speak extemporaneously; and the better way is to begin in the first place…"
>
> I spoke probably twenty or twenty-five minutes; but I attended to every proposition of my text, and finished my discourse. Mr. Ballou then arose and closed the service…I heard no more of Mr. Ballou's headache…He made no complaints in the afternoon, but preached like an Apostle. I told him afterwards, and I always believed it, that his headache was feigned.[1]

In this case, things seem to have gone just fine. But consider this account by the Unitarian nineteenth-century minister James Freeman Clarke of his first sermon at his first church, in Louisville, Kentucky:

> I was trying to prepare for Sunday. In regard to this I made two great mistakes. I had heard that the people in the West preferred extempore speaking, and I thought I must preach an extempore sermon. As I had been accustomed to speak often in debate without difficulty, I imagined that I could speak without notes. But I found it was one thing to answer an opponent in debate, and quite another to address a congregation. All the thoughts I had arranged in my mind disappeared, and I found that I had nothing to say.
>
> So after talking in a very desultory way for fifteen or twenty minutes, I brought my sermon suddenly to an end. I knew I had made an utter failure, and, mortified beyond expression, I left without saying a word to anyone, and went back to my room. No one in the society said anything to me about this failure, nor did I speak to anyone about it.
>
> Some twenty years after…I met a gentleman who told me he was in the Louisville church when I preached my first sermon. "You heard a pretty poor one," I said. "That's so," said he; "about as bad a one as I ever heard."
>
> "Do you know what the people said about it?" I asked. He answered, "Yes; after you had gone some of them stopped and talked about it. One man said, 'We had better let him go back at once to Boston, for he will never do anything here.' But another remarked, 'Do not let us be in a hurry,—perhaps he will do better by and by. I noticed that there seemed to be some sense in his prayer.' So they concluded to wait a while before speaking to you."
>
> After this experience I took care to write my sermons for Sunday morning.[2]

Not all preachers make the same decision. After all, some of the best preaching is extemporaneous. In the "I Have a Dream" speech of Martin Luther King, Jr. (which we tend to consider a sermon in content and style, if not in its secular setting), when he shifts midway from his manuscript to directly addressing the audience, there is an extraordinary increase in the power and beauty of King's preaching. ("Extemporaneous," as the word is often understood, overstates the spontaneity—though not the genius—of King's creativity on that occasion, since many of the passages he delivered were ones he had developed in previous presentations.)[3]

There are many preachers who are good at composing on the spot. If one can do it well, there are advantages: the eye contact, the spontaneity, the time during the week freed for preparatory thought and reading or other pastoral tasks (though some, like Charles Simeon, say that "it takes more time to prepare properly for an extempore sermon than to write one"[4]). Phillips Brooks contended that "the extemporaneous discourse has the advantage of alertness. It possesses more activity and warmth. It conveys an idea of steadiness and readiness, of poise and self-possession, even to the most rude perceptions. [People] have an admiration for it, as indicating a mastery of powers and an independence of artificial means."[5]

Even preachers who are not especially adept at it, and therefore (one would hope) do not do it often, may find that when they do there are some parishioners who prefer seeing their struggles at finding the right word or idea to their usual, more polished presentation.

But not all. Brooks again:

> Sometimes to an extemporaneous preacher his very extemporaneousness proves a dull, dead cloud, which wraps itself around him, and separates him from the people who are crowded up close about his feet…The struggles of thought are on him. He is busy with the choice of words. His mind is watching its own action as it seizes on thought after thought. There is a process of memory and a process of anticipation in the present act. He is forced to recollect himself, and so he does not feel the people.[6]

There are other drawbacks for preachers for whom extemporaneity is not natural or easy. R. C. Sproul recalls:

> When I was a young man, I wrote out all my sermons and memorized them. Then I came under the influence of Robert J. Lamont, the former pastor of the First Presbyterian Church in Pittsburgh. Lamont talked to me about extemporaneous preaching. It was a fateful day in my life because it was the day my digestive system was destroyed…
>
> He encouraged me to preach like that—and it was terrifying! That's what I did.
>
> I speak anywhere from three hundred to five hundred times a year. I sometimes think of how dreadful it would be if I had to write every one of them down. But not having a manuscript—not even a printed outline—evokes in me all kinds of anxiety. That's what I mean when I said Lamont's advice to me literally destroyed my digestive system. I don't think I've properly digested a meal

in thirty years because of losing the security of having that manuscript.[7]

The manuscript preacher enjoys another advantage cited by Brooks, "exemption from those foolish fluent things that slip so easily off of the ready tongue. The writer is spared some of those despairing moments which come to the extemporaneous speaker when a wretched piece of folly escapes him which he would give anything to recall but cannot, and he sees the raven-eyed reporters catch the silly morsel as it drops."[8] The reality for many preachers is that, while they may seem to do well off the cuff, it takes a severe toll on them, and not just in the despairing moments cited by Brooks. There are also those moments in the pulpit when for seconds that seem like an eternity the next words do not occur, and those many moments afterward when they realize how they might have better made a point or imagine ways that their words could have been badly misunderstood.

And yet for all of that, in recent decades extemporaneous preaching has held an allure, especially for new preachers. Perhaps it seems more authentic and real. For most preachers, however, relying on spontaneous inspiration to be with them on schedule is iffy at best. A minister once remarked that his best and most authentic sermons were indeed ones that he gave extemporaneously, but at such odd hours as Tuesday morning just after reading or driving to the hospital Friday afternoon. He saw his task as noticing, appreciating, recording, and using such inspiration to create the pages, notes, or outline with which he could recreate the original insight and emotion in the pulpit.

Some preachers can do that on the spot without the intervening paperwork. Having witnessed many such efforts, we would suggest that, at the very least, extemporaneous preachers will want to know in advance what their topics are, what their basic viewpoints are, what alternative views they will want to honor, what their basic structures are, some stories that are apt to work well, and most of all, how they expect to bring their sermons to a close when it is time.

Brooks caught the ambiguity well:

> I think that the best sermons I have ever preached, taking all the qualities of sermons into account, probably have been extemporaneous sermons, but that the number of good sermons preached from manuscript have probably been far greater than the number of good sermons preached extemporaneously; and he [or she] who can put those two facts together will arrive at some pretty clear and just idea of how it will be best for him [or her] to preach.[9]

Brooks himself "wrote out complete manuscripts of his sermons" for much of his distinguished career, but "in his later years Brooks began to preach frequently without a manuscript, taking only notes with him into the pulpit and seldom referring to them. Those who heard him in these years remembered the sermons as being among his most compelling preaching."[10] It is a progression that has worked well for others too. Yet there are those who reverse the transition, over time becoming more committed to manuscript preaching. And then there are those who stay with one pattern throughout their entire careers. When it comes to "the vexed question of written or unwritten sermons," Brooks concluded, "the different methods have their evident different advantages"[11]—and disadvantages too.

Extemporaneous preaching (which can be great, but at its worst can be amorphous rambling) and preaching from a fully prepared text (which can be great, but at its worst can be a tedious lecture) are only two among the options available in any week to the preacher. Memorized sermons, for example, offer many of the advantages of both fully prepared and extemporaneous sermons, though they require special talent and time. Perhaps this is why Brooks found it "a method which some may practice, but which I hope nobody commends."[12]

And yet we would commend it, too, for those for whom it works well. J. Alfred Smith believes that

> the sermon body can be memorized without stress or strain on the preacher. Just as the muscles of the body can be trained so that one can jog several miles without tiring or the swimmer can swim with enjoyment several laps every day, so can the preacher develop the muscles of memory. Here are some tips for memory exercise which I have used:
>
> 1. Memorize some literary gems, humorous events, and quotations. Memorize Scripture.
> 2. Select carefully the items to memorize.
> 3. Concentrate on the items that are to be memorized.
> 4. Memorize the ideas or the concepts in a logical or sequential pattern.
> 5. Visualize what you are memorizing.
> 6. Rehearse audibly the chief ideas of the sermon.
> 7. Don't fret over a memory lapse while in the pulpit, but accept the new and fresh concept given to you while you are speaking.[13]

Other preachers have done well (or not) with organized notes or with an outline with some sections of the sermon fully scripted, either written out or memorized. And many preachers vary their choices, as much as they are able, depending on the week.

As so often is the case in the practice of preaching, there is no one right way of doing things. The retired Lutheran minister and homiletics teacher Alvin Rueter wrote recently that after

> study and observation, I came to see that preaching without notes—
> a method I still prefer—is not the only way. Whether it's reading
> a manuscript, speaking from an outline almost as detailed as a
> manuscript, memorizing a script, not memorizing but still speaking
> without notes—whatever system you choose, you can find great
> preachers who've employed your method.[14]

6

GETTING STARTED:
Those First Words on Paper

Many ministers find that a sermon takes about twenty hours to prepare, or about an hour of preparation for every minute of delivered sermon. As it happens, we also believe this, and we agree with our colleague Peter Raible, who says, "The only vehement truth I have to convey on 'doing sermons' is schedule generous time...and never surrender keeping such hours on the schedule."[1]

But that does not mean twenty hours at the computer that week on Sunday's sermon, even for those of us who preach from a full manuscript. We imagine composition time is more typically six to ten hours.

During the week, hours have started to accumulate toward other sermons that may not be given for weeks or decades: you read a book, ponder an idea, a show suggests a sermon illustration, a lecturer provides a new perspective, a chat line challenges a long-held idea. You finally get around to filing a stack of articles you've clipped from the paper, and you notice new connections between some of them. You try out an idea over lunch with a colleague. And, of course, you go on ministering in all the ways that will show up as what you hope to be wisdom or insight in a sermon some day.

After all the thought and research, though, for most preachers the time arrives when they must start composing whatever it is they are going to take into the pulpit, whether it be a manuscript, an outline, note cards, a single card, or a set of ideas in their minds.

"I'd like to remind you again, Winfield, that daydreaming is only a part of the creative process."

This moment arrives at different times for different people. We know a colleague who begins writing sermons more than six weeks ahead of time, and we know others who begin writing on Sunday morning. Of course, some go into the pulpit with nothing but their trust that inspiration will come, but we don't recommend this for most.

Over the last decade, we have had students conduct interviews with more than one hundred settled priests and ministers of many denominations, including questions about work habits. Not surprisingly, the results suggest that most preachers, busy as they are during the work week, only get around to writing as the Sunday deadline draws near, on Friday or, more often, on Saturday.

Calvin and Hobbes   by Bill Watterson

CALVIN AND HOBBS © 1992 Bill Watterson. Reproduced with permission of UNIVERSAL PRESS SYNDICATE. All rights reserved.

Many feel apologetic for composing their sermons only in the final days and nights as Sunday morning approaches. There seems to be some bias at work here, suggesting that *good* preachers compose their sermons methodically and early, much as Dietrich Bonhoeffer advised:

> It is a good idea to write the sermon during the daylight hours. Anything written at night often cannot stand the bright light of day and looks strange in the morning…It is a good rule to begin the sermon at the latest on Tuesday and to conclude it at the latest on Friday…The usual sermon prepared on Saturday evening reveals an attitude that is unworthy of the work."[2]

Phillips Brooks, whose words we quote often in this book, concurred: He believed that Saturday night sermon writing is "the crowning disgrace of a [person's] ministry. It is dishonest. It is giving but the last flicker of the week as it sinks in its socket, to those who have paid for the full light burning at its brightest. And yet [some] boast of it. They tell you in how short a time they write their sermons, and when you hear them preach you only wonder that it took so long."[3]

On the other hand, those preachers who favor the last-minute approach to sermon writing will take comfort in the words of Francis de Sales, who said in 1567, "Our preaching must be a spontaneous action, in contrast to the constrained and studied action of the pedants…As to preparation, I am in favor of making it in the evening, and in the morning of meditating within oneself on what one wishes to say to others."[4]

Every person must find his or her own unique strategy for getting down to the glorious, but arduous, even torturous, task of starting to conceive, depict, and write a sermon. Pulitzer prize–winning author William Styron wrote, "Questions having to do with writing schedule are misleading and uninteresting. I find that always comes up, and that's the least important thing about writing. It is far more important to talk about…the intellectual and emotional components of writing."[5] Be that as it may, each person needs to deal with these questions—and not once and for all, but week to week.

"Starting patterns" are many, even for the same preacher, who one week may sit down, outline in hand, and begin at the beginning, and the following week may have trouble with the opening paragraph, begin somewhere else, and come back to the first page later. Some people write a quick first draft on occasion, and then destroy the whole thing and start over. There are few processes as mysterious, frightening, or important to most ministers as how to stop mulling and get down to the business of getting ready to address the congregation.

For many, a weekly rhythm helps. The retired minister Harry Meserve once said that the

> answer to the question "How do you do a sermon each week?" is simple, namely, "Sunday morning arrives"…The moment comes when preparation must be done. Whether that moment of completion be months before or, more likely, the Saturday night prior to delivery, the act of getting ready soon establishes its own rituals, much like a child's getting ready to go to bed. This seems true whether the preacher be "full manuscript" or "off the cuff."[6]

There may be a year where every Thursday from 5:00 to 5:30 you sit waiting in the kitchen of your son's piano teacher, and that's when you routinely focus your sermon idea and settle on a form. Or perhaps you always stay home alone on Friday mornings clearing your desk (and thus your mind) of phone calls, pastoral concerns, e-mail, and paperwork, so that you can concentrate on Friday afternoon's sermon research before you take your mother to her weekly appointment at the hairdresser. Perhaps you outline your sermon first thing Monday morning, two weeks ahead. Maybe you read for your sermon whenever you nurse the baby, or you discipline yourself to type the first three pages by midnight Friday night or before your shower Saturday morning.

Even though ministry, family life, and life in general can conspire to disrupt routine, trying to maintain a pattern often proves beneficial. Fred Craddock advised in an interview, "Have a regular, habitual discipline of study, reading, prayer, and reflection. Do a little bit every day and do not allow yourself to give it second place by that immensely intimidating task of 'getting up a sermon.' Do a little every day."[7]

Author Anne Lamott tells a story about her brother's feeling overwhelmed by a big writing project:

> Thirty years ago my older brother, who was ten years old at the time, was trying to get a report on birds written that he'd had three months to write, which was due the next day. We were out at our family cabin in Bolinas, and he was at the kitchen table close to tears, surrounded by binder paper and pencils and unopened books on birds, immobilized by the hugeness of the task ahead. Then my father sat down beside him, put his arm around my brother's shoulder, and said, "Bird by bird, buddy. Just take it bird by bird."[8]

A little self-indulgence helps too. The favorite coffee mug and a bit more caffeine than usual, comfy composition clothes and your favorite CD, a writing location that includes all you need for inspiration and concentration, chewing gum or jelly beans, the promise of breaks for ten-minute naps or walks around the block (even washing a load of laundry can begin to look attractive)—make whatever deal with yourself is necessary to get you to the yellow pad or computer.

Whatever they are, you will want to know your own best and most effective natural starting patterns and routines. To be sure, you will need to adjust them to the spouse who just has to have you along dancing on Saturday night when you'd really rather write, or the chair of the Social Action Committee who insists that you join the others at the soup kitchen Friday at noon regardless of your readiness to compose and the two weddings you have on Saturday. In spite of all forces to the contrary, you'll want to know what works best for you and do all within your power to conform to that scenario.

At this point, you are in possession of an idea and have carved out the time and achieved the state of mind and spirit to begin the work. Now the theme must be whittled down or worked up to sermon size, a form selected, and the emotional tone determined.

Again, personal styles differ. You may be one who spreads notes, books, quotations, scraps of paper, and Web site addresses all over the bed, along with the order of service, the hymn book, and other information about the liturgy of the day. You make a list of elements you want to remember to include; the specific, bounded theme emerges along with a form; you put the points on the list in sequence; and off you go to your word processor.

Or maybe you're in your study at church or in the sanctuary, and you get to thinking out loud—literally standing in the pulpit or pacing around the office—and you try different approaches and moods, recalling a story you might use here and a quotation there, acknowledging dangerous tangents as they occur and mentally eliminating them as you jot down your ideas.

Or you're more businesslike, sitting in your study, reference books and CD-ROMs neatly stacked in order of their probable use, outline and notes in hand, beginning with page 1, anticipating your feelings and the tone of the various parts of the sermon as you create the pages.

Perhaps you've been popping small sections of the sermon into your computer all week long, and now the job is to sift, select, order, and glue it together in an emotionally and spiritually cohesive presentation. Or you've been cogitating on the topic for so long that you just sit down and write. Or you write what you can, and then find that you have a little more research to do or that your present mood is all wrong and needs work. Some preachers regularly write a few pages to get warmed up and find themselves deleting their inevitable false start.

One extemporaneous preacher, Mark Belletini, begins by pondering the liturgy:

> On the Thursday or Friday before the sermon I sit down to compose the invocation and prayer, which are rarely thematic, but which help me to remember what the theme *is not*. By this time I've chosen the hymns/songs/chants/rounds for the service. All of these liturgical exercises help me, because I try to make the service *sufficient without any need for the sermon*. This gives me room to fail, and relaxes me some…On Saturday night, before I fall asleep, I tell my brain and heart that they *have* to come up with the basic framework by morning. Then I ask myself to *feel* where *I* am on the subject at that moment until I fall asleep.[9]

The point is, each of us has a personal style in ministry, and that style includes one's own way of sermon preparation. Know your style. Understand what works for you, what best honors your congregation, and enjoy the process.

7

PREPARING A SERMON

Much goes on in the minds and hearts of preachers as they compose the sermon: sequence, mood, message, enthusiasm, sentence construction, story, conviction, rhythm, form. That's all to the good; but throughout the preparation process, other factors, more general in nature and always in the background, need attention.

THE SERMON NEEDS TO BE RELIGIOUS—not pious or constrained, but related to the greater good. In the 1930s, Ernest Tittle said it plainly: "For a preacher to discuss any subject from a definitely religious viewpoint is…simple fairness; for the preacher is, after all, the responsible [spokesperson] of an institution that is definitely and distinctly committed to the religious conception of life."[1] Whatever the theme of the morning, be it gun control, Mother's Day, the glory of autumn, or loving one's neighbor as oneself, the point of the sermon and the experience of the sermon should be a spiritual one, broadly defined.

A colleague in Seattle points out, "Sermons that are lectures, or inconclusive examinations, or simply 'feel good' exercises miss entirely what a sermon is meant to be, i.e., a religious experience."[2] Perhaps hope is what you have to offer, or inspiration, transformation, renewed ethical commitment, or solid grounding in the natural world. The congregation is coming to *church* on Sunday, and the preacher needs to honor that.

A SERMON IS PART OF THE LARGER WORSHIP SERVICE. The church service may have one or more themes; hymns, anthems, and other music; special announcements, "joys and concerns," or congregational input for a pastoral prayer; readings; prayers or meditations; and special ceremonies such as baby namings, the honoring of a person or group, a sharing or communion, and so on. The service will have a tone, its own energy and mood. How will you link the various aspects of the service in your sermon? Will you refer to the anthem's words, the pep of the volunteer Sunday school teachers to be honored that day, or the disturbance at the peace talks you mentioned in the prayer? Will you foreshadow the choral benediction by using its words in your message? If the reading or hymn that immediately precedes the sermon is poignant or jubilant, perhaps you will build upon that atmosphere or begin with a knowing contrast. When you are writing the sermon, you are writing a piece of the whole.

THEY WON'T LISTEN TO EVERY WORD. Most ministers have received perplexing, if not startling, comments over the years after telling a story, reading a text, or making a comment in a sermon during the church service. The story was about, say, a chap who climbed Mount Everest, and the parishioner comes through the receiving line and says, "I never knew you climbed Mount Everest!" Or the preacher somehow mentions in the sermon that Edith Jones is recovering nicely from pneumonia and that she appreciated all the visits, and one church member hears that Edith has *died* of pneumonia, and she wants to bake macaroons for the funeral. Be as clear as you possibly can.

Even if you are clear, at any given time some parishioners are pondering your previous point, others are fretting over something that happened at breakfast, one or two may be daydreaming or, indeed, literally dreaming. Leave leeway in your sermon, reentry points, when you pause and begin a new story or thought, so that those whose minds have been wandering can "drop back into" your sermon.

INCLUDE THE CONGREGATION. Unreflective linguistic assumptions about gender, sexual orientation, race, education, socioeconomic background, body weight, theological viewpoint, age, physical ability—about who's included in our use of the word "we" and who's left out—can be serious barriers to communicating a fundamentally loving and inclusive message. Think about who's excluded by phrases such as "We who are so privileged...," "Let us dance the dance of life...," "Any of us might one day marry...," "We are God-fearing people...," "Our mothers deserve honoring...," "We remember Vietnam...," "In this church we feel welcomed and cared for...," "You may have read this poem by T. S. Eliot in college...," "We all want the same thing: a Scout troop for our children..." Cast a wide net.

WHEN PREPARING A SERMON, IMAGINE THE PEOPLE IN THE PEWS. As Fred Craddock put it, "You have located the Word of God at the ear of the listener rather than at the mouth of the preacher."[3] This is the time to love them, regardless of the interpersonal frustrations and ups and downs that may have transpired during the week just past. A sixteenth-century theologian said, "I like preaching that issues from love of neighbor rather than from indignation at them, even in the case of the Huguenots…"[4] Or in the words of the nineteenth-century preacher Charles Simeon, "Let your preaching come from the heart. Love should be the spring of all actions, and especially of a Minister's. If a man's [or woman's] heart be full of love, he [or she] will rarely offend."[5]

THE SERMON WILL BE ORAL. Although the job immediately ahead appears to be a writing task, Sunday morning's sermon will be preached! We must write for the ear, for the congregation who is listening (or half-listening) and has but one chance to assimilate our words.

Phillips Brooks once observed, "In general it is true that the sermon which is good to preach is poor to read and the sermon which is good to read is poor to preach."[6] Writing for oral presentation is a knack, and it takes some getting used to. The comedian Stephanie Brush confesses, "It's taken me about ten years to get to where I don't sit down and think about how I'm going to say something, I just say it on paper. But it takes a tremendously long time to get it to sound kind of conversational and off-hand."[7]

THINK TWICE ABOUT INCLUDING ETYMOLOGY, STATISTICS, OR DEFINITIONS. It is the rare parishioner who comes to church to hear that the origin of the word *worship* is "worth-ship," how many gallons of oil were spilled in the past decade, or the dictionary definition of the word *gender*. When tempted too many times in a row, remember the broader purpose of the sermon and your larger calling as a minister.

SERMON TIME IS LIMITED. The congregation has a tradition that includes how long the preacher preaches. Whether the standard is a five-minute homily or an hour-long sermon, preachers who ignore the local custom do so at their peril. No matter how brilliant and inspired the preaching, all is easily lost once the allotted time is past, the church school has been dismissed, and the roast in the oven is burned.

Centuries ago, Francis de Sales claimed, "It is always best that our preaching be short rather than long. In this matter I have been at fault up to the present time; I pray that I may correct this." And then he refers to "the feast of our Lady, when they rang the bell before I had finished."[8] Three hundred years later, a nineteenth-century writer notes that a colleague of his "in one of his works, goes on, 'Sixty-fifthly,' as if any person could remember the sixty-four preceding heads."[9] A sermon simply must not go on and on!

ASK YOURSELF QUESTIONS. You may want to have some standing generic questions in mind as you write. You'll have your own—along the lines of,

What is the message of this sermon summed up in one sentence? What emotions am I trying to evoke at this point in the sermon? Or, How does our particular religious tradition view this topic?

Henry Grady Davis, professor of practical theology at the Chicago Lutheran Theological Seminary from 1937 to 1967, suggested these five questions: "1. What are you talking about? 2. What are you saying about it? 3. What do you mean? 4. Is it true? Do you believe it? and 5. What difference does it make?"[10] Some find it helpful actually to post one or two standard questions on their computer.

IMAGINE YOURSELF PREACHING. Some tips: (1) Type "in your own voice"; anticipate how the line will sound when you deliver it, how much breath you'll need, how your face will look, and what your hands might be doing. (2) Even the most formal of preaching manuscripts can include sentence fragments, asides, and repetition. (3) Preachers can make excellent use of colloquialisms and informality.

Simplicity will be important. To return to Francis de Sales, "[The sermon] must be clear, simple, and natural, without display of Greek, Hebrew, novel, or fancy words. The structure must be natural, and without prefatory and ornamental phrases."[11]

DON'T PLAGIARIZE. Include complete citations of quoted material, ideas, stories, liturgical material, and the like in the manuscript (if you have one), but abbreviate those references in your oral presentation. The oral reference to the story you found in the June 1, 1998, edition of the *New Yorker* titled "American Chronicles: The Man in the Flying Lawn Chair," by George Plimpton, on pages 62–67, might become, for example, "Maybe you read the story in the *New Yorker* last summer where George Plimpton talks about a lawn chair—an ordinary lawn chair purchased at Sears."

Preaching is never a license to plagiarize.

USE APPROPRIATE GRAMMAR. In many congregations, some will be distracted by nonstandard grammar, pronunciation, and word usage. If you say "different than" instead of "different from" or use the word "revolve" when you mean "rotate," those parishioners are lost to you, at least that morning. You may decide to consult reference books as a regular habit or flatter the resident church grammarian by asking for regular feedback.

Composition Tips

While preaching is fundamentally an oral art, composition is always critical, whether written or created on the spot. If you feel you would benefit from review in this area, basic composition texts and courses are readily available. While every preacher decides sometimes to ignore proper common practice, several standard composition techniques are well worth noting.

Verbs should appear in the "active voice" unless the passive voice is absolutely necessary. The active voice forces you to create more efficient and interesting sentences, while the passive voice robs the action you describe of its immediacy and requires wordier sentences. "It was hoped by Jesus that love would abound," gains energy in the active voice: "Jesus hoped that love would abound." Try to use the passive voice only when the "subject" of your sentence is unknown. You won't always succeed, but your writing will benefit from the effort.

Minimize use of the verbs "to be" and "to have" in any of their tenses. "Is," "was," "has been," "had been," "will be," "will have been," "has," "had," and "will have" offer no precise information or action and result in flat, stagnant prose. Try to find an active verb. For example, "Habitual meditation will have the effect of making us better people." One might say instead, "Habitual meditation will make us better people." Again, simply paying attention to the problem helps.

Use empty intensifiers sparingly. "Truly," "incredibly," "very," "delightful," "wonderful," "terrific," and similar expressions of emotional agitation offer nothing for your listener to get excited about. In sermons, preachers often use the words "deeply moving," "spiritual," and "powerful" in much the same way. Find more precise language.

Vary your sentences in structure and length. You can write more interesting prose by varying the way in which you begin your sentences, for example, use a prepositional phrase ("In my moment of panic…"), a subordinate clause ("When the steeple tumbled down…"), or a participial phrase ("Preaching into the ineffectual microphone…"). Such variations will almost automatically result in varied sentence lengths as well.

Keep your focus on your subject, not on yourself. If you describe your subject and refrain as much as possible from describing your *reaction* to your subject, you allow your listeners to imagine themselves in the presence of what you are describing. Instead of "I was deeply moved when the waves crashed," you may want to say, "The waves crashed, thundering, foam flying through the air."

Be careful of your metaphors and common turns of phrase. When you use metaphors such as "beat a dead horse," "keep your eyes peeled," "bit his head off," "blood bath," and so forth, some in the congregation will imagine the picture all too vividly. When you say you were "literally blown away," you have told your church members that the wind actually picked you up and whisked you off. To say, "I'm an Aries," strongly implies that you believe in astrology; similarly, to say "It was meant to be" tells the congregation that you believe in a preordained universe.

Crafting sermons can be a creative, exciting, and satisfying process. Somehow, in spite of all the pitfalls and cautionary notes, even though we need to take so much into account, most preachers deliver coherent, loving, inspiring messages when Sunday morning rolls around.

8

FEELINGS THAT GET IN THE WAY

"We are apt to become men [and women] of moods, thinking we cannot work unless we feel like it," wrote Phillips Brooks. "There is just enough of the artistic element in what we have to do, to let us fall into the artist's ways and leave our brushes idle when the sky frowns or the head aches...And so the first business of the preacher is to conquer the tyranny of his [or her] moods, and to be always ready for his [or her] work. It can be done."[1]

Sermon preparation is under way, and your brain cells are percolating with matters related to composition. At the same time, you are bringing your spirit to the task as you write. That is to say, you have an emotional life to bring to bear on your work, and this is not necessarily good news.

Some of us—not all—feel anxious about the enterprise. As the author Paul Theroux wrote, "Writing is pretty crummy on the nerves."[2] Of course, one antidote for this anxiety is to actually sit down and write, but as Anne Lamott noted in her rather frenetic, yet recognizable, description of the challenge of getting started, it isn't always easy:

> What I do at this point, as the panic mounts and the jungle drums begin beating and I realize that the well has run dry and that my future is behind me...is to stop...I let my mind wander. After a moment I may notice that I'm trying to decide whether or not I am too old for orthodontia and whether right now would be a good time to make a few calls, and then I start to think about learning to use makeup and how maybe I could find some boyfriend who is not a total and complete fixer-upper and then my life would be totally great and I'd be happy all the time, and then I think about all the people I should have called back before I sat

down to work…Then I think about someone I'm really annoyed with, or some financial problem that is driving me crazy, and decide that I must resolve this before I get down to today's work. So I become a dog with a chew toy, worrying it for a while, wrestling it to the ground, flinging it over my shoulder, chasing it, licking it, chewing it, flinging it back over my shoulder. I stop just short of actually barking. But all of this only takes somewhere between one and two minutes, so I haven't actually wasted that much time. Still, it leaves me winded.[3]

The minister may fret less about orthodontia and more about whether or not the substitute organist will really appear; he or she may worry that nobody will show up to hear a wonderful sermon or, conversely, that a whole lot of people will show up and hear a terrible sermon; or that the service will run way too long or short. In any number of ways, in this mood, the minister anticipates a certain measure of humiliation.

THE SUDDEN, SURE KNOWLEDGE THAT
ONE'S BEST EFFORTS HAVE COME TO NAUGHT

Author Edmund White described a similar state of mind: "At first I'd feel lonely, afraid, itchy, very afraid to go on with my story, afraid it wasn't any good, afraid it was terrific and I was about to spoil it, afraid it was better than I understood and I would never know how to equal it again, afraid it was cold, repellent, inhuman, and my friends would see through me and realize I wasn't such a nice guy after all."[4] One minister summed it up by saying, "I wish I did not hate preaching so much…The degradation of being a…preacher is almost intolerable."[5]

For Better or For Worse®   by Lynn Johnston

© Lynn Johnston Productions Inc./Dist. by United Feature Syndicate, Inc.

Of course, some readers won't relate to such feelings at all. Perhaps for you the joy of sermon writing is easily accessed, enthusiasm is conveniently tapped, and pulpit confidence is natural. If you are such a person, count your blessings. But beware: The preacher who fantasizes not degradation but grandeur is equally imperiled in the job. Ministers who think they are somehow more than most, ever delightful and wise in the pulpit, may find that they are alone in that assessment. Philip of Macedon kept a man in his service to tell him every day before he held audience, "Philip, remember thou art mortal."[6] This is good advice.

But for those of us daunted by the task of preaching, it's easy to forget that sermon writing ought to be fun! Historian Mark Kishlansky described it this way:

> On those occasions when my fingers are flying, I am subject to a variety of physical sensations. My pulse elevates and occasionally my heart pounds…Every once in a while, when I am in the process of writing something I know is really good, I will get shivers and chills. I sometimes laugh out loud when quite unexpectedly I write something funny, and I frequently chuckle. At these times I am lost in a reverie so deep that I will literally jump if spoken to. It is one of the few experiences I have in which I lose all sense of time and I can discover that hours have passed since I first sat down…This is also the time that I have the most pure fun with my writing because—in case no one else ever tells you this—I also write to amuse myself. Alongside all of this high purpose and deep meaning, this terror and frustration, there is, every once in a while, pleasure.[7]

Regardless of emotional state, the truth is that the person preaching must not get in the way. It is the message that's important, not the preacher, and whatever anxieties, ego needs, or concerns the minister may have simply must be set aside. One student wrote, "When I have a message to share, then I can preach. When I have something to say that is worth saying, the words come…But without a spark, all the aids surrender against self-criticism and fear. The voice coaching and the readings and all the practice collapse like an elaborate scaffold into a tangle of broken beams."[8]

Focusing on the congregants also helps. Be in touch with how much you enjoy talking with your parishioners. Imagine yourself preaching to a particularly friendly fan of yours. Or picture yourself on the back porch with a couple of friends, far from pulpit and pew, telling them what you hope to say on Sunday. Remember a mood when you were eager to prepare your sermon on this subject for your congregation. Recall what fun, or how satisfying, it can be to preach a sermon that rings true to people you care about. Remember that with only a slight emotional adjustment, a case of nerves can be transformed into adrenalized feelings of excitement for the opportunity ahead. Go back to a time when you thought practicing ministry would be a nifty idea.

Whatever your state of mind, hard work is at hand. Perhaps Isaac Stiles overstated the point in 1755, yet his message endures: "Exercise and Labor of the Mind, and Sweat of the Brain, more than any other Kind of Labor, tends to Exhaust the radical Moisture, waste and drink up the animal Spirits, dry the Bones, consume the Flesh and Body, break the vital Cord, and deprive Men [and Women] of the Residue of their Years—to mention nothing else that adds Weight to their Burden."[9] The point has persisted in various forms over the centuries: John Gregory Dunne, for example, described writing as "manual labor of the mind: a job, like laying pipe."[10] Mark Kishlansky also finds writing exhausting, "something that is hard to explain to anyone who doesn't do it. 'Let me see if I have this right—you sat in a comfortable chair all morning, staring at a screen and occasionally tapping a keyboard, and now you're *too tired* to do the shopping?'"[11]

Good preaching does not come easily to most. True, it is said that Henry Ward Beecher, the foremost American preacher of the mid-nineteenth century, would not begin to prepare his sermons until Sunday morning. This fact caused the Presbyterian minister Steve Brown to observe in a recent interview, "You get a guy like Beecher who says that's how he preaches, but you have to remember that they don't come along but once in a generation. We're in dangerous territory when we look to impossible models as preachers…You gotta work. You gotta put your fanny in the chair and work your tail off."[12] Martin Luther made the same point when he said, "Out of forty-five years of experience, I can testify that the

"So that's how he's able to crank the stuff out."

problems and perspectives on preaching will change over the years, but that it never gets easy."[13]

Writer Annie Dillard describes the assignment:

> Every morning you climb several flights of stairs, enter your study, open the French doors, and slide your desk and chair out into the middle of the air. The desk and chair float thirty feet from the ground, between the crowns of maple trees. The furniture is in place; you go back for your thermos of coffee. Then, wincing, you step out again through the French doors and sit down on the chair and look over the desktop. You can see clear to the river from here in winter. You pour yourself a cup of coffee.
>
> Birds fly under your chair. In spring, when the leaves open in the maples' crowns, your view stops in the treetops just beyond the desk; yellow warblers hiss and whisper on the high twigs, and catch flies. Get to work. Your work is to keep cranking the flywheel that turns the gears that spin the belt in the engine of belief, that keeps you and your desk in midair.[14]

The prospect of imminent hard work can trigger another negative emotion for some, the feeling that may appear when it's Friday of a busy week, not a word of the sermon is in place yet, and one too many store clerks enthusiastically insists that you "Have a nice weekend," or when you get that once-in-a-lifetime weekend invitation that you have to turn down, or when the car radio makes too much of the fact that it's Friday afternoon and time to party, or when friends or family just don't understand that you actually work weekends. In order to prepare well for preaching, you have to exercise a little emotional fortitude. Sure, sermonizing is hard work, and perhaps a minister's schedule doesn't really suit you. But writer's block is not an option in the face of Sunday morning, and bitterness is poison to all ministerial arts.

In the words of Anne Lamott:

> You simply keep putting down one damn word after the other, as you hear them, as they come to you. You can either set brick as a laborer or as an artist. You can make the work a chore, or you can have a good time. You can do it the way you used to clear the dinner dishes when you were thirteen, or you can do it as a Japanese person would perform a tea ceremony, with a level of concentration and care in which you can lose yourself, and so in which you can find yourself.
>
> The best thing about being an artist, instead of a madman or someone who writes letters to the editor, is that you get to engage in satisfying work.[15]

The point is, preaching is a delightful privilege. Really!

> Therefore, count it not merely a perfectly legitimate pleasure, count it an essential element of your power, if you can feel a simple delight in what you have to do as a minister, in the fervor of writing, in the glow of speaking, in standing before men [and women] and moving them, in contact with the young. The more thoroughly you enjoy it, the better you will do it all.[16]

Tend yourself enough to feel the privilege. Do whatever it takes: daily meditation, therapy, collegial support, spiritual direction, solitary walks, workouts, treats. Some measure of spiritual and emotional well-being is a prerequisite for good preaching, and we owe our congregations and our callings that balance and zest.

How lucky we are to be able to read, ponder, and love enough to preach to our church members about important matters of the heart, soul, and mind. Somehow we have found a profession that lets us focus on the fundamentals of life and, with luck, to improve it a little in conjunction with our parishioners. This is good news!

SHAPING A SERMON

Form, the philosopher says, gives being and soul to a thing.
Say marvelous things, but do not say them well, and they
    are nothing.
Say only a little but say it well, and it is very much.

Francis de Sales[1]

A true story:

A family of four adults went to a folk music concert. Upon leaving, all agreed it had been a wonderful performance. One asked the others which songs they liked best.

The first person said it was the song about the woman whose lover went to sea and did not return. She remembered a story.

The second person said he did not recall that song, but there was one he especially liked, and he sang it without the words. He remembered a tune.

The third person could not bring either of those songs quickly to mind, but she fondly cited words that had touched her. She remembered a poetic passage.

So the three of them asked the questioner, which one had he enjoyed the most? Oh, he said easily, the one in which the first line of every verse developed a theme with a repeated phrasing, until the fourth verse, when the singer offered a startling variation, one he returned to in a clever way at the song's conclusion. He remembered a form. The other three stared at him as if he were daft.

Many people do not pay attention to form, but there are few human enterprises that are not embodied or expressed in a form of some kind. Even if they do not notice, most people respond to any creation in part because of the effectiveness of its form. This applies to poetry, bathtubs, short story plots, advertisements, floral arrangements, museum space, car design, paragraphs, skyscrapers, fairy tales, pirouettes, and gardens. It applies to sermons, too.

Students often want to know what the sermon forms are. They want to know if sermons are supposed to have three points, which has long been a popular ideal. They want to know what the outline should look like. They want to know the way to construct a sermon.

The fact is, thankfully, there is no prescribed sermon form, nor a list of required templates, nor ten standard variations. It is hard enough to define what a sermon form is, much less create a list of suggested forms appropriate for all topics, moods, and circumstances.

True, a form may be a three-point outline, but it may also derive from a flowing river or a rabbit warren. In this chapter, we can only tell you that form is crucial, and cite some attempts that homileticians have made to identify some sermon forms. But we confess, readers will not be satisfied if they seek a chart of "what form to use when," or even a single, clear definition of what a sermon form is.

People who preach or who write about preaching conceive of form in several different ways. Some think of how a sermon tries to achieve one aim or another—to explicate a text, for example, or to build up the congregation's sense of community. Without invoking the word "form," our Section 2 will engage such considerations.

Others use the word to describe how a sermon works internally, how it begins, builds, pauses, re-gathers, and concludes (or doesn't). Some preachers can outline, chart, or symbolize the emotional level they seek or expect to achieve in a sermon, or the development of the sermon's ideas. The result is what they consider the sermon's form.

For others, form consists of a particular pattern or mold. Fred Craddock suggests such forms have been part of the preaching tradition in Christianity from the start, and cites many of them in Christian scripture: the farewell speech, the conversation, "formerly but now," the journey, courtroom scenes, the master and the servant, the employer who went on a journey of uncertain length, the split story, and the refrain.[2]

However you define it, form is important for at least two important reasons. First, forms have an implicit power. As Craddock writes, form not only "gains and holds interest, [it] shapes the listener's experience of the material,"[3] creating expectations that preachers can frustrate or put to good use.

For example, a preacher's tone of voice, facial expressions, body language, choice of readings or prayers, and the way the sermon begins might promise the listener a gentle, measured consideration of some painful part of the human condition such as loneliness. If, instead, the chosen form involves mounting passion, culminating in a call to support a social cause (presumably one that addresses loneliness somehow), that can still be effective, but only if the preacher anticipates the effect and works on the transitions.

Or take an opposite example, where the preacher seems to be working in a form that will result in a denunciation of social injustice and a call to action. If the preacher has no such aim in mind, he or she is in trouble. Ignoring the power of form to shape expectations can leave congregants frustrated or confused.

Second, cultivating a variety of sermon forms can help preachers free themselves from habitual patterns of address that become boring over time. It is hard to overestimate the importance of changes of pace. Good preachers will feel it in their bones when they have been using one sermon form time after time, and know that it is time for a change. Maybe it is time for more structure, message, and demand; or maybe it is time for a looser, more casual form—the important thing is to avoid monotony.

Over-reliance on any one form can be stultifying for the congregation, and also prevent the preacher from discovering the form most appropriate to a particular subject. And it can convey a truncated version of the wide range of concerns that religion is about. As Craddock wisely points out, "few preachers are aware how influential sermon form is on the quality of the parishioners' faith."[4]

Among his examples, Craddock notes that "Sermons which invariably place before the congregation the 'either/or' format as the way to see the issues before them contribute to oversimplification, inflexibility, and the notion that faith is always an urgent decision. In contrast, 'both/and' sermons tend to broaden horizons and sympathies but never confront the listener with a crisp decision. Form is so extremely important."[5]

Form is so important, theological school president Rebecca Parker says that it is the implicit message of any sermon. Parker contends that the form holds meaning, and if the structure is strong enough, it can hold most of a sermon's message.[6]

The importance of form is obvious to some preachers. They deal in form instinctively, and assume from their earliest days in the pulpit that their most important task in designing a Sunday morning is to find the form the sermon will take, and the form of the surrounding service, forms that will make the morning work best for the congregation they will address.

Having chosen their topic, having done the reading and conversing, having pondered long and hard, having decided what they think and feel about the topic, for them the next and critical question is obvious: What is the form of the sermon this Sunday? Will it be a declaration, a celebration, a pondering, a consoling, or something else altogether? Will it start soft and conversational, or grab the congregation hard from the beginning? Will it build toward some emotional high, or aim for a more quietly thoughtful resolution?

With such choices made, other decisions may fall into place. Perhaps the preacher will feel the need to provide some actual information after eight minutes; or two stories, one at the beginning and one near, but not at, the end; or lots of humor, or none. Any choice has implications for the whole structure.

Some preachers of this sort will work out the structure in detail before writing anything other than notes or an outline, if that. Others will begin with a general sense of the sermon's form, and let it develop and become more clear and complete as they work toward the final version of the sermon. They will trust their intuition to notice that for their chosen form to work well, the sermon will need certain things at certain points, like a gentle moment or an energetic one, or more or less attention to reason or emotion.

For many, however, the whole question of form is just bewildering. They have a topic and some things they want to say about it as time allows. Period. Still, even this is a form, one identified over a half century ago by Halford Luccock as the "Roman candle" sermon, "which consists of a succession of statements or observations which follow without any particular design except that they are all related to the subject. A Roman candle throws out sparks for a few seconds, then discharges a ball, then more sparks and another ball. So a sermon of this general form may consist of an affirmation or a point or suggestion, followed by a discussion of that, as the sparks come after the ball in a Roman candle, and then another point, and so on."[7]

Luccock thinks that "this sort of 'planless' treatment,"[8] like other forms he cites, can be effective, and he cites examples, such as a chapel talk by Dr. J. Edgar Park on "How to Hit the Nail on the Thumb." "The outline was a succession of directions for doing things in a manner sure to miss their value entirely."[9]

We even suggest that on rare occasions, a preacher could offer a sermon of generally unrelated observations, snippets, and mini-sermons. We call this the note board form. Preachers use it on occasion in sermons with titles like "Ideas That Never Quite Made It to Sermons" or "A Variety of Things I Meant to Say by Now." One may be worth doing once in a while for the sake of breaking patterns, like the pattern that demands that every idea must grow to a certain length to be worth voicing in church, or that every sermon be unified and polished.

But most topics profit from more structured, coherent forms, and most congregations appreciate their use. Over the years, many writers on preaching have set themselves the task of finding names for such forms. Many of the older lists may seem dated or staid, and some newer lists may seem no more helpful at first. But the point is to become more inventive and aware and free. If any ideas, of any vintage, work for you as insight, inspiration, and prod, keep them in mind and look for ways to use them.

Among the more traditional lists are those that sound like W. E. Sangster's from 1951: exposition, argument, faceting, categorizing, and analogy.[10] In 1958 Henry Grady Davis offered two sets of forms, those that are functional, specifically proclamation, teaching, and therapy; and those that are organic, of which he identified five: a thesis supported, a subject discussed, a message illuminated, a question propounded, and a story told.[11] Many preachers still find such traditional break-downs useful.

But while such lists never quite go out of style, they are limited when it comes to describing the more exciting ways that sermons can behave. Even traditional theorists of form at times employ metaphors and analogies to characterize the more elusive and suggestive ends of preaching. John Killinger speaks of the sermon as being rather like architecture, a play, or a journey,[12] and Davis does a lot with the image of the sermon as a tree, as in his poem, "Design for a Sermon":

A sermon should be like a tree.
It should be a living organism:
With one sturdy thought like a single stem
With natural limbs reaching up into the light.
It should have deep roots:
As much unseen as above the surface
Roots spreading as widely as its branches spread
Roots deep underground
In the soil of life's struggle
In the soil of the eternal Word.
It should show nothing but its own unfolding parts:
Branches that thrust out by the force of its inner life
Sentences like leaves native to this very spray...
Illustrations like blossoms opening from inside these very twigs
Not brightly colored kites
Pulled from the wind of somebody else's thought
Entangled in these branches.

It should bear flower and fruit at the same time like the orange:
Having something for food
    For immediate nourishment
Having something for delight
    For present beauty and fragrance
    For the joy of hope
    For the harvest of a distant day.
To be all this it must grow in a warm climate:
    In loam enriched by death
    In love like the all-seeing and all-cherishing sun
    In trust like the sleep-sheltering night
    In pity like the rain.[13]

That kind of approach is carried on by writers like Andrew Watterson Blackwood, who compares sermons not only to a tree, architecture, music, and drama, but to a building, to weaving, to a river in its movement, or an oriental rug in its complex symmetry.[14]

A contemporary minister, Roy Phillips, offers forms of a sort in his eight implicit models of preaching, which picture the minister in such different roles as a professor lecturing to a class; a Bible scholar in a theological school exegeting a text; a speaker reviewing a book, play, or film; a television news analyst commenting on a current development in world events; a social critic decrying a deplorable wrong; an action organizer trying to mobilize a program of social reform; a salesperson encouraging a purchase; or a physician examining a patient, describing the symptoms and causes of a disease, and prescribing a treatment for a cure.[15]

There are other professions one might name as analogous to preaching, like those of nurse, entertainer, scout, boxer, sleuth, or magician. One might even have in mind such unlikely images as a pile driver—not often, but maybe when a message needs to be driven home—or a homemaker. At one workshop, a minister said his most guiding and helpful image in writing a sermon was that of cleaning every corner of the topic's "room."

One of the best, and most eclectic, lists of sermon forms comes from Craddock:

What is it? What is it worth? How does one get it?
Explore, explain, apply
The problem, the solution
What it is not, what it is
Either/or
Both/and
Promise/fulfillment

Ambiguity, clarity
Major premise, minor premise, conclusion
Not this, nor this, nor this, nor this, but this
The flashback (present to past to present)
From the lesser, to the greater[16]

Few writers on form have done much better, however, than Luccock back in 1944. His list catches the spirit of what is most interesting about this subject: What do sermons feel like? How do they work? Are there images that help us understand these implicit forms so we might better use their potential power?

Luccock names ten forms, or as he called them, types of outlines. They include several of the traditional bunch, like classification, jewel (i.e., faceting), and analogy sermons. Of the analogy sermon, "talking about one thing in terms of another,"[17] Luccock speaks with some ambivalence, however. He notes that Jesus used it often (e.g., "I am the vine") and others used it well. But he also cites "the trap for the lazy preacher" in this form. "Superficially, it is so easy to do that, unless it is handled with skill and costly effort, it readily becomes commonplace and tiresome, a succession of juvenile and wooden didacticisms—'life is like this' or 'life is like that'—till most of the congregation set out on their own mental travels."[18]

Luccock goes on to make some useful additions, like the Roman candle sermon already mentioned, and the ladder sermon, which "takes one from point to point like the rungs of a ladder. It is a type well adapted to argument, persuasion, and the appeal to reason."[19] Luccock's skyrocket sermon "begins on the ground, in life; it travels up to a spiritual truth which has meaning for that situation on earth; … and then, like the skyrocket, [it will] break into separate observations, pointing out reliances or suggesting action."[20] Other forms include the "twin sermon"—that is, not this, but this, especially regarding two contrasting ways of understanding something (although one of us, a parent of twins, dislikes the good twin/bad twin connotations); the rebuttal sermon, to be saved for those occasions when there is need for "a spirited and pertinent refutation of a lie";[21] and the surprise package, another "to be used sparingly," in which the sermon, "after it gets started and the ending, or at least the general direction, seems predictable, makes a surprise turning into unexpected territory."[22]

This leaves only the chase sermon on Luccock's list, but it is a particularly good one, "getting an audience to explore a problem and pursue a solution rather than merely announcing the result to them… The form of the 'chase sermon,' reduced to its baldest terms, is something like the familiar parlor game:

"Is it this?"

"No"

"Is it this?"

"No."

"Is it this other thing?"

"Yes."[23]

The "chase" reappears decades later on Craddock's list ("Not this, nor this, nor this, nor this, but this") and is still a lively, engaging form.

Like Luccock's impressionistic examples, the list we use in preaching classes is based on images like that of a skyrocket or a jewel that help convey a sense of how a sermon can develop or unfold.

We begin with images drawn from manufacturing trades and crafts, like *carpentry* or *masonry*, where one board is nailed to another, or one brick placed skillfully upon another, to build a wall or a roof or a floor. Take *weaving*, for example. Andrew Watterson Blackwood turned to this image a decade ago. "Practically, the young preacher can learn much by watching a grandparent at the spinning-wheel and later at the loom. If...an artist, the grandparent can spin and dye the threads, then...can weave the cloth out of which to fashion the garment to adorn a person. So the preacher takes from a text and the surrounding verses the strands of truth out of which to spin the warp of a pattern. These stiff threads run throughout the cloth, thus imparting strength. More fragile threads will supply the woof."[24]

Making a *patchwork quilt* can also provide a useful analogy. Among the most charming quilts are those made up of the contributions of many people. As Scott Alexander observed in *The Relational Pulpit*, preachers do well when they put together sermons that way, receiving input from their congregations, both by hearing their concerns and insights in general and by specifically soliciting them about some subject.[25]

There are other ways of envisioning how a variety of points is sometimes presented—*displaying a collection*, for instance, which happens to be the form of this chapter. Still another kind of collective sermon resembles *burrowing through tunnels*, as would a mole. (The namer of this form, one of the authors, had just read *The Wind in the Willows*.) It is like displaying a collection, only harder work. You have to struggle down each tunnel, and some end up as dead ends, while others turn back on themselves. In the end you may find yourself back where you started, having progressed hardly at all, but having gained a sense of the surrounding terrain.

Sometimes sermons resemble a *drama* in three acts, involving a kind of set-up and pay-off. The pay-off is the climactic scene in Act 3, but it only works because it pulls together all the elements that the earlier acts have introduced. Likewise, entire services can work from the beginning to introduce not only a subject and a tone but the ideas and the very phrases that the skilled and careful preacher begins to reclaim at the climax of the sermon and in the denouement that follows, concluding with the benediction or closing words that send the congregants back into the world, inspired and refreshed.

The set-up, by the way, includes what one might call "booby-traps." (Remember Luccock's "surprise-package" sermon.) These are often dangerous, leaving a congregation resentful and hurt. Used with care and in appropriate circumstances, however, they can have a stunning effect.

> A biology professor delivered about the most powerful sermon I ever heard, at chapel at the college I attended. For at least ten minutes he talked about some protein found in muscle tissue. Such dry information was not infrequently the subject of our daily chapel talks.
>
> So there we were, mildly interested at best and just barely paying attention, when the biology professor mentioned how hard-earned were the discoveries he was describing. The problem is that muscle tissue breaks down quickly, and one must therefore have many pounds of it to derive an adequate amount of the protein to be studied. Luckily for science, though (the professor rolled right along), most of this work took place in Germany in the early '40s.
>
> It is hard to imagine how he created the moment so that it had the effect it did. Partly it was his delivery, as though he were mentioning a rather humorous irony. Partly it was that most of the audience was half-listening at best. But the thing was, the audience laughed—not uproariously, but we laughed.
>
> He stood silently until the laughter quickly turned to horror, and then he finished his sentence, noting that the Nazi death camps provided all the muscle tissue a scientist could hope for. He had caught us, booby-trapped us, and during the time that remained no one, no one, was not glued to his message, which was that all human activity depends upon larger social realities, and is subject to the standards of basic human decency.
>
> Some of the listeners were incensed, of course. That is the price you pay. But many heard that message more clearly than any other in their four years of college.[26]

Finally, there is the adventure story, often expressed in the image of a perilous voyage, like Homer's account of Odysseus' journey home from Troy. Some have said that this is the fundamental human myth: a person ventures out in the face of possible dangers, has adventures, survives them, reaches a destination—often home—and in the process, grows.

Sermons that work this way conduct the congregation out toward life's awful and frightening realities, those things from which we try to shield ourselves most of the time, but that we must in some place, at some time, confront: the realities of death, loss, contingency, meaninglessness, despair, and failure. As we picture the form, the captain must first reassure the passengers and crew that they are safe in his or her care. Throughout the service, by means of humor, tenderness, thoughtfulness and concern, we convey a love for our congregants and an impression of self-confidence that will encourage them to climb aboard intellectually and emotionally, and then to let themselves be guided out into those perilous waters, close by the eddies and shoals, and safely past.

That is how powerful a sermon form can be. Selecting one deserves careful, creative attention. As Anthony Burgess once said, "You can't create unless you're willing to subordinate the creative impulse to the constriction of a form."

Which forms will work best for you is for you to work at and discover for yourself. There are many ways of thinking about form, and many images and categories to describe the possibilities. Some will work better for particular preachers than for others, some will work better for certain subjects than for others. To think about sermons in terms of forms should not be confining and prescriptive. The goal is, rather, to increase your options, your flexibility, and your pleasure in the task.

What is important is that you think of the sermon as a unified or at least a consistent whole, a complete and living organism, suited to achieving specific aims or effects with a particular congregation. Thus, when you sit down to write a sermon, you should choose a form based on whatever analogy or image or function you think will give it a unified structure appropriate to your goals and the occasion. And don't agonize too long over your initial choice. Use your imagination. Innovate. The form your sermon eventually takes may not look like what you started with. But in general, it helps to start with some form in mind. And it matters a lot that by the end, your sermon has a form that is coherent, dynamic, and engaging to you and the congregation alike.

10

MORE THAN A MESSAGE:

The Use of Story, Examples, and Evocative Illustrations

"When the minister told that story about the waiter in the restaurant, it reminded me so much of my uncle who just died. I cried my eyes out. It was a wonderful sermon."

"Remember that poem she used about the stars? That really got me thinking about infinity."

"I figured if that little homeless boy could do it, I can do it. Starting now."

"You know that story about how the different children in the Sunday school class imagined God? It raised so many questions for me! I loved it."

"Couldn't you just smell the ocean and taste those fried clams? Maybe there really is a heaven on earth!"

The question is an old one: Should preachers use examples or should they stick more closely to the matter at hand? The pendulum swings back and forth, depending in part on what the religious leader thinks the sermon is for. For Jews prior to the destruction of the temple in 70 C.E., for example, preaching and teaching were one and the same. Missionary homilies, propaganda addresses, legal halakic discourses, and extremely loose haggadic instructive sermons were all characteristic.[1]

Later, medieval Christian friars were inclined to accept entertainment as part of their charge in preaching, and so they unselfconsciously "deliver'd in expressions of peculiar levity, and intermix'd with frequent stories unsuitable to the solemnity of the place and occasion,"[2] that is to say, they told of "all the marvels of creation,...in earth and sea and firmament, mighty 'gestes' of the Romans, wondrous miracles of the saints and martyrs."[3] They "played to the gallery."[4]

In seventeenth- and eighteenth-century New England, sermons were a medium of communication, a channel of information, combining religious, educational, and journalistic functions. Sermons extended to all facets of life—social and political, as well as religious.[5]

American preachers of the early twentieth century often understood the function of preaching just as broadly. "Who do you think this preacher is?" asked John Haynes Holmes.

> A reporter, merely, who gives us facts in serene and pleasant voice? Not if he remembers and responds to the call of his ordination. The true preachers are advocates, who defend great causes of human need; they are artists, who depict with glowing colors the beauty of holiness; they are minstrels, who sing songs of the soul's melody; they are seers, who reveal reality seen only "in the mind's eye"; they are messengers, who come from afar to bring the good news of the kingdom. These are the parts that they must play— and, if they are to play them effectively, they must command the language, the color, the music, the inspiration of them all.[6]

Henry H. Mitchell, author of the 1970 book *Black Preaching*,[7] says that good preaching functions as communication that addresses the whole person. Gayle White elaborates on the point: "That's done by art rather than by argument. Stories, metaphors, character sketches, stream-of-consciousness, recitation of familiar psalms and hymns can all create a kind of vicarious experience for the worshiper."[8]

Finally, if the purpose of preaching is, as Lucy Atkinson Rose suggests in the 1990s, "first and foremost an encounter," then poetic language becomes important. Citing Thomas H. Keir, she supports the use of images, analogies, parables, metaphors, and paradigms, distinguishing between abstract language and poetic language, "the language of the human heart, of the lover and the sage."[9] Poetic language, she believes, is capable "of connecting human existence with a reality that lies just beyond language, a Word or voice that seeks to come to expression in language."[10]

During the course of history, then, sermon illustrations have often been promoted. But not always.

In Christian antiquity, John Chrysostom adopted a sermon style that included "an overflow of words, of images, of ornamental figures, which called forth the enthusiastic but unwelcome applause of his hearers, who flocked to the church for aesthetical amusement more than for edification."[11] He was roundly criticized.

Robert South inveighed in 1660 against "Quibbles and Trifles,"[12] and the Royal Society embraced "a constant Resolution, to reject all amplifications, digressions, and swelling of style: to return back to the primitive purity, and shortness..."[13] Shortly thereafter, the Rev. John Tillotson secured the universal triumph of the edifying style of plain, judiciously modulated prose.[14]

Charles Smyth, writing in 1940, cautioned that the preacher "would be ill-advised to emulate the medieval predecessor in entertaining the congregation with stories of Brer Rabbit and Brer Fox and Cinderella, however aptly moralised." He also notes that more than one curate in recent years had moralized on the nursery rhyme "Pussy-cat, Pussy-cat, where have you been," though "one would have been quite sufficient."[15]

Along the same lines, Francis de Sales, in the sixteenth century, warned against "over-use of allegory, unseemly analogies, and references to pagan fables." He was particularly upset at "the practice of giving elaborate imaginary descriptions of a Scriptural scene, or worse still of putting fanciful conversations into the mouths of scriptural characters and assigning the speaker's own paltry ideas to their minds."[16]

If one believes, as Phillips Brooks did, that a sermon exists for the purpose of persuading and moving souls, then all artistic diversion must be avoided. "Art knows nothing of the tumultuous eagerness of earnest purpose...And yet we find a constant tendency in the history of preaching to treat the sermon as a work of art."[17]

Karl Barth agreed. Although he believed that "God may speak to us through Russian communism, through a flute concerto, through a blossoming shrub or through a dead dog," he also felt, according to Bernhard Lang, "that when people go to church, they must leave behind the vague sentiments of God's presence inspired by art, nature, history, or work." The divine word can be recognized "only in a clean, aseptic laboratory situation in which the pure word of scripture is read and the uncontaminated message of Christ proclaimed."[18]

Today we are living and preaching during a period where examples are much in favor, though the line is drawn, it seems, at using them for pure entertainment or in bad taste. Preachers no longer conceive of illustrative material as "exempla," strictly speaking, aids for instruction in doctrine or supporting moral arguments;[19] rather, our examples clarify the quandary at hand, illuminate the options, and evoke the listener's thoughts, feelings, and spiritual development. Such additions help connect the sermon content to the listeners and their lives, the theology to the people, the theoretical to the immediate.

One author, John Dufresne, reminds us that as people, we "want to know about life, about what it's like to be a human being. About how that feels. It's a recognition that people are more important than ideas (including ideas of the Divine) and that all history is local. It is an acknowledgment that we come to understand the world one three-decker at a time."[20]

Preachers supply or inspire detail, color, imagery, and feeling. With the use of story, poetry, quotation, anecdote, example, and references to near-common experience or popular culture—even music within the sermon, art on the cover of the bulletin, props such as sculpture and posters, or just about anything else—we do our best to add life to the sermon. We bring the raw material of the sermon as close to home as possible, without dictating the congregation's reactions or providing the "correct" interpretations. Our listeners take it from there.

And when they go home and report on the sermon, they will say that for them, "the story was so funny" or "so real" or "the poem made me feel so calm." "I felt transformed by the line of the song she used," or "it raised so many questions," or "he told it just for me." That vignette was "so typical," or "such a relief in the midst of a boring sermon," or "so motivating."

Tips When Using Stories and Examples

Humor

- Humor is complicated. Note that each joke used in the monologue on *The Tonight Show* on television requires the work of people in six highly specialized professional disciplines: *The Tonight Show* employs twelve "clippers" who track newspapers for material; a "comedy engineer" who decides what shape the joke should take; a "comedy stylist" who fashions the raw joke; the "polish man" (usually a woman), the joke's editor; the "timing coach"; and, finally, the "talent," that is to say, you![21]

- Don't hesitate to script everything if that method works best for you—ad-libs, rejoinders, recoveries—all of it. Comedy can be "as formal and structured as anything found in traditional kabuki," according to the cartoonist Garry Trudeau. "The stakes are too high for it to be otherwise."[22]

- Don't make fun of people, except, perhaps, yourself. When the city of London wanted to give George Bernard Shaw its Order of Merit, he said, "I would have accepted it. I would have recognized the opportunity for a world-class joke, but would never allow myself to be funny at the cost of making somebody else feel like something the cat drug in. Let that be my epitaph."[23]

- Some people won't understand the humor. Make room for them.

- Gratuitous jokes—jokes for their own sake—don't work. Further, actually "telling a joke" is very risky—if it doesn't succeed, everyone is embarrassed.

- Don't get too funny—know the limits of your congregation.

- Some people simply don't like humor in church, though most people do.

- If the crowd is laughing, don't move on until most of them stop.

Irony
- Some listeners will take whatever you say at face value. If you say, with appropriately ironic voice tone and facial expression, "The church, of course, has unlimited funds," a few people will believe that somehow the congregation has come into millions of dollars.

Pop Culture
- Many people read the latest best-sellers, see current movies, listen to public radio or the popular talk shows, know what music is being listened to, and watch TV. But some don't. Try to include everyone.

- If you find yourself describing a long movie plot, talking about characters on television, and so on, you might consider finding an illustration that is more immediately recognizable.

Imagery
- Make use of all the senses without implying that everyone can hear, see, smell, and so on.

- Leave room for your listeners' imaginations. As Fred Craddock said, use "images which awaken images."[24]

Poetry
- Poetry is much more available to a listener when it is read well. If reading poetry aloud is not your strength, ask someone else to deliver the passage when it occurs in the sermon.

- The parishioner only has one chance to "catch" the poem during an oral presentation. Choose accessible poems that aren't overly complex.

- Don't be afraid to repeat the same passages of poetry during the sermon.

Using the Material of Others

- Feel free to add to your own material by borrowing good ideas (citing sources) wherever you can find them. As Alethea Hayter put it, "Any writer's stock of imagery is a mixed bag of wild game which he [or she] has shot for himself [or herself], and tame, even tinned fowls which are obtainable in shops."[25]

- You have to write your sermon yourself. In the time immediately following Augustine's preaching years, nobody expected the average preacher to deliver original sermons. Those who were good at sermonizing provided the "weaker brethren" with manuscripts.[26] In 1330, the Franciscan John of Werden offered advice to other preachers in his collection of sermons, *Dormi Secure (Sleep Soundly)*: "Sleep soundly, and don't worry about your sermon tomorrow: there are plenty to choose from in this book."[27] But times have changed.

- These days a minister can get into big trouble for plagiarism. However, off and on throughout history, the practice has persisted, even when it was understood to be unethical. When, in 1734, a Reverend Hemphill was caught plagiarizing, Benjamin Franklin remarked, "I rather approved his giving us good sermons composed by others, than bad ones of his own manufacture."[28] Unless Dr. Franklin, and only Dr. Franklin, is sitting in your pews, manufacture your own sermons.

Quotations

- People think they don't like too many quotations in a sermon, but if the quotations are woven well into the text, you may have a successful sermon nonetheless.

- You must credit the author, even though the reference may spoil the art and rhythm of your prose. Names are preferable to "a colleague once said." Surely the author would appreciate the credit—in fact, don't hesitate to send the writers you quote a postcard or e-mail letting them know and thanking them.

- Be clear about exactly when the quotation begins and ends. It is, of course, unethical to allow the vague impression that the quote must have long since ended and that these current paragraphs are your own. Either pause and change your position and voice tone at the end of the quotation or actually say, "end of quote."

- The church is not paying you to quote extended (more than, say, a double-spaced page) pieces written by somebody else.

Diversity

- Articulate the experiences of people different from yourself. Those in other economic categories, of different races or genders, people who are disenfranchised, or whose interests are different from your own will appreciate stories they can relate to.

- Puritan preachers were trained to address four different aspects of the human personality: "the will, the understanding, the imagination and the affections."[29] The point is well taken. Some listeners never understand poetry but respond well to metaphor, others love a gushy story or a clever analogy, some love to laugh. Some listeners appreciate an intellectually rigorous quotation, others want to hear a dream sequence.

- Each of us is bound by our culture, place in history, language, theology, learning style, and community. From time to time, acknowledge that fact.

Distractions

- Prose itself can be distracting. Geoffrey Stokes described the problem when he responded to the following passage:

  "It was a stainless-steel day, polished and sharp. The light was glazed, falling in hard tines through a rack of thin, high clouds." This, I'm afraid, is Fine Writing, and it stopped me. There I was, reading along quite happily, but these two sentences got in my way…Let's see, "stainless-steel" day; that's a kind of handled silver, dulled like luncheonette flatware—maybe an all-over gray day. Oops, nope, "polished and sharp," so it's more like the knife blade, a day so bright the glare waters your eyes. "The light was glazed," now what the *hell* does that mean?…[And] I'm a little disturbed that the knife has become a fork.[30]

- Don't work at it too hard. As Somerset Maugham wrote, "You would not believe a man was very intent on ploughing a furrow if he carried a hoop with him and jumped through it at every other step."[31]

- Sometimes an illustration or story is unusually powerful or moving on its own. Know that if and when you use such an example, in most people's minds when all is said and done, your illustration will have become the sermon.

Taste, Discretion, and Going Overboard

- If you use even slightly off-color language, somebody will be offended. Why take that risk?

- Standards of good taste for you, the preacher, are higher than for ordinary members of polite company, especially when in the pulpit. As Phillips Brooks put it when speaking of poor taste in humor in sermons, "It is a purely wanton fault. What is simply stupid everywhere else becomes terrible here."[32]

- Some images can be too vivid—a near drowning experience, the mess in the toilet, torture experiences in the concentration camp, the time you put your eyeball out. If you don't have reliable natural instincts about what's useable material and what isn't, for heaven's sake, ask someone who does.

- The example is only the example. Don't let it get too long; don't let it overpower the sermon.

Integration

- Make sure that the time and attention you give to your example during the rest of your sermon is proportional to the weight and impact of your example.

- The story should fit thematically into the sermon. Sometimes you've come across a story or quote that's just *so* good, you want to jam it into whatever sermon's at hand. Resist the temptation.

- Tend to your transitions.

The sermon's supporting material, the images, story lines, poetry, and humorous, all-too-true vignettes, give our sermons their humanity, their reality. They provide the link between ivory-tower theology on one hand, and religion as experienced by real people—by our congregations and by us—on the other.

In writing about Anton Chekhov, John Dufresne said,

And he knew the awful truth at the center of our existence, which is the truth that we are dying and we don't want to be, that everything we love will vanish…Yet we go on loving; we find comfort in community. We gather in kitchens, we pick up books, we administer the sacrament of fiction—our every story a sign of the human heart and a victory of hope over experience.[33]

11

"THE HOUR DRAWS NIGH":
Immediately before You Preach

You have a topic, a service prepared that leads up to the sermon, and on paper, on note cards, or at least in your mind, the sermon itself. The time of its delivery approaches. It will help at this point if you have also prepared yourself physically, spiritually, emotionally, and intellectually, so that you can feel truly present with the sermon and with the congregation. These are highly individual matters, but it is worth attending to your own best pattern.

For example, some who preach at morning services find that they are more ready for the pulpit if they go to bed early the night before, rise early, and go through a preparatory routine, perhaps including prayer, meditation, exercise, a final rehearsal, a favorite breakfast, or some combination of these activities and others. Other preachers find it works better for them to stay up late the night before, fussing over all the details, and the next morning get up, dress, and head straight for the pulpit (just not at the last moment, we hope, especially if one is a guest preacher, with caring lay leaders waiting nervously).

There is nearly an infinite number of styles, and we would not presume to name any one of them as ideal. But we would insist that such concerns are important, mundane as they may seem. If you find that you are repeatedly less than lively, engaged, and sharp when it comes time for the sermon, you may want to reconsider how you spend your time prior to preaching. As Dietrich Bonhoeffer optimistically wrote, "The hour of worship should be kept free from the rush and uneasiness that delayed preparation can cause. Sunday ought to be a day of joy for the pastor and not one of fatigue and heated exertion."[1]

For some preachers, final preparation will include techniques for overcoming their nervousness, anxiety, or fear. For instance, to address and reduce tension, Patty Ann T. Earle suggests,

> Just prior to the beginning of a service, set aside five minutes of time alone where no interruptions can occur. This time is important for "fine-tuning." The essential ingredient is intentional relaxation. Begin by assuming a position that is comfortable, and allow hands to rest in the lap and feet on the floor. Begin with the feet, then legs, then arms, then hands, trunk, neck, face, and finally, shoulders, intentionally tensing each set and consciously relaxing the muscles. Continue until total relaxation has been achieved.
>
> Allow breathing to become regular and obvious. Concentrate on the in and out flow of breath until it becomes natural. Then, with eyes closed, imagine a blank screen.
>
> Then place yourself on that screen, rehearsing mentally each step leading up to the beginning of the delivery. The essential imagining here, however, is visualization of a situation in which you are relaxed, competent and inspired.[2]

From her own theological outlook, Earle's next advice is to "offer a prayer of thanks for what God is about to do in this service and through the sermon. Then take three deep and rhythmic breaths, open the eyes, and sit still for about thirty seconds."[3]

If it is any comfort to the anxious, you are not alone. Fear of public speaking is among the most common of fears. Many actors, singers, and preachers never entirely master their nerves, and yet they have successful careers. An interviewer once asked Nora Dunn, a regular performer on the television show *Saturday Night Live*, if live television was really worth all the panic and anxiety it causes. Dunn replied, "Before the show goes on you don't think it's worth it, but once the show starts, and it's live, and the writing is good, it's worth it. Actually, the panic drives you, and it can be a wonderful thing, very exhilarating."[4]

Indeed, up to a certain, manageable degree, anxiety is a helpful way the body has of drawing forth reserves of energy and focus. "Some anxiety is natural, of course, and may even make the delivery more effective," notes Earle. "When the pressure becomes extreme, however, the effects may be so disconcerting as to interfere with viable delivery."[5] Preachers need to develop their strategies for coping with this paradox.

Mister Boffo

by Joe Martin

THEY SAY PUBLIC SPEAKING IS MOST PEOPLE'S NUMBER ONE FEAR ?... BUT THIS HAS TO BE RIGHT UP THERE !

For now, let us assume that you have learned the various patterns that best prepare your mind and soul, body and spirit, for you to preach—and that you have followed that pattern, despite all the distractions, large and small, that unpredictably arose. (Examples could fill a book: Your printer refused to work, your child was up all night, and your car wouldn't start in the morning. Then coming across the parking lot, a parishioner caught up with you to ask if you think she should divorce, while two committee chairs waited nearby for the chance "to touch base with you," one about the arrangement of tables for the church picnic and the other about the checks that the church has been bouncing. One of this book's authors once went into the pulpit having just been informed that her father had died.)

For better or worse (and even for very good preachers, some weeks just work out worse), the time of the service nears, and you, the preacher, arrive. Especially if it is not your usual venue, you will want to arrive in plenty of time to "case the place." There are a lot of technical details to notice. They may seem trivial, but they affect your chances of giving a successful sermon.

What things about the setting that morning might merit your appreciative comments, like the flowers, the weather, and any recent church events? Guest ministers may want to pay special attention to such details and add thanks for the congregation's welcome and their admiration for the choir or the beauty of the building.

Is the pulpit a good height for you? If not, you might adjust by adding an impromptu platform underfoot (phone books? lasagna pans?) if you are short; or if you are tall, by adding books on the pulpit to elevate the written material. If you wear bifocals, do they work at the distance you have available?

Is the pulpit of sufficient size to hold your papers (there are podiums so small that one cannot move pages across without causing notice, if at all) and of appropriate angle? If not, how will you deal with it? Is there a pulpit light? If not, can your written words still be seen? And for those hard of hearing in the congregation, is there a system that augments the delivery of sound? Is there a microphone? If so, is it on the pulpit or for your lapel? Do you have a lapel? Did the rental group on Wednesday evening change all the settings on the equipment? Just how well does sound carry in the space in which you're preaching?

In practice, such matters of setting are as important to the success of the preacher's efforts (and as seemingly trivial) as are the details of any other profession. No matter how brilliant the sermon may be that you have written, it may still fail if you cannot see the manuscript well or if the congregation cannot hear your words easily (and the congregation includes those listening on supplementary sound systems, such as parents in a room for infants and those who will listen to tapes of the service).

The preceding also is applicable for established preachers, appearing in their customary places. They still need to show up every Sunday in time to attend to the practical aspects of the service's potential success. Sometimes when they least expect it, someone has fiddled with the pulpit space.

So even if you are fairly sure of the pulpit's height, you will do well to check that the pulpit contains whatever you expect to have there, such as water, a Bible, a hymnal, the order of service, your watch, your readings, and any props. You will want to develop a strong mental (and maybe a written) list of such necessary elements. Include on the list the pages or notes of the sermon, lest you forget that upon arriving you set them down on the table in the front hall, where they still reside—unless some helpful soul has tidied up the front hall and thrown them out. (More than one preacher has arrived early and deposited the manuscript right on the pulpit, only to find as the service approached that someone had thoughtfully cleaned up the pulpit area, including all paper!) Even well-tended, those pages are worth giving time to before the service, to be sure that they are in order and that all of them are there. Many are the preachers who didn't notice when they grabbed their printed pages and headed for the pulpit that their printer's paper supplies had run out on page eight, of eleven, leaving them on their own for the rest.

While mentioning details, we might pause a moment to consider questions of personal appearance, even though most books on preaching do not even discuss them. However, in most church settings, they matter. Perhaps that should not be the case. But in the real world, many congregants listen more or less well, take you more or less seriously, depending on how you look.

In some cases, their attitudes are only ugly prejudice, devoid of merit. We are not going to concede a centimeter to bigotry in its various forms. Parishioners cannot be honored for listening less well or taking a speaker less seriously because of his or her sex, sexual orientation, gender expression, color, class, marital status, handicap, weight, or beauty.

But after all those factors are eliminated from the realm of legitimate concern (and we are all working for the day when they will be eliminated in fact), there remain matters of appearance that congregants perceive as within the control of the preacher, where aspects of personal presentation can seem to reflect either professional incompetence or, worse still, an indifference or even hostility to the feelings of the congregation.

These matters can be small: men (or women) who cannot keep their shirts tucked in, women (or men) who cannot keep their hair off their faces for long—some apparently minor infractions can cause more than a few listeners to become altogether distracted, even annoyed. Or the concern can be more general: styles of dress that consistently miss the mark by being way out of style; repeatedly unflattering or ill-fitting; oddly formal, casual, or unsuited to one's age or position; or too meticulously fashionable, raising questions about where the preacher's energy and caring are most deeply invested.

A pleasant appearance, one that gives evidence that the preacher cared enough about the occasion and the congregation to try to look appropriate, can invest a sermon with an extra measure of congregational confidence and respect. If you as a preacher receive hints that the way you present yourself may detract from your larger goals on Sunday morning, you might check in with trusted colleagues or laypeople for feedback.

And so before donning his tie-dyed T-shirt or the blouse that so flatters her cleavage, or the dangling earrings or the tie that always provokes compliments, the preacher may want to ponder a question like, How important is the sermon I'm about to give, and how much do I want to draw attention away from it and on to me? The fashion critic Richard Blackwell once commented on Barbara Walters, the television newscaster, "Her clothes are invisible, the smartest trick anyone has ever pulled on TV. You never remember what she wore, only what she's telling us."[6] Chances are, a preacher would prefer the same. "After all," in the words of Rebecca Young, violinist with the New York Philharmonic, who favors regimented dress at performances, "the audience comes to hear music without the distractions of a fashion show."[7]

Some preachers, too, appreciate the consistency provided by a robe or by conventional business clothes. Others feel more comfortable in somewhat more informal or varied dress. And, of course, expectations differ among congregations (within them, too). The preacher has to decide how far to honor, or to deviate from, those expectations, weighing the hope of the congregation's hearing the morning's message against an inclination to look odd, sloppy, or even offensive.

As the newspaper columnist Judith Martin, also known as "Miss Manners," wrote in response to a father whose grown-up son had chosen "to neither cut nor comb his hair for more than five years":

> Miss Manners is probably the only person in the world who wouldn't automatically agree [with your son] that people should be judged by their personalities and not by their physical appearances.
>
> Or rather, she insists that those aspects of appearance in which there is some play for self-expression are fair game for social judgment. This does not include race, beauty, or health, of course, nor monetary value of clothes, but only those other areas in which one has at least some choice.
>
> Your son has chosen to keep his hair in a state that he knows gives people offense…He is deliberately annoying people by trying to make them deny the obvious fact that how one presents oneself in public symbolizes one's attitude toward that public.
>
> Defying the known standards of society when one is easily able to comply with them demonstrates contempt for those standards and for the people who hold them. This is a hostile act…Deliberately provoking people is—well, provoking. And mean.[8]

So you probably don't want to show up in sneakers or Bermuda shorts unless that's the sort of congregation you serve, just as in many a congregation a preacher would seem to be flouting parishioners' feelings by appearing in a pulpit gown.

It is not that congregational expectations need to be slavishly followed. The preacher will also want to ask, How far am I willing to accommodate and hide my own true self? There may well be instances of appearance that one may think worth upsetting people over. A beard may seem part of who you think you are, as might hair that flows to your waist over a peasant dress in which you like to preach. What is important is to be aware of the dynamics (it is their church) and deal with them with honesty, thought, and care. Most parishioners simply want their preachers to appear to be "together," their appearance conveying competence, confidence, and care, eliciting in return a sense of calmness, safety, and respect.

Before moving on, we need to note that the distraction of clothes is not just the congregation's concern (which, in our experience, usually wants nice, simple, classic outfits for women and men alike), but also our own sometimes. Are our zippers and buttons holding fast? Will our makeup run? Does our hair or beard (or both) look funny? Will static cling mold our skirt to our legs?

Such details can matter. The press reported that

> not the least of the problems that have kept Ferruccio Busoni's "Doktor Faust" out of circulation is the phenomenal difficulty of its title role…The New York City Opera…was fortunate to find a baritone of exceptional artistry and stamina for the role: William Stone…
>
> Fellow singers said they have been impressed that Mr. Stone simply gets to the end without collapsing…In describing how he got through it, Mr. Stone quoted Birgit Nilsson on the occasion she was asked for advice on how to sing Brunnhilde: "Wear comfortable shoes."[9]

We want to develop a sense of what deserves our attention beforehand.

But let us continue to assume that things are going well. You look fine. The service and sermon are ready to deliver. You know the setting and at least something about the congregation. The prelude concludes and you rise. You look at them warmly, caringly, with that sense of competence or presence that we will speak more of in a later chapter. You make the transition that Queen Elizabeth II made when she "took up her crown with an aplomb that startled those nearest her. 'I no longer feel anxious or worried,' she told a friend. 'I don't know what it is—but I have lost all my timidity somehow becoming the Sovereign."[10] Presumably, you are not a sovereign (as a few preachers seem to need reminding), but as the service begins, you do become the worship leader, one would hope with a fair measure of "aplomb: complete composure or self-assurance."[11]

Your opening words establish a tone and perhaps the morning's theme. Your readings are given with conviction, even dramatic flair. Your prayers elicit reverence, growth, rededication, and healing. You (or the music director, collaborating with you on the mood and the message) have picked the hymns to help set up the sermon. Eventually, whatever it is that precedes the sermon ends, the congregation is seated, and after a final glance down at the papers or notes on the pulpit, if there are any, you look out into the congregants' eyes and begin to deliver the sermon.

12

SERMON DELIVERY

For days or weeks or even years, you have been thinking of what you would say in your sermon's twenty minutes or so, and now those twenty minutes have arrived. There was a time when you cared about each idea and each story so much—or at least you acknowledged to yourself that they had to be included to make the sermon whole—that you decided you had to deliver them, and now you can.

If everything is going as well as we have been imagining, you will be "reexperiencing the message as it is being spoken."[1] You will be in touch with the creative spirit at work when you composed the manuscript, outline, or notes on the paper before you, or in your mind. The ideas and experiences that were so powerful, lovely, or true that you included them will come to life again in your recounting. Citing Bezzel, Dietrich Bonhoeffer contended that "the sermon must be twice-born, once in the study and once in the pulpit."[2]

It is an odd sort of remembering, of reliving, of making a moment of insight, conviction, and expression come alive in your mind and speech anew, so that the congregation can know it with some measure of the power that you once felt and that you experience again in the telling.

Such times are sometimes referred to with words like congruence, authenticity, magic, and flow. They can inspire some of the preacher's most natural and effective techniques, as when the preacher pauses in silence to catch up with his own words, or when she fights to put a difficult point across with repetition and forceful gestures; in either case (or in numberless others) because the preacher is in moment-to-moment, one-to-one contact with the words and message of the sermon, and with the emotions that inspired them.

The effective use of such emotion is necessary to most good preaching, but some preachers find it hard either to access their emotions or to contain them.

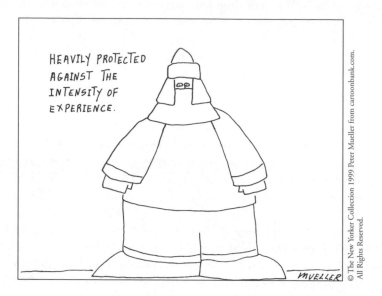

On the one hand, many preachers seem unable to get in touch with their deepest feelings in the pulpit. It is one of the most common complaints of church members, who often say they wish their preachers shared more of themselves from the pulpit. Emerson complained, "I once heard a preacher who sorely tempted me to say I would go to church no more…He had not one word intimating that he had laughed or wept, was married or in love, had been commended, or cheated, or chagrined."[3]

In our chapter on self-revelation, we caution against giving in too easily or completely to this congregational desire. But a compelling sermon usually displays some measure of the preacher's feelings, his or her compassion, sorrow, delight, anger, hope, indignation, excitement, or chagrin.

Of course, preachers have to have such feelings in the first place if they are going to display them effectively in the pulpit. To become good preachers, some people will have to work on developing their emotional lives in general. But for most preachers, who experience a normal, healthy range of emotions in their lives, those emotions can add conviction and drama to their sermons.

On the other hand, such intimate contact can become problematic when the words and the message are heavily freighted with emotion for the preacher. Genuine emotion in a preacher's voice and bearing can also be effective. But such emotion is far less so if the preacher is rendered speechless or visibly upset for very long. Further, most congregations will find it disconcerting if their preachers seem in tenuous control of their emotions on a regular basis. When dealing with passages that are deeply powerful or personally disturbing, preachers will want to draw on their stores of distancing tactics to keep their emotions in reasonable check.

Three strategies stand out for dealing with passages fraught with emotional weight. First, read a difficult passage aloud over and over again until it no longer makes you weep when you say it. Some passages may take several dozen recitations spread over days. Second, in delivering such passages, "breathe deeply and keep your breath flowing freely to help prevent constriction of the throat," recommends a voice coach.[4] Third, when you feel emotion threaten to take away your ability to speak, shift to thinking of the words as just words that you're reading; let your awareness of their meaning recede. With practice, you will be able to allow yourself just enough contact with the emotional charge of the words that it will be carried over powerfully, while you retain control of your pastoral demeanor. Held in that kind of professional check and balance, it is a great asset for preachers to be in touch with the emotions and convictions that created a commitment to a sermon, its points and illustrations.

Even when we are *not* feeling congruent with our texts—when our minds have for the moment gone blank, when we are worrying about whether we said the last point right, or we have drifted off to consider the condition of the ceiling or some episode from junior high (which is to say, the mind is strange)—if we just say the good words we once did well to conceive, congregants hear the good in them nonetheless, to a remarkable degree.

Many ministers have stood in the greeting line after a service, at the subsequent social time, or in conversation the following week, and heard praises sung of words they themselves had found befuddling as they heard themselves deliver them. "What a wonderful message," they hear, and are tempted to respond, "Oh really? How nice! And what in the world did it seem I was trying to say?" This experience is one of the reasons the authors tend to favor sermons prepared in advance, in some detail (indeed, in both of our own cases, a full text to deliver), rather than extemporaneous preaching—but that is a decision best left to individual choice, and is the subject of another chapter.

Whichever style best suits your skills, there are some techniques that seem to help in general, like making eye contact with the members of the congregation. This technique is so effective, it is rarely, if ever, overlooked by guides to preaching, to the extent that one master teacher of the craft,

Fred Craddock, finally warned that indiscriminate eye contact is discourteous, and total eye contact can feel "too close to staring."[5]

Eye contact may not be the end-all of sermonic assignments, but few techniques are more effective (and natural, given the preacher's warmth of regard not just for his or her message, but for the people listening as well) than seeming to look at every congregant, not neglecting any section of the room, spending as much time as possible focused not on the pages on the pulpit but out on the members of the congregation.

In practice, some preachers may find it too intimate or distracting to look directly into the eyes of everyone present, given all the relationships and issues involved. Remember your own experiences in the pews: Did it really take more than a look in your direction, one that seemed to focus on you directly (though the preacher in fact may have been looking only in your general direction or at some point just above your eyes or halfway there), to make you feel that you had been personally included in the preacher's concern?

Meanwhile, congregants look back, as they are able. If you slouch or rock back and forth, shifting your weight from one foot to the other, some will notice and find it distracting. Some will be bothered by other mannerisms you may have—a tendency to fuss with your hair, perhaps, or to gaze inexplicably toward the ceiling as you preach—and you may wish to work on controlling these. One of the authors was kindly instructed by the organist at his first church that his preaching would be easier to listen to if he would wave his hands around less, advice he took to heart. Then again, in a reflective moment in a sermon, he is still apt to fuss briefly with what's left of his hair, and parishioners seem not to mind or even much notice by now, or so they say.

When it comes to personal quirks of this sort, the kind that one could hope to change if one decided to, it's good to know what your own are and how bothersome they are to listeners. Some you may want to alter. For others, you may want to follow the advice that the Baptist pastor Ed Young gave his ministry-bound sons. "When they took classes in speech, I said, 'Don't let them mess with your style, with who you are…Just be yourselves.'…When I was in seminary…I heard George Buttrick speak, and Buttrick would pull on his earlobe; he did a lot of crazy things. Be yourself; that's what I would say."[6]

But the congregation will see more than the preacher's behavioral eccentricities. Most of them will also see the preacher's expressive gestures of body, hand, and face. Such gestures can matter, conveying subtleties of meaning and emotion. Or not: Francis de Sales said that "our preaching must be…dignified, in contrast to the rustic ways of some preachers who make a show of striking their fists, feet, and stomach against the pulpit, shout and utter howls that are strange and often improper."[7] But "dignified" need not mean unduly constrained. Many effective preachers have discovered how to use motions of the hands, shoulders, eyebrows, mouth, and other instruments of expression without including among them the stomach.

Like many other books on preaching, we have stressed the oral nature of the art, as opposed to its being literary. But most who hear a sermon also *see* it being given. Preachers who do not use their movements, their gestures, and (if the room isn't too big) their facial expressions deny themselves great resources for communication. Albert Mehrabian, author of the book *Nonverbal Communication,* reports that his research shows that "what is most important in terms of an audience liking you as a speaker is your facial expression," more than your voice and content put together.[8]

Of course, gestures and expressions will not serve your purposes if they are artificial or exaggerated or if they are inconsistent with the message. Harry Farra contends, "If there is a discrepancy between the ideas you communicate verbally and your non-verbal communication, audiences will believe your non-verbal communications over your words."[9] At the least, such incongruity will confuse or distract the congregation. Common instances include the preacher who smiles when nervous, even if the message is sad or serious, or one who gesticulates randomly.

By contrast, the former White House speechwriter Peggy Noonan made this observation about the effectiveness of a gesture used at the Democratic National Convention in 1992 by then-Governor Mario Cuomo:

> Mario Cuomo is also a great actor. You have to act a speech. It's a paradox of modern politics: to "act" is to be phony, but because of the demands and limitations of big-room oratory, if you don't act the text you'll look wooden and—phony. Natural politicians understand and master this intuitively, without thinking.
>
> When Cuomo puts out his hand to maintain his command— that movement that says, "Don't clap yet, the applause line is coming"—it is the short, blunt hand of a masseur. He's not only controlling the crowd, he's massaging them. He's touching the audience's shoulder and saying, "Like that? Wait'll I get to your back."[10]

The members of the congregation will also attend to the sound of the preacher's voice, as much as they can. For them, much of the sermon's effectiveness will depend on such matters as articulation, emphasis, pacing, phrasing, volume, and command. Preachers will want to make themselves heard, draw attention to the points that most matter, and use their voices to convey meaning, acceptance, and care. By the way, don't be surprised if there is verbal response to your preaching in some congregations, or if there is none in others; practice varies.

At least a few sessions with a voice coach can be of great benefit. Phillips Brooks was one of the most respected preachers of his day as rector of Trinity Church in Boston. "Dissatisfied with himself, however, Brooks sought elocution lessons for a decade during the Boston years."[11] In our own classes, students (including preachers of considerable experience) are grateful for the voice work given by professional coach Pamela Gore.

Focusing on such practical concerns as posture, breathing, enunciation, inflection, and even facial warm-up exercises, Gore helps students develop what she names as the characteristics of a good speaking voice:

- Adequate loudness
- Clarity and purity of tone (not fuzzy, hoarse, breathy, or throaty)
- A pleasing and effective pitch level (neither Coke-bottle low nor squeaky high)
- Ease and flexibility (responsive, with variety and melody)
- Vibrancy or resonance (not a flat, dull monotone)
- Clarity and ease of diction (clear, effortless enunciation)

It hardly substitutes for an in-person session, but Gore generously agreed to share some of her tips for public speaking:

On focus:

- Always look up at the congregation on your first sentence. Your voice comes out of your eyes as well as your mouth. But don't be afraid to keep your head down while you read the first half of subsequent sentences or phrases. That way you can deliver the second half looking at the people, all the way through the last word.
- Look *down* to *memorize* and look *up* to *talk*. *Tell* us what you've just read; don't *read* to us.
- Keep your energy focused. Look at one part of the room for at least a phrase or sentence before turning to speak to another section. Avoid whipping your head back and forth as though spraying the whole room.

On exhalation:

- Every sentence must be fully vested with air.
- Let go of your air. Holding on to your breath is like holding on to money at 0 percent interest. Spend! Spend! Spend!

- Imagine that your sentence is one of those sausage-shaped balloons. Keep it fully inflated *all the way to the end*. Don't let the last few words die, leaving a little tail on the fully inflated balloon.

On inhalation:

- Taking a breath is a cue to your listeners that another phrase or thought is beginning. Help your listeners to understand your phrasing by taking frequent enough breaths.
- Don't inhale too fast. Your listeners process what you've just said during your pauses. Give them time to digest your message.

On pace:

- Speak at a normal pace, but remember that your listeners need to process your words emotionally as well as mentally. Their comprehension comes through your breath-pauses, not through slow-paced delivery.
- Your pause *is* your breath. Don't pause and then breathe; if you do, your pause will be too long.

On style:

- Write so that you preach for the listener, not the reader. There are no rewards in heaven for overly long and complex sentences spoken without a breath.

On emphasis:

- Emphasize only *one* word per sentence or phrase. Try slowing down to emphasize rather than dropping the pitch of your voice or your air flow.

On volume:

- Exhale your air at a constant rate to achieve adequate volume and a sense of sharing a vital part of yourself (your air) with the congregation.

On intensity:

- Your preaching voice is *not your conversational voice* with a lot of breath pushing it; it is your *enhanced* or *stage* voice traveling on a steady, fast outflow of air.
- *Project air*, not sound. The air must have a direction; send it out of your mouth toward the people. Wrap your air around your listeners. Touch them with your air; then your spirit will touch them as well.

On confidence:

- The aura around you is like a Michelin-man space suit. Fill that aura with air as you speak. Keep your Michelin man inflated; it makes it easier for people to see your spiritual self. It also feels better to you.

A few final concerns: papers, sound systems, and humor. Regarding papers, Gore has four good pieces of advice:

- Try writing on one line only that part of the sentence that you can read with one pass of your eyes and one intake of air. Eight to twelve words per phrase is about right. This format will help you to keep your head up through the last word of the phrase, because you won't have the anxiety of looking for the beginning of the next sentence or phrase. It will always be at the left-hand margin. (This will also help you to regulate your breathing.)

- Try larger font sizes if you read better this way. Many preachers do. For example, we always use at least 14 point, like this; or even 16 point, like this. Or you could use 18 point, or even higher.

- Try filling only the top two-thirds of your page with text. Then you won't have to bend your head and squash your throat to see the bottom lines of the page.

- If you type on a computer, try using **boldface type** to emphasize certain words.[12]

We have an even more mundane concern: What do you do with a page once you're finished with it? Some people prefer having their pages in a notebook, which offers the advantage that they are more apt to be in order and all there (unless, of course, you've left the notebook itself in the car). But turning the pages becomes a conspicuous act, more distracting than it needs to be. If the pulpit is of adequate size, pages that have been read can simply be slid across from one pile to another.

If the church has a sound system (microphone and amplification), be sure you learn its dynamics in advance and know matters such as how loudly to preach and how far from the microphone to turn or wander. Some of Pamela Gore's tips require refinement, too, when one can be heard to the last pew without a stage or enhanced voice; indeed, with many systems, a skillful speaker can get great power from words that are little more than a whisper spoken directly into the mike.

We already encouraged the use of humor, in discussing sermon preparation. To develop masterful delivery, it helps to study master comics, especially those whose style you can imagine yourself emulating. If you are inclined to a broad style, watch tapes of how Jackie Gleason, Lucille Ball, or Red Skelton made it work for them. If you think quirkiness is your métier, study Gracie Allen, George Carlin, Gilda Radner, Paula Poundstone, or Robin Williams.

For a deadpan style, you could learn from the likes of Bob Newhart, Steven Wright, or Jack Benny (whose "look of pained innocence" *M*A*S*H* writer Larry Gelbart describes as "the expression of a calf that has just found out where veal comes from"[13]). Each of the authors has stood in the pulpit on many occasions with a look of dull bewilderment and a brave confidence that the congregation would catch on to the joke.

Watch the timing of the masters. Watch how they move and how they use their eyes and voices. We required Harvard Divinity School students to spend an evening with us at a local comedy club, so they could experience and sense their own reactions to professional comedians working with a live audience. Such observation can help preachers develop their own personal styles. Laughing easily at one's own jokes is effective for some comics and preachers, just as some comics and preachers do best by looking dazed and innocent.

Don't step on the laughter, beginning your next line so soon that the first few words are lost and the congregation feels guilty for having not kept up. Neither let the laughter die down until the mood is lost, unless that's what you want because you have a change of mood in mind. Give at least subtle clues that a joke is at hand. And when they laugh when you didn't expect them to, pause long enough to make an important decision: Should you take the time to undertake the difficult (but sometimes essential) assignment of explaining that you did not mean your statement as humor, without coming down too hard on those who just enjoyed a good laugh?

Two last observations about sermon delivery: First, the sermon begins as soon as you step up to the pulpit, and only ends when you leave it. The moment before you begin to speak is part of the congregation's experience,

FoxTrot   by Bill Amend

and can contribute to their sense of your authority and competence or subvert it. The moment after your sermon ends can do the same.

And second, as Craddock says, "The final word about delivery has to be 'passion.'"[14] Jana Childers notes that "when questions about what is missing in contemporary preaching are put to laypeople, they yield an age-old and suprisingly consistent response: Passion.

"Call it passion, life, authenticity, naturalness, conviction, sincerity, or being animated. Call it fire, electricity, mojo, spiritual lava, or juice. It is what listeners want in a preacher."[15] Surveys may note the importance of other factors, but usually nothing will matter more to the success of a Sunday's sermon than the parishioners' sense that the preacher really cares about them, and about the morning's message.

13

PREACHING WHEN CHILDREN ARE PRESENT

When it comes to children and worship, congregational practices vary widely, even regarding questions as basic as when and whether children attend worship at all. In some congregations, children attend all or part of the worship service with the adults every week. In some, children have a service of their own, even one they may lead themselves. In some, children almost never join in worship. And some congregations use a combination of approaches.

There are a sizable number of such variables. For instance, which children attend? What are their ages, and how many are there? Such factors make a big difference, as do other considerations, such as who else attends, who leads the worship and who helps (perhaps some of the children themselves), where it is held, and for how long.

If children's worship is part of the all-church service, are the children seated with their parents (if they are there), clustered as classes in the pews, or gathered as a group around the preacher? If the children come forward to surround the preacher, does the sound system enable the rest of the congregation to hear (including words the children themselves may contribute)?

And while for convenience we will keep referring to "messages and stories" in this chapter as the forms of presentation, by "message" we mean a wide range of possibilities. Usually, a message is a homily, often of four or five minutes and inadvisably longer than seven. But it could be a pageant, a skit, a drama, a presentation by a Sunday school class, or a performance by the children's choir, occasionally or often.

Such practical details can multiply to fill many a committee meeting, and most deserve such consideration on occasion, although rarely is only one way of doing things the best or the most child-friendly, despite the passion of its proponents. While the minister may offer her or his own opinions, often a more critical role is to temper the discussion, reminding people that perfect and lasting solutions are almost always unattainable. Some that should work don't, and even those that do work well for a season may need to be rethought by the next. Generally, the best the church can hope to do is to adopt some set of ideas that look promising, given the circumstances as they seem to be, then and there.

Luckily, most congregations have religious educators (directors or ministers of Christian or religious education) who bring understanding and experience to the decision-making process. As one minister of religious education, Norma Veridan, wrote after reading a draft of this chapter,

> To make the experience of being together as a congregation of many
> ages as positive as possible for as many as possible it's helpful to
> have input from the experienced religious educator. She or he can
> be helpful in suggesting what is age appropriate in terms of length
> of time in the service, what ages, what aspects of the service are
> important to include (music, yes, especially if it is lively; numer-
> ous lengthy announcements, no [but that's true for any age]). This
> "expert" advice is especially helpful if parents of quiet girls aged
> four want to include *all* four-year-olds and parents of active four-
> year-old boys see that as potential for disaster. As you state, "per-
> fect and lasting solutions are almost always unattainable."[1]

Besides all the details, there are a number of larger concerns that face preachers, however their preaching assignment to the children is structured, whether they are preaching on occasion in the children's chapel or prima-rily to the children when adults are also present at worship.

For one thing, such opportunities are precious and should be gladly accepted. They provide a chance to pass on religious messages and a sense of the importance of worship. They help to establish the pastor-parishioner relationship that the minister has, not just with the adults of the congrega-tion, but with the children as well. And they may make children feel part of a congregation, a worshiping community, either the one in which they gather together with other children or the one in which they and the adults unite for a time (or, in some settings with more complicated schedules, with both, depending on the week).

We prefer to have children attend the first part of services with the adults (although in practice, there are good reasons for congregations to have children worship on their own, too, at least on occasion—"especially if the children are just learning how to be in the worship service," points out Norma Veridan[2]). In church life it almost goes without saying that any practice alienates some, and this one is no exception. There are people who do not like having children present in what to them is a weekly hour of adult time. (Not all the kids are wild about it, either.)

Then again, many adults in many congregations welcome the chance to have the children of the church community join them for at least a part of the service, for a variety of reasons, among them: to gather individual families and the fuller church community; for most adults to see the children, to enjoy their presence, and to follow their growth; for most children to see the adults, learn their faces, and feel their affection; and of course to teach or inspire the children. (If the format allows the children to interact with the minister, they will often provide teaching and inspiration of their own, and a chance for insight into their religious perspectives.)

Either way, whether together with adults or among themselves, in most congregations children will be there, someone will deliver a message for which they will be the primary audience (although many adults will admit that at least on some Sundays, they most enjoyed and profited from that part of the service themselves), and often that someone may well be the minister.

Of course, the congregation's religious educator may often play that role, and it is important for the congregation, young and old, to experience the religious educator as a worship leader, storyteller, and preacher. The congregation is apt to include parents, teachers, some of the older children, and others who are especially skilled at leading the children's worship. The minister may be tempted to defer altogether to such expertise, but shouldn't.

Playing this role on regular occasions gives ministers a chance to make themselves better known to the children, and vice versa, along with the other advantages already cited. Still, some preachers don't find it easy. Other preachers take to it naturally, of course, and can hold a gaggle of ten-year-olds captive through yet another recounting of the tale of the good Samaritan. Most preachers find themselves in the realm in between, neither wholly intimidated nor entirely confident, neither inept nor yet proficient.

All of them can improve their skills. The better ones can become terrific; and at least as important, nearly all can become skilled enough to do a good job. Take advantage of the growing number of chances to watch expert storytellers at work. Read some of the books on the subject. Best of all, practice—to yourself, to a group of Sunday school children, to your child or a niece or nephew. Watch their eyes, feel their energy rise or fall, listen to their questions, and ask your own. How do stories or messages work (or not)? What engages and gratifies listeners, and what leaves them perplexed, disturbed, or just bored?

After years of observing people attempting to preach to children, with dramatically differing results, and trying to do so ourselves, we have developed some opinions about offering messages to children (and others who may be there). They are not offered as rules to be slavishly followed. We have seen nearly every one of them broken to fine effect by someone who knew what he or she was doing. But more often by far, we see preachers misunderstand the setting and the assignment, thereby missing a rare opportunity to foster religious growth.

And be assured: It is indeed a rare opportunity a preacher is given to convey a religious point of view to children, who spend vastly more time being offered messages by the rest of the culture, usually (though not always) of far different import. We need hardly rehash the numbers: how many hours North American children spend watching television, how much violence they see, how many appeals to material acquisition they are exposed to, and so on.

As their preacher, you have maybe fifteen minutes a week, for the thirty Sundays the family comes each year. Yes, the Sunday school program and the family will provide the bulk of the children's religious training, but isn't it also important that the message or story means something *religiously?* that it strengthens their sense of what it means to be part of your congregation's faith tradition, and that it passes on the group's most cherished stories, names, lessons, and values? that it conveys to them the religious community's love, esteem, expectations, and inclusion? that it helps the children know what it is to be religious? Our strongest opinion regarding worship time with children is that the time spent have a religious point.

Religious liberals that we are, our definition of "religious" is broad, as readers have probably noted by now. You will see further evidence in the second section of this book, when we review the many tasks to which a sermon might be set. We think a message to the children—as to any of their parents—might serve just as broad a range and still qualify as religious, in that it may inspire them, stimulate their thinking, help them heal, carry on the heritage of the faith, make them feel part of a community that loves them, understand that community's need for their support, alert them to issues of peace and social justice, and awaken or amuse them. But whatever the particular subject and approach, the message or story should be religious.

Many worship leaders, faced with an upcoming children's message, dash to the children's library in the hope of finding a story that will suitably illustrate the theme of the morning's service. Chances are slim, though, that a story explicitly about the Lutheran view of nature will be readily available, or about the Unitarian Universalist perspective on racial justice or the Episcopal view of ritual. Why not invent your own message?

In our preaching workshops, we ask participants to prepare a children's message to be given the next day, as if the theme of the service were (a) the welcome of new members, (b) denominational polity, or (c) the annual appeal for financial pledges—not many children's favorite topics. But using creativity, wit, passion, and props, preachers always rise to the occasion with messages that relate directly to the topics, their faith traditions, and the age group we name. This is good ministry.

In accomplishing the goals of this ministry, it is as important as ever to picture the setting, to imagine the various perspectives of those in the room, to consider what has the best chance of going over with that congregation that day.

As an example, if you are leading worship for a reasonably small group of children in a space of their own, the quality of the artwork in a book whose story you're telling may help hold their interest and deliver the message. But if the whole church family is worshiping together, the only members of the congregation who can see the pictures in the book (unless you have had them reproduced large enough to show) are those in the very first rows. This will include the children if they are gathered there, but for almost everyone else the strategy is pointless at best, if not insulting, implying that those other members of the congregation don't matter.

Any number of such situational concerns are important, considering all those who may be gathered, such as those with hearing limitations. A general guideline might be applied: Everyone there should be able to understand, appreciate, and learn from the story or message presented. For the adults, if they are to be present, this may require more attention to such basics as placement and amplification.

For children (and actually, most adults as well), whatever the setting, accessibility will require that the message be not only religious, but also enjoyable, interesting, comprehensible, effectively delivered, and basically true (whether literally, metaphorically, mythically, spiritually, or psychologically; more about "truth" will come later).

Helpful advice on how to accomplish those aims can be found in books and from local experts. For instance, one storyteller, Sandra Gutridge Harris, notes that a story that is good for the telling has

1. a beginning phrase that announces that something important is about to happen;
2. a character that you, the teller, care about;
3. a "hook" or attention grabber early in the story;
4. uncommon events;
5. simple story line;

6. minimal description with vivid sensory details;

7. suspense;

8. a mixture of narrative and dialogue;

9. repetition (of colors, of characters, of events, of language: verses, chants, phrases);

10. an ending phrase that concludes and satisfies.[3]

Here's our own list:

TELL THE STORY OR MESSAGE, DON'T READ A STORYBOOK. If it is a written piece (whether by yourself or another), read it over and over the week before, but learn it. This is not the same as memorizing it, though for some people it may come close. Some storytellers use a five-step program, passed along to us by Sandy Hoyt, a children's librarian:

1. Read the story.

2. Read the story out loud.

3. Draw pictures in the margin that depict important points in the story.

4. Cover the words and tell the story from the pictures.

5. Tell the tale without the pictures.[4]

However you learn best, come to know your story or message so well that you can (and may well) tell it to a friend, partner, child, or relative stranger before you stand in front of a group and try to put it across. This is not a reading; it is a telling.

One uncommon exception is a work of truly great prose or poetry. Even then, reading from a text to children is like reading a sermon to adults: It only works well if you can avoid the appearance that you're reading.

A GOOD STORY OR MESSAGE IS ONE THAT THE CHILDREN (AND OTHERS WHO LISTEN) WILL FOLLOW, UNDERSTAND, AND REMEMBER, WHICH IS TO SAY, IT SHOULD BE COMPREHENSIBLE. In selecting, preparing, and delivering a message or story, keep asking yourself, If I were a child listening to it, would I know what was going on? Could I follow the plot? Would I know the characters and events referred to and the meanings of the words and concepts? If not, would I be able to learn or guess them? even if I were the youngest child there (besides the infants)? If I could figure out the story or message, would I care about it? Would I want to know how things work out, enough to keep listening, even enough to forget that as an eleven-year-old, I may be trying to be skeptical, cool, and difficult?

Obviously, one measure of your success will be that the story or message has been enjoyable and interesting. Humor helps; so does surprise. Always, but especially as some of the children tend toward adolescent savvy, one does well to overcome the dullness of predictability.

PROPS CAN IMPROVE A PRESENTATION if they are not distracting or handled awkwardly. If used well, drawings, music, puppets, hats, and other props can help hold attention, convey the message, and make it more memorable. The authors can bring to mind an abundance of examples—childhood lunch boxes, sketches of youthful hairstyles, a fake arm protruding from a trunk—perhaps none more memorable than the melting ice cream sundae.

The title of the sermon that morning was "It Doesn't Always Look like the Picture." The message to the adults and to the children alike was that life doesn't always provide what we expect. The preacher had two props: a large, picture-perfect menu from a local restaurant, one that specialized in fancy sundaes, and one of their actual, flawed sundaes, set on the corner of the pulpit, which steadily melted into a mess as the preacher delivered her message.

Give-away props can work well, too, and help children hold on to the message. Examples are coins, balloons, flowers, and acorns. But watch out for the timing of the give-away: Do you really want to put throwable objects into the hands of that pair of eight-year-olds who last month sailed paper airplanes back and forth? Maybe yes, maybe no; it will depend on many factors, like the setting itself. Often, the give-away happens best after the story, as the children are leaving. And, of course, the give-away props should not be items that easily encourage warfare, stomachaches, or other impediments to learning in upcoming Sunday school classes.

A STORY OR MESSAGE SHOULD ALSO BE *TRUE* IN SOME SENSE OF THE WORD. This is an important point, but one that needs to be stated carefully. After all, most good stories are fictitious. Most experts and their research support the basic tenets of the point of view put forward by Bruno Bettelheim, that fantasy is a good thing; that it helps children deal with their psychological issues; and that through the encouragement of their imaginations, it helps them to develop the ability to distinguish fantasy from fact, and to deal more creatively with both.[5]

Still, children have a right to expect that church is a place where they will not be deceived. Judith Boss cites one such obvious danger: "In telling children Santa Claus is a real human, we are not engaging children's imaginations. We are simply lying to them."[6] Such duplicity can occur in a number of ways, as when fantasy is presented as if it were fact or when the preacher, teachers, or parents are not subsequently prepared or willing to deal honestly with curious or skeptical questions.

The current wisdom is that before they are long into grade school, children are able to enjoy imaginary worlds that they know are only "real" in some other way than the world in which they actually live. While every child is different, elementary school teacher Denise Gianola observed that "by third grade, children are pretty sophisticated about fact and fiction. They know that a story is only make-believe."[7] Others put the age as early as five.[8]

But concern about care and integrity suggests that preachers, given the large authority with which they are invested, must provide sufficient signals as to which world children are to understand themselves to be in: the fantastical, where elephants fly, stars alight over stables, and servants are magically made the elite; or the everyday, where they themselves live. We believe children deserve a clear signal as to whether we're telling them a make-believe story or a report on their world.

Norma Livo and Sandra Rietz state the situation very well in their book *Storytelling: Process and Practice*. As they put it, "*Storytelling is a game…*The storyteller is obliged to conduct the game, to provide for audience entry into it. The storytelling is initiated by ritual (liturgical or protocol) that announces a shift in realities—from this time to the 'other' or 'story' time, from today's truth to 'story' truth."[9]

The transition may take no more than a phrase; some would say that "Once upon a time" would suffice. Others would argue for a cue more overt such as, "This is the sort of story where pigs can talk and angels fly around." One minister, Makanah Morriss, says,

> If I am choosing a fantasy story, I introduce it with a bit of a disclaimer as to its connection with reality. "I want to share a story with you which is not a story of facts as much as it is a story of ideas and pictures you can make in your head," or something like that. I try to end with a tie back in to reality, as the story does have a real message for them, while again acknowledging that it is not a "real story"…I think there is nothing wrong with using fantasy as long as it is simple enough fantasy for young children to understand and as long as it is not scary.[10]

This raises one of the issues that people still debate regarding Bruno Bettelheim's positive assessment of fairy tales. Most scholars seem to agree with Bettelheim that children profit from scary, even violent stories. They may be right, but we share Morriss' disinclination to use them in a worship service with children, except with the greatest reserve.

It is easy to scare children, and that cannot be an appropriate role for the church. While some children may enjoy being scared and even be helped in learning to cope with life's actual dangers, as experts contend, other children are simply upset and even psychologically scarred by the kinds of stories that preachers sometimes employ, with little apparent concern for the consequences.

You might want to consider an upcoming story in this light: What does it imply about the world in which the children live? If in your story, little Johnny comes home to find that his parents have been murdered and his wicked aunt has sold him off to vagabonds, how are you going to deal with the feelings of children for whom such a possibility is a very unpleasant thought—and one that you may have newly, inexplicably, and inexcusably created?

Besides the violence and general scariness of many traditional folktales, the issue that some people (such as the authors) have trouble with is their stereotypical roles. Any conscientious pastor today will be wary of stories that assume a traditional role for anyone because of her or his sex, occupation, wealth, color, place of birth or residency, age, or the like.

CONSIDER WELL THE ATTITUDE YOU CONVEY TOWARD THE CHILDREN. It starts with things as basic as eye contact, which is especially important with children. (This is one of the reasons that routinely reading a story is such a waste of potential connection.) It continues with a sense of warmth and concern, a connection of your care with the responses you see in their eyes.

AVOID ANY TRACE OF A CONDESCENDING TONE. You can avoid this danger even if you use words or concepts that you have to explain. Children are glad to learn, as long as your spirit conveys a sense of the joy of discovery, without any hint that they are lacking or foolish for needing to be told.

NEVER, NEVER MAKE JOKES AT THE EXPENSE OF THE CHILDREN OR THEIR COMMENTS. This is easy to do, and sad to say, it is done more often than one might imagine.

It is often inadvertent. For example, one Easter, as youngsters hung symbols of the season on an Easter tree, one first-grader announced that she was hanging an egg to stand for fertility. "Fertility" is an unusual word for a six-year-old to say, and the congregation laughed appreciatively. But for years thereafter, despite repeated attempts at explanation from her parents, the child was troubled by the fact that she had stood up in front of the entire congregation, delivered her line exactly as she had rehearsed it, and everybody had laughed at her.

Such sensitivity in children is not uncommon. Yet incredibly, we are told of preachers who even set up a situation in which children will respond in a way that will draw congregational laughter. Indifference to feelings is unprofessional and all the more monstrous when the butt of the humor is a child.

ENGAGE THE CHILDREN AS BEST YOU CAN, WITH YOUR EYE CONTACT, ENERGY, AND WARMTH. In most settings, it works to engage them with questions, even in discussion. But pick your questions well: There are few ordeals as excruciating for congregants of any age, the introverts in particular, as the silence after a preacher has asked children for an answer that is not obvious— or the even more painful silence after an irrepressibly eager youngster gets the answer wrong. As we keep saying, picture the setting, the participants, and the likely responses.

CONSIDER THE CHILDREN TO BE AS MUCH A PART OF YOUR MINISTRY AS ANYONE ELSE IN THE CONGREGATION. Learn their names, pay attention to them, send them cards on special occasions, and when it comes to worship, remember if and when they will be there and prepare accordingly.

Three matters not dealt with yet could fall into this penultimate category. First, we like to include children in the service, even though we understand the concern of some adults that children not be put on display in church merely to be cute. Children are part of the congregation, and their participation in worship can be a very positive thing.

Second, the person planning the service will need to keep in mind that children may be there, and not necessarily patiently, when they decide whether and how to have the volunteer in charge of the fund-raising campaign deliver the annual appeal. And third, more generally, if children are going to be present at worship, particular care needs to be paid to such matters as the music, the transitions, and especially, how the message or story is brought to an end.

Finally, and most important, CARE ABOUT YOUR STORY, YOUR MESSAGE. At best, you will like it so much that you are a threat (or better, a potential blessing) to every friend, acquaintance, or fellow bus passenger for days before Sunday, so enthusiastically ready are you to tell the tale or relate the lesson. The wonderful news is, Sunday morning will arrive, and with it a congregation of youngsters and others ready to listen, to hear you make your message or story come alive and put its meaning across.

SECTION TWO

PREACHING AS MINISTRY

Imagine: You're the minister in town. You go into the shoe store, and there's your parishioner whose mother died last week. And while you're offering her words of comfort and support, it occurs to you that it has been over a year now since matters of loss and grief were the focus of one of your sermons. As you leave the store you're remembering that in that time several other parishioners' loved ones died.

Or you're leaving the church after a visit to the Religious Education Committee and in the parking lot you're caught by a certain parishioner who again this week has a complaint to register about the vase that was used to hold the altar flowers on Sunday. In your own impatience, it occurs to you that it's been over a year since a sermon remembered that in our faith communities, we try to cherish everyone, even the tasteless and the cranky (although those may not be exactly the words that you will use).

Or the paper reports that a local grade school teacher refuses to recognize same-sex or single-parent families. Or at a class for newcomers, a young mother and a retired farmer both express a hunger for greater balance and calm. Or passing you at the post office, a judge in the congregation relates an ethical quandary about scientific evidence.

It seems to us that preaching is not just one of many different and distinct jobs in the pastoral workweek, but that it is an extension and expression of all those other ways that we as ministers interact with a congregation or whatever group we serve: attending committee meetings, counseling, visiting, leading groups, engaging with the needs and issues of the community and world outside, socializing with the membership, and all the rest.

The situation is somewhat different for ministers serving outside a local parish and for laity, but it is closely related: An effective message by a guest preacher will still grow out of the learning of the workweek. But to relate that message to a particular congregation that is not one's own, the preacher must fit a guest sermon into that congregation's preaching schedule and its life experience, or related stories about its members.

Effective sermons are a reflection of effective ministries and of their aims. Specifically, sermons may attempt to heal, to tend the institution, to move to action, to build the loving community, to inspire a sense of spiritual wholeness and well-being, to teach a religious tradition, to stimulate thought, and to startle, awaken, or amuse. In the second section of the book, we consider each of these aspects in turn.

These categories are not entirely distinct in theory and are certainly not so in practice. On any given Sunday, a sermon is apt to try to accomplish several of these tasks, in differing degrees, depending on events in the life of the congregation. But among them all, the effective preacher has hope of ministering to the many deep needs of a congregation and its members.

14

SERMONS THAT HELP THE HEALING

Some sermons heal.

Parish ministers know that on any given Sunday, members of the congregations they serve are especially drawn to worship because a favorite uncle has died, a romance is coming to an end, the sixteen-year-old has run away again, or the medical test results are in. On any given Sunday morning, some parishioners count on a measure of solace, whether they derive it from the music, the quiet of the sanctuary itself, the pastoral prayer or meditation, or the attention of a few empathetic church members over coffee after the service.

It could be said that these incidental cases of healing are the most a parishioner might expect from a Sunday morning: that preachers preach in order to proclaim, and nothing more. But as Phillips Brooks said in his *Lectures on Preaching* to those who thought it impossible to be both preacher and pastor, "I assure you you are wrong."[1] One of twentieth-century America's most prominent liberal Protestant preachers, Harry Emerson Fosdick, went so far as to describe preaching as "counseling on a group scale." "People come to church on Sunday with every kind of personal difficulty and problem flesh is heir to. A sermon was meant to meet such needs."[2]

To be sure, whatever our intentions on a given Sunday morning, our services are apt to include that phrase, that illustration, that reference that acknowledges the degree to which all lives are touched at times by hurt and anguish. But on some Sundays, ministers preach specifically in order to heal. We talk directly about giving love to partners, parents, children, and others and about how tough it can be. We preach about grief or the loss of love; about stress, self-esteem, anxiety, and too-busy lives; about a wide variety of pain. Take, for example, this excerpt from a typical Sunday morning sermon:

> Let me acknowledge this about pain: that it has a powerful potential to isolate, whether a person chooses to try to tell about it or to bear it out alone. Public discourse is unreflective of people's interior lives…for example, death, grief, sex, and pain.
>
> Isn't that true? I mean, there are times I meet with you when you talk about what really weighs on your mind. But I think that most conversations that most of us have, you and me included, would leave an observer from another planet all but totally in the dark as to what goes on in our minds. And mostly, I think that's just fine. I do. It is not dissembling or phony; it is appropriate and caring and discreet.
>
> But maybe it needs on occasion to be acknowledged some- where, like here, like now, that that is what goes on. The visitor from outer space may report back that human beings do most of their thinking about weather and sports and home improvements. But we who are inside those mysterious minds know otherwise.
>
> We know that we are thinking about our teenager's curfew, our parents' failing health, our baby's delayed verbal expressive- ness, and—lest the list sound negative—our baby's smile, our parent's affection, our teenager's surprising act of understanding.
>
> I said there was a lesson I had learned from my own pain since I damaged my back. It is not arcane or complicated. It is, in fact, a confirmation of the primary lesson I received from my ministerial trainer, Wallace Fiske, the senior minister of the church in Connecticut that helped put me through seminary.
>
> On his desk, Wallace kept a hand-lettered copy of words of his own that began, "Above all, let us be kind to one another. Nearly everyone we meet is fighting a hard battle. We are all sometimes troubled, anxious, hurting and heavy of heart. Let us all be kind to one another and to everyone as far as we can reach."[3]
>
> May we know and remember how hard the way can be, how deep and how hidden the pain, and proceed in respect for the silence, the hurt, and the struggle and the will to endure.[4]

Some sermons seek to heal a common congregational hurt or to lay bare a distressing wound in the life of the congregation as a whole and seek to salve its pain. The wound can be internal to the congregation—a dissension, perhaps, or the tragic death of a member—or it can be something outside that has bruised the spirit of the congregation in common with others, as when Martin Luther King, Jr., was shot, or the Federal Building in Oklahoma City was bombed, or the community one serves has suffered a shocking, tragic injustice or loss.

In preparing any sermon designed primarily to heal, the minister recognizes that the goal of healing largely defines the tone, the style, and the message of the sermon. We may well castigate the racism that killed Dr. King or proclaim that the witness of his gentleness and love may yet ultimately triumph over hatred and violence, but we do those things as part of an effort that first of all aims at solace.

We recognize the personal pain, fear, anger, and despair of the folks in the pews, and we try to bring those feelings out so that they may be held in the hands of our words and our silence, held in the spirit of prayer, reflection, and communal fellow feeling.

One example of preaching that heals also illustrates the fact that our preaching may change when children are present, as they were when the congregation gathered in Reading, Massachusetts, after a well-known, much-loved children's librarian was shot and killed in the library by her husband, an elementary school teacher in town.

When a special person like Mrs. Zalubas is killed, we're likely to have all kinds of feelings about it. We're surprised, for example, that anybody could be shot in Reading. We are not in the movies or on TV—this is our town, and it's scary to see violence up so close. It's important to understand that this was the kind of tragedy that does not repeat itself.

A lot of us feel puzzled about why Mrs. Zalubas was killed. And that's fine, because it doesn't make sense. She did not deserve it; it was not fair. It's awful, we feel awful about it, but we will get used to it, our insides will heal up, and in spite of the mysteries of the way things happen in our world, we will be able to remember her with happiness.

Some of you are angry that Mr. Zalubas would do such a thing. The Mr. Zalubas you knew and may have felt close to as your teacher at Birch Meadow School has changed. If you loved him then, you will want to continue to love what he was. People sometimes change without wanting to. He changed and became dangerous, and now we must learn to care about him in a different way. Dangerous changes are so rare, that I can almost assure you that it will not happen to anyone in your family, or in your neighborhood, or in your school, ever again.

We are sad when someone we like dies. But you know, if you think about the kind of person Mrs. Zalubas was, you'll understand that by listening to her stories, by reading the books she offered you, by smiling back at her smile, you made her happy. And that's a nice feeling.[5]

Sermons that seek to heal both sound and look different from other forms. They look and sound more as we do when we try to offer comfort during the phone call when we first learn of a crisis or when we counsel one-to-one. More than other sermon forms, sermons that heal grow out of a relationship between preacher and congregation. The job is to say out loud the congregation's feelings of pain, reflecting back what we know they feel. And we know that they feel what they feel, not because we think we understand them, but because they literally tell us what they feel during the week in the trusting relationship we have. To return to Fosdick's viewpoint, the key to being a good preacher is to make oneself available as a counselor to parishioners.[6] We must listen before we begin writing.

If the relationship is working, when members of the congregation experience our healing sermons as authentic, empathetic, appropriate, and true, we will, as William Willimon puts it, have engaged in a "precounseling activity." "People make themselves available to pastors who have made themselves available to the people. People listen to preachers who demonstrate that they have listened to their people."[7]

Similarly, it was said of the late Dr. Norman Vincent Peale that "the secret of his success is simple: he knows what the people are worrying about. He knows because they tell him."[8] More recently, Frank Harrington said, "If you're not in constant touch with people—knowing their hurts, their hopes, their dreams, the rigors of the reality in which they are living—you may find yourself in the pulpit answering questions that no one is asking."[9]

Once our parishioners have talked with us, we need to be able to preach to them in a warm, practical, and personal way that heals. Søren Kierkegaard urged preachers "to present a human being as he [or she] is in daily life" rather than as some abstracted, ideal type: "The speaker who does not know how the task looks in daily life and in the living-room, might just as well keep still, for Sunday glimpses into eternity lead to nothing but wind."[10]

Just so, as preachers who heal, we need to be in honest conversation with our parishioners; and if we offer platitudes at all, they must be platitudes that are true. So we use our words, our vocal tone, our pauses, our gestures, our looks, and our bearing to reassure and soothe, to offer perspective, and to point the people to sources of strength and solace beyond or deep within themselves.

Many years ago, Joseph Parker told a group of young ministers to "preach to broken hearts…There's one in every pew."[11] There are still broken hearts in the pews and wounded spirits and psyches in pain. There will always be a need for the sermon that helps the healing.

SAMPLE SERMON

When the Reverend Patrick O'Neill delivered this sermon in the large church he serves in Wilmington, Delaware, he spoke in a low-key, sincere, and sympathetic tone. He seemed to be saying, "I've encountered these feelings, I'll bet you have too. So I've been thinking about them, and remembering some of my emotions, and doing a little research, and here's what I've come up with. Together we can handle this kind of thing." O'Neill does not judge or admonish, but he sides with us in a way that feels authentic. He leads us to the place where healing may begin.

Forgiveness: The Hardest Act of Love[12]
PATRICK T. O'NEILL

In the crowded urban neighborhood where I spent my earliest growing-up years, there was an amazing array of people for a young boy to encounter and observe. One of the nicest and most exotic personalities of that long-ago place, I remember, was an elderly immigrant Frenchwoman who lived in our building.

Mrs. Boutellon was always very elegantly dressed, and she always carried herself with an upright posture and stately demeanor. She spoke with a very thick French accent, and she was my sister's piano teacher. She and her husband were both shy and very quiet, and how tolerant they must have been, living next door to the boisterous racket of seven O'Neill children wrestling past them night and day.

My mother once told me that the Boutellons were Jehovah's Witnesses. This fact only added to their mystique, as far as I was concerned, for that sounded like a very select group indeed.

I was to have one very important encounter with Mrs. Boutellon. I was very young, first grade maybe, and several older boys—second grade thugs, I suppose had run by me and pushed me face-first into a snowbank. It was a great indignity, and I sat there on the stoop crying tears of outrage and frustration.

Mrs. Boutellon had witnessed the incident from her upstairs window, and she came down and collected me from the stoop and brushed the snow and tears from my face, and brought me into her kitchen for a cup of hot cocoa, and fussed over me in French-accented maternal phrases that seemed to right the universe again.

"You are angry at those boys for what they did to you, Patrick, and it is natural for you to feel that way. But now you must let it go," she said. "This day has other things to give you."

It wasn't until years later, after Mrs. Boutellon and her husband had both passed away, that my mother mentioned her name in conversation, and I told her of the day Mrs. Boutellon rescued me from that hard experience on the front stoop. "That sounds just like her," said my mother. "You know, don't you, that the Boutellons were both survivors of the Nazi death camps in the war?"

I had never known that. But it gave even more power to the words Mrs. Boutellon had offered me on that cold day when I was still a young boy. "This day has other things to give you." Imagine hearing that from a death camp survivor.

Besides the hurts and indignities of an unfair universe, this day has other things to give you. Besides the anger that you want to carry in your heart for all the wrongs done to you—this day has other things to give you. If you are ready to let go of your anger, to forgive what has happened in the past, this day has other things to give you. I heard that from someone who knew a thing or two about pain and hurt and injustice and indignities. I heard that from a survivor.

At a workshop I attended not long ago where one of the topics was helping people deal with their anger, a therapist was holding forth about how important it was for people to learn to forgive others and sometimes to forgive ourselves for the wrongs that have occurred in our lives or for wrongs that have been done to us. The therapist rightly pointed out that the willingness to forgive is one of the most powerful tools we have to help us move on from some of the most deeply wounded places in life.

Just after the therapist finished saying this, one woman raised her hand and said with wonderful honesty, "But I'm not really ready to forgive the person who has hurt me. Can't I skip this forgiveness part for a while and still move toward healing for myself?"

Forgiveness is hard. It's hard to do. It's hard to give, it's hard to receive, it's even hard to talk about. Forgiveness is hard business. It is soul work on the deepest level.

Forgiveness is hard for a lot of reasons, some of which are healthy and understandable, some of which are very unhealthy and damaging. Despite all the practice we've had over a lifetime of telling each other we're sorry for all the intentional and unintentional hurts and harms we do to each other in this limited living space together—forgiving each other is hard.

Let's be clear that we are talking about an adult activity here. When children practice forgiveness, they are practicing adulthood and maturity. And when adults refuse to forgive, they are quite often acting out of a very childish stance. Forgiving is the act of a thoughtful and mature civility between people, the opposite of aggression and vengeance. As one psychologist puts it, forgiveness is about "preventing the pains of the past from distorting the joys of the present and undermining the promise of the future."

If there is one fundamental misunderstanding about what forgiveness is and what it does, it is this: A lot of us still think forgiveness is something we give to other people, to people who have wronged us and who may or may not be sorry for what they did to us. But that is only part of what forgiveness is, and it completely misses the true nature and power of forgiveness in our lives.

Forgiveness is first and foremost a gift to ourselves. It is an act of self-love, self-care, self-respect, self-healing. It is the permission we give ourselves to let go of the pain of the past so that it does not define us for the future.

Mrs. Boutellon always wore high-necked, frilly blouses with long sleeves. But one day at the piano my sister saw the number that was tattooed on Mrs. Boutellon's forearm. It was her identification number from the prison camp. And when my sister innocently asked what it was, Mrs. Boutellon patiently explained that the number on her arm represented her past identity as a prisoner, but now she covered it over not because she was ashamed of it, but because that was not her identity anymore. It was not her present, and it was not going to be her future. She had moved beyond the victimhood of her past, and her future was different.

What people like Mrs. Boutellon understand is that forgiving is the intentional act of moving away from a place of woundedness, letting go of that woundedness, letting go of the hurt feelings we harbor from that woundedness, and leaving it in our past in order to receive unencumbered the gifts of future growth.

Let me say that again, because a lot of people never think of it quite this way. Forgiving is the intentional act of moving away from a place of woundedness, letting go of that woundedness, letting go of the hurt feelings we harbor from that woundedness, and leaving it in our past in order to receive unencumbered the gifts of future growth.

That honest woman in the workshop (to whom we can all relate) wants to move on to new wholeness in her life, but she is not ready to put down the burden of the hurt that has been done to her; she isn't ready to forgive. The wounded child in her wants to carry the psychological cargo of that hurt around for a little longer. She's moving in the right direction, she's aware of what she's doing and what ultimately she ought to do for herself, but she's not yet ready to forgive.

"Can't I skip this forgiveness part for a while and still move toward wholeness for myself?" she asks. Which is exactly what all of us do whenever we choose to harbor a hurt rather than forgive it. "Can't I carry this pain with me for just a little longer? Can't I keep this grudge growing inside of me for a little longer? I don't know if I'm ready to part with all this anger yet—I'm used to it now, and I'm used to having this as part of my story. It's part of how I explain and justify my life now. Can't I carry it for a while longer?"

When we do that, of course, we may indeed move forward in life even carrying our cargo of unforgiven hurts with us, but we do so only with diminished capacity. Of course, you would be amazed at just how much emotional junk some people manage to carry around with them every day. There are people who carry within their hearts the freight of every pain and hurt that life has ever dealt them. That such people can even get out of bed in the morning is a stunning act of strength. Some people do it. And they do it for years and years. Hold on to that pain, hold on to that anger, carry that old hurt, never forgive, never put it down, never clear it out.

The problem is, you see, there's only so much room in the human heart, literally and figuratively. And if all your heartspace is taken up with a collection of unforgiven hurts and the junk and clutter of unprocessed anger and the pain of bitter resentments that you have never managed to clear out through forgiveness, then your heartspace is all occupied, unavailable when the good stuff comes along. This day has other things to give you—if you've made room in your heart to receive other things.

The tragedy of some people's lives is that they've never given themselves the gift of forgiveness. It isn't an all-or-nothing kind of deal, we know that. And it isn't a quick fix-all, we know that too. The heart gives up its bitterest cargo only piece by piece, and the process can take years, we know that. But how tragic to watch someone allow some terrible event of the past to take up so much of their heartspace that there isn't any room left for new love to touch them, for new hope to lift them, for new faith to call them out of their pain.

Can you move through life "skipping this forgiveness part," carrying the cargo of unforgiven hurts? Of course you can. But it will cost you. It will cost you heartspace. It will cost you energy and joy and freedom and love to keep carrying all that junk. In some senses, it may even cost you your life.

One book on forgiveness illustrates this principle by telling the story of how national park rangers in Africa catch monkeys in the wild. Maybe you know this already.

> The ranger brings a plexiglass box, which has a small round hole on one side. Into it he slips a banana. He places the box underneath a tree in which there are some monkeys, then retreats into the distance. Inevitably one of the monkeys gets curious and comes down out of the tree to explore the situation. He finally puts his hand through the hole and picks up the banana. But when he tries to withdraw his hand, his fist, holding the banana, will not fit through the hole. The monkey jumps up and down squeaking and squealing, trying to get free. In the meantime, the ranger appears and captures the monkey. So the question is, what did the monkey need to do in order to get free? *Open his fist and drop the banana.*[13]

Learning how to open our fists that have been clutched in rage or anger for a long period of time is not as simple as it sounds. We have a lot of wrong ideas about what forgiveness is and how it works, a lot of misconceptions. Forgiveness is not forgetting. Forgiveness is not tolerance. Forgiveness does not mean denial of a past hurt. It does not mean that the feelings of anger are not real or justified. Forgiveness means simply that I will not allow myself to be defined only by those things. Forgiveness means I will not allow my foot to be nailed to a spot in the past from which I can never move again.

When the great prophets and teachers of history speak of the human heart, their teachings begin and end with the lessons of love and its great and powerful tool of forgiveness. "Forgive us our trespasses," one of them taught us to pray, "as we forgive those who trespass against us." In my opinion, the world would be vastly improved if churches spent less time teaching people how to repent and more time teaching people how to forgive.

"This day has other things to give you": a lesson about heartspace and survival and liberation from an old French Jehovah's Witness. I hope you pass it on.

15

SERMONS THAT TEND THE INSTITUTION

As a settled minister, or as a guest preacher, you are serving an institution or organization. Whether you are preaching transformative messages of hope or prophetic messages of social change, whether you favor addressing pastoral concerns or spiritual inspiration, the context in which you preach is institutional—a church, hospital, school, prison, fellowship, or agency—and sometimes that institution needs tending. It's as simple as that.

This preaching function might be called "mucking out the stables," as when horseback riders have to pay for enjoyable days of posting and galloping by doing the necessary labor with pitchforks in the straw.

There are times when money must be raised and sermons given with novelty and conviction to kick off annual drives and capital fund campaigns. Or your congregation or agency may want you to preach a special sermon annually for "Founders Day"; or the first Sunday of the church year; or in honor of a local hero, this year's Sunday school graduates, the new members, the volunteers, the departing ministerial intern, or the scout troop that meets in your building. One minister, whose church stands on the Lexington Green in Massachusetts, is expected to preach each year on Patriots' Day Weekend about the Battle of Lexington, which is so much a part of the congregation's identity.

Such Sundays are hard work for many of us, especially if we have been in a congregation long enough to be raising money or welcoming newcomers for the tenth or twelfth or eighteenth time. But the time comes again every year to notice with apparent excitement: Here it is, canvass time again!

But that work, of course, is what they pay us for, in no small part—not just for our perspicacious outlook on the Middle East or Algonquin prayer, but also for our ability to muster the humor, style, passion, and conviction, the lay testimonials, historical vignettes, and other touching tales, the visuals, rituals, honorary awards, and whatever else it takes to get the congregation enthusiastic about another class of commencement graduates, another report from some denominational office, or another appeal to increase pledges by more than many think they can afford.

And indeed, despite life's wearying ongoingness, we all know in our collective heart of hearts, enthusiastic is exactly what we *should* be. Unless we believe that, why have we given our lives to the effort? And so, for example, one might come up with a gigantic scroll that lists the alphabet soup of denominational agencies, or dare to suggest that we could close up shop and convert the church building into a roller rink. We expose our personal finances, drag out the communion silver from the original seventeenth-century meetinghouse, celebrate a longtime member, or, as our colleague Bob Schaibly did, award colored eggs on Easter morning to a dozen good eggs from the membership.

Which is to say, we pull out the stops, looking for the funny, the startling, the poignant, and the profound when our listeners are most apt to expect the predictable and dull. For example, here's an excerpt from a sermon addressing the annual fund-raising campaign by using an incident from local church history:

In the 1930s, of course, times were tough. At that time, our church members were accustomed to pledging either twenty-five cents a week, fifty cents, or one dollar. During the 1929–30 church year, all of the church members fulfilled their pledges of thirteen, twenty-six, or fifty-two dollars.

But as the Depression began, our ledger books begin to show tiny numbers at the bottom of each page. Five cents. Two dollars, twelve dollars. And then a little "s." Five cents "short" of the pledge. Twelve dollars "short." Just what one would expect.

But imagine this: Imagine that more numbers appear at the bottom of the ledger. Four dollars. Eighty cents. Seven dollars. Thirty cents. And after these numbers, the tiny letter "o." Four dollars "over" the pledge. Eighty cents "over." I can find no evidence of a special appeal from the Governing Board, no traces of public discussion, only the quiet generosity of the people of our church.

I read lots of historical material this week, but nothing touched me more than the dusty ledger book from the thirties, from high up on the shelf: In our church during the Depression, for every pledge that had to fall short, one of many generous people over-paid his or her pledge to compensate.

I love the history of this church. Gandhi was never a member. Mother Teresa never belonged either. Just regular folks. They dedicated their babies, they worshiped, they reached out to do their part in the world, they cared for one another, they kept this place going, they tried to live their best lives.

A long time ago, Samuel Eliot stood on our corner here on Summer Avenue and Woburn Street and dedicated this church. He said, "My friends, let us not forget that the church of the spirit must be forever building. You are linking your personal religion to the spiritual life of this whole community, and in this high endeavor, I bid you Godspeed." So may it ever be.[1]

We need to inform, teach, and inspire our listeners about the institutions of which they are a part. Increasingly, parishioners weren't raised in congregations, and it's our job to tell them how our churches and affiliated agencies work—who holds what power, for example, or what is expected of them. From time to time the preacher adds a line or two in a sermon that describes the polity of the local church or the fact that our homeless shelter has a board of trustees. Newcomers will want to know whether the church is run by the minister, a CEO, the Pope, or some mysterious office downtown or someplace in the Midwest. They may be interested to find out in a sentence or two what in the world the minister does all day. The people in the pews often welcome a perspective on conflicts in the church, or the addressing of rumors head-on, or clarification in the midst of simple confusion. They need to know to whom to complain and who deserves thanks, who cleans up, how religious education is handled, who's responsible for choosing the music, and how one contributes something to the newsletter. With luck, our congregants will want to know why and how they should volunteer to help.

Similarly, they'll want to know where the money comes from and how much they are expected to contribute. Ministers can and do talk about money in church, though current wisdom suggests that people respond better to articulated visions and dreams than to precise pitches for budget items. Experts abound just now in the "how to's" of church fund-raising—although in our experience, enthusiasm, heartfelt commitment, and good humor are the keys to success, regardless of the current popular techniques.

On occasion, institutions are fraught with controversy that needs to be addressed in fair and loving ways from the pulpit. Typically, people want to know the facts, they may appreciate a perspective or two, they want to know that their voices can be heard, and they want to know how to move ahead together in a helpful and healing direction.

This is how one minister handled a controversy in the congregation about the denomination's sex education curriculum, a controversy sparked by a segment on a national television program:

> We have used this sexuality curriculum in our churches for almost thirty years and we have thousands of graduates, some of them grown-up now and sitting in this room. My own mother taught it. It badly needs updating—we've known that—and the brand-new curriculum, jointly developed by the United Church of Christ and the Unitarian Universalists, is in press. Each congregation, each church's Religious Education Committee, may decide whether or not to use the curriculum.
>
> If and when parents and the young person feel that he or she is ready, the young person may take this completely voluntary course in a safe, loving environment. It is taught by trained teachers from within our midst whom most of us know and trust, in the context of open and honest conversation and religious values.
>
> Here's what I think, for us, in this congregation. If you disagree with the person sitting next to you, or with me, or if you're not quite sure what you think, or if one minute you think sex education would be good for our children and the next minute you don't like the idea, or if you feel a little nonplussed, or if you can't imagine what the fuss is about, please know that that's okay and we can talk about it. And we like it when we question one another. In fact we have scheduled a meeting at 11:45 in the Austin Room today so we can hear each other's thoughts. It's just us, people in a religious community who care for the generation of young people growing up today. We all want what's best for them, and there's room for us all.[2]

Whether we hope to tend the institution by addressing the recent firing of the music director, the booming Sunday school program, the pathetic results of a finance campaign, or the intricacies of local church government, a little goes a long way: No one attends a worship service to hear whose fault it was that both the wedding and the aerobics class counted on using the church hall on Saturday at three o' clock.

Finally, the institution is nothing without the people who care for it, and those people must be honored. Two volunteers spent the year revising the bylaws—bylaws that most people don't care about. Other people painted the eaves, audited the books, enhanced the Web page, or arranged carpools. Brief yet abundant thanks are in order, thanks in keeping with, and integrated into, the larger mood of the worship service.

But there is a danger. Once we begin tending the institution from the pulpit, our fundamental purpose can easily appear to be just that: addressing conflict, defending this or that, raising more money, corraling or appreciating volunteers, promoting meetings and events, maintaining the building. The institution itself is not the point. We need to tend our institutions well, but sparingly, and always in relation to their higher purposes, the reasons for which they exist in the first place.

SAMPLE SERMON

Sometimes we confirm the hopes of our most faithful congregants that their efforts on behalf of the institution are important. Other times, we sanctify and enliven denominational rites. An example of the latter sort of sermon was offered at a worship service for continental delegates, a service that celebrates the ministers each year, new, retired, or dead. It is the central act of the church assembly's worship life.

The preacher took up an issue of long-standing concern in her faith tradition, a common problem among religious liberals: how to balance or reconcile competing commitments to communal convictions and individual freedom. The problem had become particularly painful to some. The preacher was able to affirm the competing arguments and suggest a way of incorporating them both into a fuller, more complex, and healthier outlook. Those who were present were struck by the force her message took on with its humor, thoughtfulness, and evident care for all in the congregation.

Those Singular Rooms[3]
JANE RZEPKA

We arrive out of many singular rooms, walking over
    branching streets.
We come to be assured that brothers and sisters
    surround us, to restore their images on our eyes.
We enlarge our voices in common speaking and singing.

We try again that solitude found in the midst of them
    who with us seek their hidden reckonings.
Our eyes reclaim remembered faces; their voices stir
    the surrounding air.
The warmth of their hands assures us, and the gladness
    of our spoken names.
This is the reason of cities, of homes, of assemblies
    in houses of fellowship.
It is good to be with one another.[4]

Indeed it is good to be with one another. It is good to be assembled in this house of fellowship. As Kenneth Patton reminds us, we are surrounded by sisters and brothers. We sing "Rank by Rank" at this service each year, and we know that "our voices are enlarged" by our common song. The spoken names we hear at this Service of the Living Tradition do have, for us, a power…But those singular rooms. "We arrive out of many singular rooms."

You have arrived from Miami and Edmonton and Boston and Phoenix. You have shown up at General Assembly with your credentials and your yellow registration receipt and your comfortable shoes and you make your pilgrimage to MECCA [the name of the GA convention site] and find GA registration. You get a big fat notebook and a name tag and some ribbons and buttons and stickers and maybe a map. And you are on the skywalks of Milwaukee and into the octagons and inadvertently in the parade, and people seem to recognize you…or they recognize the person behind you, and then, finally, you make it to the Astor Hotel or the Pfister or the Marc or Marquette and you arrive at your SINGULAR ROOM!

For once it's true. If ever we join together in worship "out of many singular rooms," it is, quite literally, at the Service of the Living Tradition.

- As religious liberals from across the continent and the world, we arrive from those rooms to form this congregation.

- As active volunteers in our home congregations, as professional religious leaders, as youth, as welcome guests, as those being recognized and celebrated today—we arrive from our singular rooms and we become this congregation.

- As rationalists and theists, eco-feminists, humanists, neopagans, agnostics, and spiritual seekers of every variety; rooted in Christianity and Buddhism and Judaism and our mother earth and Universalism and Native American tradition and Unitarianism and religious and cultural foundations of all kinds; from those singular rooms we unite this morning as one improbable congregation.

- As people who live in different kinds of bodies, who love in different ways, people who are new to the world or who've seen it all before; as Unitarian Universalists who express our visions and our dreams as one people, we arrive this day out of our many singular rooms and join together in this place as one amazing congregation.

One amazing congregation. A well-trained minister would launch into some warm "one big family" talk about now. Certainly we do on occasion imagine ourselves as sisters and brothers of a sort, but "family"? Is that what we are—a family? A family as in Cain and Abel? Cordelia and Lear. Lizzie Borden. Think about Woody Allen. The Simpsons! Hallmark may write the cards, but Hallmark never writes our scripts. Why on earth would we want to turn a perfectly marvelous group of people like this one into one big family?

We are not a family. No matter how warm our sentiments—or how cold—the Unitarian Universalist Association has at its core not the casual fluidity of family feeling, but purposes and principles and bylaws. To belong is simple: Those congregations that subscribe to our principles and pledge to support the Association may apply to belong. Simple and clear.

Simple and clear, maybe, but questions of plurality continue to drive us nuts. When we are open and inclusive, we loosen our connection with our Unitarian Universalist traditions and our theological identity. When we clearly define ourselves, on the other hand, we alienate those congregations—among them some of our oldest and most traditional and some of our newest and most innovative—we alienate those congregations that find themselves on that definition's edge. A number of Unitarian Universalists arrive here at General Assembly, look through the schedule of events, and find programs so far removed from the theology back home that they begin to wonder who the real Unitarian Universalists actually are. For us, plurality is an issue. But before I move ahead, a word or two about perspective and degree.

I've just been on my sabbatical with my husband and two middle school boys in Nepal. We happened to be on the last plane into Kathmandu as a revolution broke out, so we spent some days under martial law in a room that served as a library of sacred Buddhist and Hindu texts. Despite an around-the-clock, shoot-on-sight curfew, one day, in walked an old swami: long, white hair; long, white beard, a little tattered, a little holy. And he lit some incense, sat us down, and began reciting our morning prayers.

- In a country where all forms of Buddhism, all forms of Hinduism, all forms of ancient animistic religions blend as one, we prayed to a universal spirit of peace.
- And as we prayed, the people were divided in the streets.
- In a tiny country where dozens of tribes speaking thirty-six languages live in one ancient valley, we prayed to the mother and the father.
- And as we prayed, the people rioted with swords, and sticks, and scythes.
- In a country of a thousand gods and goddesses who sit together in the temples, we learned to pray in Sanskrit, "You are All my God of gods."
- And as we prayed, the army fired into the crowd over and over again.

Sitting there in Kathmandu, I tried to think about this sermon, a sermon on pluralism. And I have to tell you, I had difficulty imagining our convention of Unitarian Universalists gathered in Milwaukee, Wisconsin, as being very diverse.

Yet it's true, even in this theater in Milwaukee. We are diverse within our own limited range. None of us completely belongs. Even as we work toward pluralism in our denomination, and in large part fail—even in our small, relatively homogeneous denomination—none of us belongs altogether. Maybe we feel we're older than most—or too young, or less monied, or too new to the denomination, more physically challenged, a person of color, or out there alone on some spiritual limb. We're vegetarians, or Asians, or Thoreauvians, or Canadians, or lesbians, or Republicans. Or maybe it's just that we love the hymns that everybody else hates, or we can't stand it when ministers wear robes—especially in numbers—or that when it's our turn to light that flaming chalice, it always sputters and goes out. For nearly all of us, just being a Unitarian Universalist makes us seem a little strange, at least to our neighbors back home.

At times, each of us feels a little weird. When I was trying to think up a title for this sermon, my first thought was something straightforward like "Thoughts on Inclusivity." How boring. So instead I typed in a different title: "How Much Weirdness Can We Include?" Until I realized that the sermon title would appear on your order of service and it would read, "How Much Weirdness Can We Include?" and then "A Recognition of New Ministers."

Be that as it may, the question remains, "How weird *can* we be and still be Unitarian Universalists?"

The question is not new: In the early nineteenth century, Universalists agonized over those among them who had differing visions of universal salvation. A little later, Unitarians wondered, "Can we accept those who don't believe in miracles?" "Can we accept the Transcendentalists?" Later still, "Do you have to be a Christian?" And eventually, "Do you have to believe in God?" We have been playing the Unitarian Universalist identity game for a long time.

And we struggle still. We struggle because there are people in this room who value a religion that knows what it is, where it came from, what its boundaries are. These Unitarian Universalists want a religion that stands for something, a religion that shows integrity and consistency and congruence. I, for one, like the notion that when my boys are old men, they could visit any Unitarian Universalist church and feel as rooted in our tradition as I think they do now. I would feel best knowing that when one of you new ministers does my funeral, you will have the same general idea as I do of what that service might look like. Some of us look at our religious institution as an expression of our way of Truth; in fact, I will call this cluster of values—this love of rootedness, theological integrity, denominational identity—for now, I will call these values "Truth."

On the other hand, there are people in this room who value a religion that is pluralistic, people who not only accept but celebrate our diversity. These people welcome innovation, anticipate the future, and appreciate a spirit of openness in our free faith. And indeed, I like to imagine that when my boys are old men, their religion will meet the needs of the time, it will have grown and expanded far beyond my recognition, and that our Association will have shared its power and its resources in order to serve a far wider range of Unitarian Universalists. In his book *The Company of Strangers,* Parker Palmer notes that "the essence of hospitality…is that we let our differences, our mutual strangeness, be as they are, while still acknowledging the unity that lies beneath them."[5] I know that a number of us firmly believe in this cluster of religious values—this open welcome, this inclusivity, this easy embrace—and I will call this cluster of values "Love."

Truth or Love. Institutionally, it turns out they're not compatible. Will we define our theology, proclaim that theology with integrity, and be guided by our denominational truth? Or will we invite and include; will we love?

We must choose both. We have always chosen both! As Unitarian Universalists we value love and we value truth even though they turn out to operate on two parallel lines. Emerson said, "So often, nature delights to put us between extreme antagonisms, and our safety is in the skill with which we draw the diagonal line."[6] "I accept the clangor and jangle of contrary tendencies."[7] Coleridge called it "Multeity in Unity"; psychologists call it cognitive dissonance; Buber called it "the totality of antinomy"; Carol Gilligan called it "the complementarity of identity and care." Indeed, we must draw the diagonal that connects our Truth and our Love, and we must live amidst the inevitable clangor and jangle that we shall always hear.

In the mountains of Nepal, we trekked for days among people who had never seen a road or a car or a bicycle or a wheelbarrow; people, however, who knew precisely how to live simply in the high country. There I was nearing the end of a day's climb, wearing the customary long trekking skirt, huge hiking boots, a down jacket, a backpack, a wide-brimmed hat, mountaineering glasses, a camera around my neck, and globs of sunscreen. It was Easter, so for the kids I had brought along a garish little Easter basket and in it a small stash of jelly beans, which I carried importantly. Periodically, when I couldn't resist the temptation to further mortify my family, I'd burst into song about Peter Cottontail and how much he liked to hop up up up that trekking trail. In fact, I was singing Peter Cottontail when I looked up and in a sobering flash discovered that we had reached the Buddhist monastery, and the venerable reincarnated high lama himself was standing in his simple robe, staring at me.

He spoke then in Tibetan to our Sherpa guide, and later I learned what he said. As I stood before him in my full regalia with my basket of jelly beans, he said: "I will never understand these Christians, their songs, or their gods. But invite them in for yak milk tea, and I will bless them."

Yes. Confident in his truth, he loved us still. And for a time, we lived, with our tea and blessings, on Emerson's diagonal line.

This morning, in this place at this time, we gather on our own diagonal line as one community. As one community we light the chalice in the spirit of truth and love alike. As one community we remember those men and women who cherished our tradition, and as one community we shake the hands of those who will carry us forward in openness. As we gather in worship on this Sunday morning, we celebrate our living tradition as one community.

> We arrive out of many singular rooms.
> We come to be assured that brothers and sisters surround us in love.
> We try again that solitude found in the midst of them who with us
>   seek their hidden truths.
> This is the reason for assemblies in houses of fellowship.
> It is good to be with one another.
>
> So may it be with us.
> Amen.

16

SERMONS THAT ENGAGE WITH THE LARGER WORLD

Religion is about all of life, and so good preaching will be too. Religion is not about a narrow range of human interests (piety, ecclesiastical dogma, and the afterlife, for instance), but about how questions of meaning, purpose, and joy apply to almost all aspects of human existence.

Therefore, preachers will want and need to struggle, on occasion, with a wide range of concerns, including immediate issues in the personal lives of parishioners, great theological quandaries, and practical matters of congregational life, to name a few.

One of the most important of those concerns will be the situation of the larger local community, the country, and the world. It would take another book to make the case well (and such books already exist), but religion must concern itself with current events, and it must be committed to positive goals and values.

People of faith will disagree forever as to how those goals may best be achieved and those values advanced, but the preacher may well seek to preserve two important expectations. First, that any disagreements will take place in the spirit of love and respect. And second, that whatever the differences may be regarding means, there should be an abiding commitment to certain goals and values: social justice, peace, and progress; opposition to oppression, prejudice, and the desecration of the planet; and the alleviation of suffering and want.

Preaching speaks in the voice of that love and respect to express those values and goals. Sermons should help bring subjects of social importance to attention and into focus from the perspective of a faith tradition's deepest convictions. They should help listeners feel more compassionately involved in the subjects, clearer as to the ways they might help, and at least a bit more hopeful that their actions can make a positive difference.

"What we are asking in this service here today is whether an individual life…can truly affect the quality of the day," said Bill Schulz, a minister and the executive director of Amnesty International USA.

Now if we are honest, I think we have to acknowledge that there is much about the world that threatens to convince us that it cannot. There is nothing more discouraging to me in the work I do with Amnesty International than the sheer anonymity of human suffering…

And yet there is something else I have noticed about the work I do and that has to do with the singularity of courage. For in every situation of incomprehensible terror there are always a few people who have cast their lot with the Honorable and the Just. Such people need not be well-educated or sophisticated. Luisa had dropped out of school at age eight and never been outside her village, but when the security forces came to her house and demanded that she give them the names of all the villagers who were critical of the government, she supplied them a list of twenty names, all the same—her own. And such people need not even be successful in their witness. The Irish poet Seamus Heaney describes one of the most harrowing moments in the whole history of the Troubles in Northern Ireland:

One January evening in 1976 [Heaney says] a minibus full of workers was held up by masked men and the occupants ordered at gunpoint to line up by the side of the road. Then one of the masked men said to them, "Any Catholics among you, step out here." Well, with one exception, this was a group of Protestants and the one Catholic was terrified that he was being singled out by what were obviously Protestant terrorists, but the Catholic made a motion to step forward, and, as he did so, he felt the hand of the Protestant worker next to him take his hand and squeeze it in a signal that said, "No, don't move. We'll not betray you." All in vain, however, for the Catholic had already stepped out of the line—only to be pushed aside by the gunmen as what was in truth a group of IRA terrorists mowed down the Protestants remaining.

Such people need not be well-educated or sophisticated or even successful in their witness; they simply need to be those who, in the face of sorrow, choose honor and blessing and life.

And when they do, they redeem if not humanity, then at least their generation. For, you see, you don't need an entire population to choose righteousness in order to prove that righteousness is possible; you need only one person. When Lydia Maria Child spoke forthrightly against slavery while thousands in her generation supported it, she proved that anyone of her generation could have chosen defiance. When Dietrich Bonhoeffer continued to preach against the Nazis when thousands of his colleagues chose collaboration, he proved that anyone in his country could have chosen that option. And when Fauziya Kasinga chose exile in the United States last year rather than allow her two daughters to return to Togo to be ritually circumcised, she proved that culture does not determine history, that anyone in any society can be an agent of the tender. For if even only one person in a generation or a country or a culture chooses honor and blessing and life—even only one—then it means that anyone could have made that choice; it means that the Radiant had not completely died in those days; it means that Glory has not been silenced.

Now, I know that you and I will probably never have to make terrible choices like these, and I know that, even if I had to, I might very well opt for expediency rather than honor, but I also know that almost every day in small and simple ways—from the way we teach our children to the way we treat our neighbors to the way we model our faith—you and I have the opportunity to choose the gentle or the cruel, the generous or the petty, the ennobling or the venal...Ministry exists to teach us, to tempt us, to tease us into choosing the former.[1]

It may seem obvious and nonsectarian that a sermon should be so engaged with matters of social import. After all, by the end of the twentieth century, many religious conservatives had taken to preaching on contemporary issues with all the zeal associated with religious liberals only decades before. And the popular press had long been fond of featuring religious social activism, from the leftist Social Gospel of the early decades of the last century to the right-wing Christian Coalition of the final ones.

But in fact, another trend in twentieth-century American preaching was a *disinclination* to address contemporary social issues. Speaking of Protestant preaching, this case was powerfully made in 1994 by David Buttrick, who argued that "the incestuous relationship" between preaching and the Bible fostered by Karl Barth and the biblical theology movement had "led to an ebbing of the prophetic word, at least in white Protestant churches."[2]

The reticence persists, and in other circles as well. It has never been a cozy thing to raise troubling matters with congregants, who probably have troubles enough of their own already. Still, if the relationship between a preacher and a congregation is healthy, the members will expect that a preacher will try—caringly, skillfully—to awaken their souls to situations near or far about which they will want to be concerned, even passionately so.

Newly settled pastors may wisely hesitate to take on many controversial issues. But as Harry Baker Adams writes,

> The preacher who has been a trusted pastor to a congregation over a span of years can speak the hard words because the congregation knows that he genuinely cares about them. When the preacher presses people to take a stand for justice for the oppressed in the community, they know that she does so not only because of concern for the oppressed but also because of concern for them. When the person in the pulpit is the same person who sat all night with the family in the hospital waiting room, the family may well disagree with the preacher's position on gay relationships but they will be able to listen to her. They will know that the stand is taken out of a profound concern for all people.[3]

Some guidelines seem in order.

INVOLVE THE CONGREGATION IN THE TOPIC, PERSUADE THEM TO CARE (without implying that they may not already). Most likely, one effective part of that effort will involve sharing the process of your own developing concern and conviction. Why do you care? Tell them. How did you get interested? What touches, upsets, challenges, angers, or imspires you about the subject? What are your own emotions, confusions, and stories?

GROUND THE CONCERN THEOLOGICALLY, DENOMINATIONALLY, OR BOTH. Be explicit as to why the subject is a religious issue for you. Doing so increases the chance of the subject's becoming a matter of like concern for members of the congregation.

Elizabeth Ellis, a minister and director of the Unitarian Universalist Urban Ministry in Boston, cited her own Christian faith in explaining the importance of the work her agency does with troubled young people:

> One of the nice things about working with a multi-cultural group of people is that you get to celebrate more holidays. Last month we went to lunch for Chinese New Year, and next week we are going to lunch for Persian New Year...

There are so many celebrations of endings and beginnings, of death and rebirth. The spring solstice is upon us this weekend, and of course Easter with its redemption and revival. The earth seems to die, but no, it has come alive again. Our spirits seem at times of darkness to hold us in the long night of winter. But no, the light returns.

These celebrations seem particularly appropriate for me as a Unitarian Universalist. For the Universalist there is always a new day. Believing in universal salvation, it is never too late. It is never too late. God holds the gate open until the last sheep comes home.

For us in Urban Ministry this strongly underlies our work. It is never too late for any one of God's children to be redeemed…to have a good life; a quality life, even within the confines of difficult circumstances. A young man in one of our youth programs got out of prison yesterday. He is not one of our successful young people. While another young man in prison has taken advantage of the time to study and mature, this young man has become more violent during his various incarcerations.

But, on coming out, he called Louis, who runs the program. Then he came over to the church thinking he would see me. We will do what we can. But most of all, we will believe that it is not too late. That it is never too late. That he can live in goodness, be revived, renewed, redeemed through the love of good people. Through the goodness of creation. Through the power that is in his own heart. Through the love of God.[4]

CONSIDER HOW YOU WANT TO USE YOUR AUTHORITY. Do you mean to be prophetic? ("Here I stand. This I believe. Go and do likewise.") Or do you mean to be pastoral and understanding? ("I know it's tough. We're busy, we're scared. You're not a bad person if you can't help out.") Or will you try to touch both bases?

PROVIDE ACCURATE INFORMATION. Know what you are talking about.

RESPECTFULLY ACKNOWLEDGE THAT THERE ARE OTHER OPINIONS. Credit those opinions with their best arguments, not dumb renditions easily destroyed.

KNOW WHAT YOU'RE ASKING THE CONGREGATION ACTUALLY TO *DO*. It may be necessary to raise the congregation's awareness of troubling conditions somewhere first; but when possible, provide a range of actions that people might take in response, lest they become dispirited if conditions remain static. Be specific. Ideally, commit yourself to the same action. For example, you might say, "I have signed up to serve a meal a week from Sunday at the local shelter. I hope you'll join me." "I've written a check to our partner church for $100 for firewood. We've put a basket here on the piano for your checks." Or, "I have found a nice children's edition of the story of the good Samaritan; I will include the reference in the next church newsletter so you can read it to your kids, and I'll see that the church library has it."

KEEP THINGS IN PERSPECTIVE. Gun control may be *your* issue, but there are lots of issues out there. Any parishioner is apt to have a passion just as strong, except it is a passion for the United Nations or for saving a rare species of bird.

LOVE THEM. KNOW WHO THEY ARE. BE PATIENT. If someone gets angry with you, listen and respond pastorally, or at least like an adult.

USE JOY AND HOPE. EMPOWER THEM.

Engage, inspire, and motivate; draw them forward, don't beat them up; grant that they are as moral and intelligent as you are, and that, in fact, some members (if not the whole congregation) may have done more to help the cause you espouse than you have yourself. This is especially worth checking in advance if you are coming in as a guest preacher, expert in some area of concern; there may be congregants who deserve commendation for their prior and present commitment.

Whatever the case, the congregation deserves understanding and respect. It is not good ministry simply to shock, except rarely and with the greatest of care. Appeals to reason, conscience, compassion, and a sense of justice work better than guilt, manipulation, and shame.

After all, you are their *minister*, at least for that morning. You are on their side. You are enlisted with them in the effort to be religious women and men, and that means caring for others and for justice and peace. They have put you in the pulpit in the hope that you will minister to them in many ways, including a willingness to share with them, honestly, caringly, and lovingly, your perception of how their best instincts might engage with a troubled world.

A preacher may need at times to raise a strong voice that she or he knows the congregation may not want to hear or is sure to disagree with. And that should be okay. The congregation does not tell you what to preach *on*, nor what your message should be. In most places, they expect you to preach on whatever might trouble the conscience.

Just as important, they tell you who you are preaching *to*. They tell you all week long, as you hear or sense the troubles in the larger world with which their souls are struggling to cope. So when it comes to a sermon on a difficult social or ethical topic, you can engage parishioners effectively as their minister—prophetically at times, yes, but with pastoral concern as well.

SAMPLE SERMON

Using memorable imagery and phrasing, personal stories, information, outlook, and conviction, the preacher uses the occasion of Mother's Day for a sermon that calls for renewed hope and effort for social change. She overtly addresses the question, What can we do? and then movingly closes by restating her central point with a return to her opening imagery. The preacher is author of the book Unafraid of the Dark.

Birthing a New World[5]
ROSEMARY BRAY MCNATT

Happy Mother's Day, everyone.

If you'd seen me this morning, before I robed, you'd have noticed that on my left side, I was wearing a red carnation. I try to wear one every Mother's Day. If you look around the streets of Montclair today, you'll see other women wearing them. People don't wear Mother's Day carnations as much as they used to, and sometimes the ones you see aren't real. But I always try to wear a real carnation, because where I grew up, that was a Mother's Day tradition. When we went to church on Mother's Day, my mother always stopped along the way to buy five carnations. The selling of Mother's Day carnations, in fact, was a kind of two-day cottage industry on the South Side of Chicago. There was always someone selling them on the street, and my mother always found someone to sell her those five carnations—four red ones, and one white one for herself.

For those of you who may not know this custom, the color of a Mother's Day carnation matters. When you wear a red carnation, it means your mother is alive. When you wear a white carnation, it means your mother has died. I turned forty-three last Tuesday. All these years, I've been able to wear a red carnation on this day. For that same number of years—for all of her conscious life, in fact, my mother has always worn a white carnation, because her mother (my grandmother) died when she wasn't much older than my little Daniel is right now. Mama's on her way to church right now in Chicago, and she's probably getting my sister's kids ready, and everyone's probably pinning on their red carnations right before they leave, and once again, my mother's hands are reaching for the white flower she wears every year.

When I was little, there were two things I always wondered about on Mother's Day: I wondered how Mama must feel to be the only one among us who wore a white flower. And I wondered and feared what it would be like when Mama died and it was my turn to wear a white carnation. But I figured I'd grow out of it, because grownups, I reasoned, were big enough not to wonder or be afraid. So now I'm grown up, and there are three things I always wonder about on Mother's Day. I wonder how Mama feels to pick up her white flower for another year. I wonder, and fear, what life will be like when my mother is gone, when it is my turn to wear a white carnation. And now, as a mother, I wonder what it will be like for my sons when I am gone, when it is their turn to wear white.

Recently I attended a consultation as part of a denominational project; it was a meeting at which an old friend was present. He's been a minister for a long time, and we've served on a couple of committees together. We hadn't seen each other for a long time, so he and I broke away from the group for lunch. As we ate and talked, we reflected on all the years we'd known each other, and how for much of that time, I was a laywoman who talked a lot about staying a laywoman. I mentioned how weird it was to think back on those times, and to find myself now, neck deep in both motherhood and seminary. I may have mentioned somewhere in the conversation that clearly I was crazy to be doing all this stuff at once, and wondered, not for the first time, how it was that I'd decided on the ministry now, perhaps at the most inconvenient possible time in my whole life. My friend was quick to answer: "Oh, that's easy. It was having the children," he told me. "That's what broke your heart open."

What broke my heart open, I thought. What a funny thing to say. And yet the more I thought of it, the more the truth of it became clear. I was, to a lesser degree, like Anne Lamott, a passage from whose book *Operating Instructions* is one of our readings this morning. I cared about life, about things, about people—but in a distant, nearly theoretical way. Joining every committee and working group that presented itself was something I had been doing for years. For part of that time, I thought I might have experienced the call to ordained ministry. But it was a thought I dismissed over and over again. Ministers had to be different, better than the rest of us. I could never do what was required; the depth and breadth and seriousness of intent that ministers needed were not part of who I was, or who I would ever be.

And secretly I was convinced I could never care enough. But even amid my refusal, I kept myself near the church. I joined task forces and the search committee and seminary boards because it kept me near the church. Near—but not too near. It was only in the months and years after Allen's birth that I could hear my call and answer it.

What was it about the birth of my children that broke my heart open, that entered in and made itself at home? It was this wondrous love. Love I had not counted on, love I could not have anticipated, love I had not earned, love I could not prove but knew was real. Daniel followed Allen and now there are these two people in my arms, climbing on my head, throwing themselves at me, clinging to my legs. There are these people who love me, even at 6:30 a.m., crabby and sleepy and distracted as I am. They do not keep score of all my failings. They see the me I long to be when I look in the mirror, and sometimes I think all my life since they were born has been the process of becoming that woman they see, the process of a woman, in Sonia Sanchez's words just now, "making pilgrimage to herself."

Mothering is about the business of worry and change and worrying about change. And though I may not be a world-class mother, I am a world-class worrier. It was the novelist Mary Gordon who once wrote in an essay that being a mother means never again knowing a day without fear. I thought she was exaggerating, but she's been right so far. But it also would be fair to say that her statement is not complete. The fear for them is real, and I expected that. But the fun of it, the joy, the incredible pride of knowing that these little people belong to you—and yet can never really belong to you—that, I did not expect. All these things—the fear and the joy—they shape and focus my life now. They imbue my life with a different kind of energy than I have known before. It is a palpable desire to make the world brand new for their sake. But it is difficult on this Mother's Day not to remember the millions of women who, along with me, would birth a new world if they could, but have lost their faith in the very possibility of that world. Some of those women have already pinned on their red or white carnations and headed for their home churches this morning, holding fast to God, but having long ago given up on humanity.

There is a writer named Lisbeth Schorr, who in addition to being a writer is also a social analyst at Harvard University. If her name sounds familiar, it's because she also works often with her husband, Daniel Schorr, the NPR commentator and former television news anchor. She's written two books; the most recent is entitled *Common Purpose,* and it was written as a kind of sequel to an earlier book of hers, *Within Our Reach*. Both these books have as their focus the intersection between social policy, good intentions, and the nature of bureaucracies. And though her analysis and her prescriptions have wide implications for a host of areas that concern us as citizens, Schorr's focus is relentlessly on children, especially poor and desperate children.

The premise of her previous book, *Within Our Reach,* is a simple one. She writes that after thirty years of social programs within the Great Society and beyond it, we know what works to change the lives of the disadvantaged people in our midst. And she is vigorous in making the point that so many of us refuse to accept about social change. What we know how to do, what we could do tomorrow if only we would, are all the things that work not to *beat* the odds, but to *change* the odds. It's long been Schorr's contention that we can't change everything in the lives of a poor child and her mother and father. But we can change enough things to give that family a fighting chance.

Schorr thus puts her finger on one of the most pernicious reasons we are failing the poor and the marginalized of this nation and this world, a reason we rarely utter even to ourselves. We are failing because we want to be perfect. Ever since the early 1980s, when Ronald Reagan declared that "we fought a War on Poverty and poverty won," we have allowed ourselves to be sucked into the pernicious view that the poor will always be with us, so why bother. We've done all we can, and some of what's wrong with people in this country is that it's just part of their nature and will never change. This is an egregious lie, one fed by the personal conservative agendas of some, the discouragement of others, and the sheer exhaustion of still others who can barely figure out what to do with their own lives, much less someone else's.

It turns out that the things we most need to change the world are some of the same things I've learned are needed as a mother and as a minister. For sure, they all take money, and you can bet they all take more money than you feel like you want to spend; sometimes they take more money than you really have. But mothering, ministry, changing the world—they take other things too. They take practicality and flexibility, patience and humor, love and the right kind of accountability. They take a willingness to stand with one another, not in judgment, but in profound and enduring faithfulness, as change takes place.

In her second book, *Common Purpose,* Schorr tells the story of a program called Homebuilders, a Tacoma, Washington, family intervention program that does remarkable work, in large part due to the concentrated time each staff person spends with the families entrusted to their care. At a weekly staff meeting, one of the workers made a request for $200 to help one of her families buy a washing machine. With an infant, two toddlers, and an incontinent aunt, the woman holding this family together didn't need therapy, an expensive home aide, or a bureaucratic song and dance as much as she needed a way not to haul clothes back and forth to the laundromat. So they helped to buy her a washing machine. In hearing this story later, a legal aid lawyer voiced the concern that the decision was irresponsible and unfair. Wasn't it a waste of money to help this family buy such an expensive item? And wouldn't every family then expect that same kind of help for some equally large purchase?

In fact, each member of the Homebuilders staff has discretionary power to effect just such purchases; that's one of the things that makes it a model program. Sometimes it means getting someone's car fixed so they can get to work. Sometimes it means getting a washing machine for a woman strained to the breaking point. Another Homebuilders worker recalls being met at the door by a new client who announced angrily that the last thing she needed in this world was another social worker showing up and telling her what to do. "What I really need to do is clean my house and get it in some kind of order," the woman said. So the social worker asked whether she would like them to start in the kitchen. And together the woman and the social worker cleaned her house and talked together about the troubles she was having with her teenaged daughter. Schorr makes it clear throughout this wonderful and useful book that, in all the programs that work, people are willing to do what's necessary to get the job done. What's necessary is not always heroic, or brave, or glamorous. But it does get the job done.

I would describe the process differently, I guess; I would say that Schorr gave us examples of hearts broken open and placed into the service of someone in need, not in that icky or condescending way that makes even the most earnest activist run for cover, but in the sensible, practical ways that mothers and fathers know, that ministers try to cultivate, that are the province of all of us who want the world to be different than it is.

When we are parenting, or ministering to one another here in this sacred space, or in the world outside, how many of us have lost our hope that things can really change? Our children often make us despair, the members of our church family don't see things our way and make us want to strangle them; the world we want to reconfigure resists and resists and resists. What, then, can we do? We can be faithful people. We can hang on. We can remember that standing with people, helping them to bear their burdens, accompanying them, is one of the tools that makes a changed life possible.

I'm lucky enough to have a faithful mother who stood with me on days when she could hardly stand for herself. I remember that about her all the time, not just today as I wear a red carnation in her honor. Because I know all too well that not everyone has a mother like that, it's what I'll treasure about her all my life. Because of her example, I work hard to be a faithful mother, and I hope it's what my children eventually think of when they think of me. I hope, too, that they learn to see my faithfulness not only in my life with them, but in my life in the world outside our home, where the need for faithfulness takes a different shape but is just as great. And on each Mother's Day, in what I hope is a very long time from now, I like to think they'll pin white carnations to their lapels and remember that they were the reasons I wanted to change the world. I pray they'll wear their white carnations and think of me—and pick up where I left off.

    Amen.

17

SERMONS THAT BUILD
THE LOVING COMMUNITY

In her book *The Cloister Walk*, Kathleen Norris worries that the church has forgotten

> that Christian worship is not, in the words of Margaret Miles, "primarily a gathering of the like-minded" but a gathering of people "to be with one another in the acknowledgment that human existence originates in and is drawn toward love." Even when I find church boring, I try to hold this in mind as a possibility: like all the other fools who have dragged themselves to church on Sunday morning, including the pastor, I am there because I need to be reminded that love can be at the center of all things, if we will only keep it there.[1]

Some sermons seek to build up the congregation's sense of itself as a community that tries to keep love at its center. The occasion may be a special Sunday, such as an anniversary of the congregation or of its building, the installation of a new minister, the first service of the fall or the last service of the spring, or even the start of a fund-raising campaign. These are good times to affirm the central importance of the care and affection that members in most healthy congregations expect to give and receive.

The emphasis on the loving nature of the congregation is apt to be a secondary theme in many sermons of other sorts too. And it is an emphasis that will often show up in other parts of the service: in the opening words, the prayer, the announcements, the welcome of new members, the time for the joys and sorrows or for the candles of concern, special recognition of a

136

longtime member, a ceremony of appreciation for an unsung congregational hero, and the benediction.

Every tradition's worship service provides opportunities to minister to the congregation by building up the sense of their religious community as a safe, warm, and caring place. We communicate this by our attitude, by the inclusive gesture, the affectionate look, the sympathetic prayer, the easy smile, all the little ways we say from the pulpit what our ministry hopes to convey all week: that they are in a community where they are accepted and valued for themselves, as they are, whatever the struggle, whatever the failing, even in the midst of all strain and all failure, even now.

When it comes to religious community, we help the congregation will itself into being by the words we use, by the claims we make on their behalf, by the ideal we state as current fact. We do it over and over, every time we celebrate—as if it were already true—the nature of the community we hope to help them become. Members of the congregation share that hope, and they not only allow us to voice the dream again, they probably expect us to.

So as the service begins, we may say, "We gather this day as a people united in bonds of respect, affection, and common aspiration." Some weeks, some congregations will hear words adapted from Israel Zangwill:

> Come into the circle of love and justice.
> Come into the community of mercy, holiness, and health.
> Come and you shall know peace and joy.[2]

Others will say a unison affirmation:

> Love is the spirit of this church, and service its law.
> This is our great covenant:
> To dwell together in peace,
> To seek the truth in love,
> And to help one another.[3]

And sometimes it will be worth taking the sermon—and indeed, the whole service—to say clearly and strongly that love is at the heart of the community's desire. As with any other sort of sermon, care needs to be given to the actual situation:

THE GAP BETWEEN STATED COMMUNAL IDEALS AND REALITY CANNOT BE SO WIDE AS TO BE RIDICULOUS. Preachers can help create by affirmation what yet should be, but not if the words of affirmation threaten to mock or come across as satire. The ideal we claim to exist cannot outreach current fact by more than a reasonable margin.

As Ronald Allen writes,

It is important for the preacher to respect the complexities and ambiguities of the various communities that become focal in the sermon. The authority of the sermon is undercut when the preacher oversimplifies or paints an overly rosy picture of the nature and functioning of communities…The preacher may wax poetically about how I am joined to all others in the church. But the distasteful fact is that I do not even like all the people in the church. The trustworthiness of the sermon increases as the preacher names and helps the congregation deal with such discrepancies in its own life and in its relationship with other communities in the world.[4]

Therefore, many effective sermons aimed at building the loving community will acknowledge that the effort is not simple, easy, or ever complete. For instance, one minister, speaking in the early autumn after a summer that included the deaths of several especially beloved church members, and during the Jewish High Holy Days, or Days of Awe, began a sermon,

There are words I sometimes say at weddings, that "Life is woven fine of sorrow and joy,[5] and even in our happiest times we remember those who can not be here, especially those who have died." So it is with church life. This is a time of strong mixed feelings: the joy of the community's coming together again, and our sorrow at the loss of treasured members of the church community.

I expect "community" to be a recurrent theme of mine this fall, and what it means to be a people who choose to some important degree to go through life—through gladness and woe—together, in common caring and concern, solace and celebration. And I look forward to our continuing and strengthening and extending the effort in all its finely-woven complexity…

The theme of community-building is a central part of my sense of assignment here: I think you have called Kimi [the associate minister] and me to be midwives to the ongoing birth of this community, this place where lives are linked in challenge and forgiveness, in meditation and action, in attention and affection.

Today I want to affirm the importance of that sense of community of the sort we try to be, a sort that seems lacking in much of contemporary life. The dictionary cites a variety of types of communities, defined by a common neighborhood, or policy, or history, or work. I suppose the definition that comes closest to us is "a unified body of individuals with a common characteristic or interest."

But I like better what Parker Palmer said in an interview in the *Christian Century*, speaking about the many forms of community. "What I'm most interested in now," he said, "is how institutions like schools and churches, where there is a chance that people's lives may be deeply touched, can help folks develop the capacity for connectedness. That capacity requires recognizing the rich resources that the other person has to offer and accepting our accountability to one another."[6]

After developing that theme for some seventeen minutes, the preacher turned to the novel *The Shipping News,* by E. Annie Proulx:

It is a wonderful evocation of the spirit of community in a fishing village in Newfoundland, as well as a touching tale of tenacity, recovery, and love. Quite funny, too.

Speaking of community, trying to describe what community was, Ms. Proulx comes up with this magnificent sentence: "There was a joinery of lives all worked together, smooth in places, or lumpy, but joined."[7]

Have I mentioned yet the lumpiness? Before I close, let me acknowledge that communities made up of people who covenant to live their lives together in mutual respect, support, and all the rest are still made up of people, who can disagree, and sometimes disagreeably; who mean well, or want to, but face their own private crises; who have their own peculiarities, not all of them endearing; and who may at times get a bit cranky.

Community is not just acceptance, service, and search, valued as they are. It also involves forbearance, repentance, forgiveness, and the other acts highlighted by the Days of Awe that have helped Jewish communities to persevere through millennia.

That is what we aim for here: to be a place where aspiring folks like you and me, just as we are, glorious in our prospects, exasperating in our fallings short, may find that precious human achievement, a community. So may it be.[8]

NOT EVERYONE FEELS INCLUDED. There are people in the congregation on many Sundays who have not yet felt welcomed; and others who once felt welcomed but have come to feel alienated from the very congregation whose warm sense of community we stand there proclaiming. We need to have them in mind, too, for our words could be painful in their ears. Still, it is often our job to remind them and everyone else that just such a welcome is what the community wants (or should want) to extend to anyone who will accept it.

One minister said in a sermon:

> I have been wondering and remembering what it feels like to be welcomed in a church like this one. You come into the front hall [and appropriate details are named] or in the back door, and then up the elevator or one flight of stairs or the other, and chances are that someone—a greeter, an usher, a stranger—has said hello or at least made eye contact before you are seated. The service begins. What welcomes you?
>
> Some of you feel welcomed when the organ plays or the choir sings. Music is "home" for a number of folks, a touchstone, a link with a depth of emotion, of spirituality, of participation, of memory.
>
> Others feel the welcome when the room is quiet, when peace descends and envelops and comforts and creates an inviting solitude.
>
> Then there are the words of welcome from a member of the governing board, and announcements (in the bulletin, too)—a sense of activity and inviting involvement.
>
> Some find the sanctuary itself a welcome. The room doesn't change much. A lot of people like the walls, the windows, the trees beyond, the morning's flowers, the care good folks have taken to make this an attractive, welcoming place.
>
> Others don't feel welcomed until someone greets them personally. Remember that. It's not as though some of us are hosts and hostesses and some of us are guests; but rather that each of us, even those who feel brand-new—each one of us is both host and guest. It may be you who extends a hand and makes a difference in somebody's morning.
>
> Some of you feel welcome here because you know we do our best to welcome other people. Free thinkers. Creative spirits. Children. People in search of healing, or sanctuary, or a swift kick, or a religious grounding, or help with their children's pesky and provocative theological questions, uttered from behind the car seat, driving along Route 28. We are people who are looking for new priorities, or a couple of friends, or high-powered intellectualism, or companions in the struggle for justice.

I feel the need so passionately to make room for us all. And yet I know that in real life, some of us are going to walk in these doors and feel right at home, and others are going to come here to church for decades and worry in the car on the way that they won't have anybody to sit with. We enter this community at our own paces: tentative, bombastic, or moderated, with our own styles, expectations, and preferences.

Moreover, we're not always at our best. We can't help ourselves. We say what we later regret, we look askance when some one of us takes a turn being fallible, raise an eyebrow, we judge, we grumble—but hey, at least we know what we're after as a religious community, we try to be inclusive. We are involved in this church, and "welcome" comes with the territory.[9]

THERE ARE ALSO THOSE IN THE CONGREGATION WHO DO NOT *WANT* TO ACCEPT THE INVITATION TO BE A PART OF A LOVING COMMUNITY. It is important that we not imply there is something wrong with that. For all our talk of religious community, the service needs to be a welcoming place for people who have come just to hear a message, the music, the readings, or to be apart from the rest of their lives for a while.

OUR CELEBRATION OF THE CONGREGATION'S SENSE OF ITSELF AS A LOVING COMMUNITY SHOULD NOT CONTRIBUTE TO A SENSE OF SUPERIORITY OR INSULARITY. As important as it may be that members of a congregation come to feel that their lives are linked in caring bonds with those with whom they share the pews (and those who would be there but can't), it is just as important that the community's sense of its loving and caring extends outward as well as inward and includes the surrounding community and humankind.

THE LOVING COMMUNITY WE STRIVE TO INVOKE IS COMPOSED OF PEOPLE WHO COME FROM WIDELY DISPARATE WORLDS. This is true even in apparently homogeneous communities, where most folks might be Nordic, Puerto Rican, or Italian by background. But not all. And even among the majority, there are countless differences in occupation, outlook, physical characteristics, well-being, wealth, sexual orientation, home situation, and much more.

Take age. Excerpts from a pair of lists illustrate the different worlds in which even members of a single family live.

Each year the staff at Beloit College in Wisconsin puts together a list to try to give the faculty a sense of the mindset of that year's incoming freshmen. Here's a recent list:

- They have no meaningful recollection of the Reagan Era and did not know he had ever been shot.

- They were prepubescent when the Persian Gulf War was waged.
- There has been only one Pope. They can only really remember one president.
- They never had a Polio shot and do not know what it is.
- They have never played Pac Man and have never heard of Pong.
- They have always had an answering machine and cable TV.
- They have no idea that Americans were ever held hostage in Iran.
- *The Tonight Show* has always been with Jay Leno.[10]

On the other hand, you're over forty if…

- You know that "Bay of Pigs" is not a farm term.
- Watching a space launch was an event.
- You've put your finger in a hole to dial a phone.
- You remember the first time skateboards were popular.
- You own a John Denver album that wasn't bought through a TV offer.
- You know what an album is.[11]

The diversity in any congregation makes it dangerous to use the words *we* and *us* without care. They are powerful and helpful words in creating a sense of community, but if mishandled, they can exclude instead. "Who among us wouldn't jump for joy about getting a new steeple?" Well, people who cannot jump. And what about the people who do not want a new steeple or think the money could be better spent—they have just been told that they're not part of "us."

In the end, the main point remains: It is worth a preacher's saying again and again that one goal the worshiping congregation sets for itself—hard as the task may sometimes seem, given the difficult variety of human personality and behavior—is to be a community with love at its center.

SAMPLE SERMON

When done well, the message of community's importance will resonate deeply in a local congregation and in larger settings as well, as when a minister preaches to a continental gathering of thousands of denominational delegates. Such was the case when Thandeka, associate professor of theology and culture at the Meadville/Lombard Theological School, delivered this sermon on the first morning of the annual General Assembly of the Unitarian Universalist Association.

Counting Our Blessings[12]
THANDEKA

A few years ago, I met a Catholic priest who had spent several months in Ethiopia doing famine work with people from a local village. The priest was a tall, middle-aged, American man whose body weight and size seemed more suited for the heavy gear of a football lineman than the willowy garments worn by a man of the cloth. I was still a television producer at NBC in Los Angeles and had arranged an interview with him as background work for a program I wanted to produce on religious missions.

During the course of the interview, the priest described a personal experience in Ethiopia that had changed his life. He had participated in a dance in which members of the devastated community spent countless hours rhythmically moving in a circle to the beat of a drum. Without food to forage or land to cultivate, the members of the village could do nothing except wait for their next shipment of food to be flown in. But instead of simply waiting, they danced a slow step that consisted of something that by the count of the priest seemed to have a "one, two, three, jump" sequence. The villagers did this for hours on end.

Wanting to be accepted as a full member of the group, the priest joined in, which immediately brought him face-to-face with a seemingly insurmountable problem: He was dance impaired. He could never jump at the right time. He jumped too soon or too late, or sometimes he simply forgot to jump at all. Needless to say, these missteps provided the rest of the members of the group with countless hours of laughter. The children, quite frequently, were so amused that they would fall out of the circle on to the ground in fits of giggling delight. All the humor, however, was good-natured. The priest said it was neither intended nor experienced as ridicule. Instead, it felt more like the bemused jesting that goes on in a community when someone marches to the beat of a different drummer.

Hour after hour the priest labored to learn to count and then jump in just the right way. How many times did he move into and then out of step with the group's rhythm? Too many to count, he confessed, but as time wore on, something happened that took him completely by surprise.

Tears now welled up in the priest's eyes and he was silent for a long moment. When he finally spoke, his voice seemed no louder than a whisper and I had to move closer to hear his words. "You know," he said, "until that experience I thought that I had known God all of my life. But only as I danced with the other members of the group did I actually feel God's presence in my life." He felt the unconditional love of the members of this group who accepted him with open arms even though his style was so very different from their own.

As Unitarian Universalists, we know something about this feeling of being accepted by a beloved community even when we are out of step with it. We, in fact, know more about this feeling than we think. We have only to remind ourselves of the other side of a major symbol of individualism in our religious tradition: Henry David Thoreau. We tend to remember him as the recalcitrant soloist: the radical individualist, evermore proclaiming himself a "majority of one" in his protests against unfair social policies. And so we picture him in our mind's eye as forever celebrating his isolated Walden Pond soul.

But we must remember that this Yankee individualist also ate his dinner with Ralph Waldo Emerson and his family and washed his clothes at their home while he lived at Walden Pond. We must also remember that Thoreau spent almost a year in Emerson's home while Emerson was in Europe. As social historian Robert D. Richardson Jr., reminds us, Thoreau not only took Emerson's place in the household while Emerson was in Europe, but Thoreau was also adored by Emerson's children and was "emotionally attached to Lydian," Emerson's wife.

Thoreau, Richardson notes,

> had written [Lydian] lofty, ardent letters [when he was in] New York a few years earlier and his journals have passages that have led a number of people to believe that in some complicated and never quite fully acknowledged way he was in love with her. "Others are of my kindred by blood or of my acquaintance but you are mine," Thoreau wrote in his journal for 1848–1849. "You are of me and I of you. I can not tell where I leave off and you begin—there is such harmony when your sphere meets mine."[13]

To be sure, such feelings for Lydian, her children, and his lifelong but tumultuous friendship with Emerson do not negate that other lifelong tendency in Thoreau to get lost in a "well of isolation." But my point is this: although Thoreau celebrated this isolation, he also knew what it meant to count one, two, three, jump and land in the center of a human community and feel loved.

Counting our blessings as Unitarian Universalists means counting on the movements of other persons inside our own heart such that their life pulse and our own life force create a rhythmic harmony of feelings ebbing and flowing in an intimate dance, creating anew the supportive feelings of life itself. And what do we mean when we say the words "life itself"?

We know, for example, that there is a long tradition of Christian theologians ranging from Augustine to Paul Tillich who describe God as "life itself." And we are aware of the Judaic tradition expressed by Martin Buber who describes life itself as the experience of relating to others and by so doing, being in relationship to an eternal Thou. "All real living is meeting," Buber reminds us. Surely this is why he describes sicknesses of the soul as sicknesses of relationship.

As Unitarian Universalists, we tend to speak of "life itself" as the source of our humanity. "Life itself" refers to our ability to relate to others in ways that affirm their inherent dignity and worth, as well as our own. Henry Nelson Wieman called such encounters "creative interchange" because he knew that the religious person, as he said, "must not only be intellectually persuaded but emotionally stirred."

Today, we have gathered 3,200 strong, because we know what it means to count our blessings. It means counting one, two, three, and then jumping into the hearts of our associational life as members of this religious movement and representatives of its congregations. It means arguing, disagreeing, becoming exasperated, and then embracing each other once again. And so as our General Assembly gets underway, I offer this prayer:

Let us remember not only to silently count our blessings while we are here, but also to actually count them aloud and then jump when a session becomes particularly difficult. Let us hop, skip, and take other leaps of faith, hoping that other persons who might also feel threatened and afraid, lost and ignored, or alienated and out of sync with the group will see in our own inimitable step a heartfelt sign that life is present ever-new, ever-renewing. Let the congregation say Amen.

18

SERMONS THAT INSPIRE

Most preachers know the experience. They have been struggling along, trying to do the best they can under the circumstances (the pastoral pressures on their time, the congregation's distraction over some dispute), and occasionally it seems as if the words of the sermon are touched with power, insight, hope, and grace—but after the service, much of the talk is about a church committee meeting, a controversial decision by a town board, the weather, the crops.

And then a letter unexpectedly arrives from a parishioner, and later, another parishioner takes the pastor aside. They say they don't know how they could have gotten through the awful time after a sister or brother died, or how they could have mustered the courage to make the bold and right decision they did, or how every day they live with greater courage, confidence, resilience, perspective, compassion, forbearance, and faith because of your sermons.

Your sermons. You spoke of the inevitability of change, and a woman finally accepted that one stage of her life was over and that it was time to move on in fresh hope. You spoke of the difficulty and importance of forgiveness, and a man finally called his child, parent, former business partner, or ex-spouse, and reconciliation began. You offered a story, a poem, an insight, a reading, a parable, a lesson, a presence, and people were more able to endure, and even to flourish, to find for themselves ways of living that were more productive, gratifying, creative, kind—more inspired.

Many sermons seek to provoke and nurture just that inspiration, that in-spiriting. As much as for any other reason, that is what many parishioners come to worship services seeking. They come when the week was long,

146

hard, and tedious, and when it was frantically busy. They come when they are feeling discouraged and weary in body and soul, and when they are feeling anxious and distracted.

They come to be buoyed, to hear words that bring a renewed sense of life's mercy, blessing, and possibility. Richard Wright put it well: "Our churches are where we dip our tired bodies in cool springs of hope, where we retain our wholeness and humanity despite the blows of death"[1] —and despite the other blows the spirit must endure.

Likewise, the playwright George Bernard Shaw once spoke of the theater as "a place for the exaltation of the human spirit and a haven from gloom and despair."[2] The church may serve just such a role.

Parishioners come for that same haven and nurture for their spirits (along with exaltation) even when all is going well for them, and they are feeling fine. Perhaps they come for a booster shot against the next contagion. Perhaps they come out of a healthy sense that material satisfactions are not what life is most deeply about. Perhaps it is the hope of keeping their spirits alive to life, as religion has often aspired to do.

"Nothing else matters much," wrote Harry Emerson Fosdick, "not wealth, nor learning, nor even health—without this gift: the spiritual capacity to keep zest in living. This is the creed of creeds, the final deposit and distillation of all…important faiths: that [we] should be able to believe in life."[3]

For many people, the concern for sustenance, hope, meaning, and zest is expressed by the contemporary use of the word *spirituality*, and preachers are appreciated (sometimes to their surprise) by parishioners who believe their sermons fill this need. If you doubt the hunger of spirits today for words of this kind, pay a visit to your local bookstore and look at the self-help or spirituality section. If there is a market for so many books that seek to feed that hunger, many people in our pews probably feel it as well.

But the job of providing inspiration for the spirit is, for the clergy, as old as the profession. That is a big part of what we are there for, to be a source of inspiration, encouraging the breath of life itself in those we serve. To be inspired literally means "to breathe in," "to take in spirit," to find a greater, stronger, deeper, fuller spirituality.

For those of us who are parish ministers, inspiring members of the congregation is a task we work at all week, whether in counseling on Tuesday or in a casual conversation at the drug store on Friday. So, too, there we are on Sunday morning, encouraging their spiritual strength and depth.

We want to help them connect with sources of spiritual renewal, whether it be the God of their common faith, the spirit of life, the community of faith, or their own personal systems of belief and practice. We want to help them transcend their everyday concerns with a sense of a beyond or a "more," to put their wearying struggles in some larger, comforting, or ennobling perspective.

The effort to inspire takes a variety of forms but, broadly speaking, perhaps only two: It can mean bringing to people—in our discussions with them Tuesday, Friday, or in Sunday's sermon—encouragement and enthusiasm for their spirits, tending their spirituality with words that enliven. Or it can mean tending their spirituality by bringing stillness, peace, and greater calm.

One of the authors humorously took on the latter task in a December sermon:

> The newsletter editor of the First Parish in Wayland, Massachusetts, recently ran her favorite *New Yorker* squib:
>
> "IMPORTANT NOTICE. If you are one of the hundreds of parachuting enthusiasts who bought our *Easy Sky Diving* book, please make the following correction: On page 8, line 7, the words 'state zip code' should have read 'pull rip cord.'—Adv. in the Warrenton, (Va.) *Fauquier Democrat.*"
>
> I worry about things like this during the Christmas season. Had I been a parachuting enthusiast, and had I breezed through *Easy Sky Diving* during the month of December, I'd still be flying through the air, picking up speed, shouting my zip code.
>
> Zip codes aren't important. Rip cords are. During the Advent season, it's all too easy to confuse one for the other. The "zip codes" of the season—the replacement bulbs, the four sticks of butter, the fruit-by-mail catalogs, the party shoes—have our attention, and before we know it, we're picking up speed and shouting out those "zip codes" without ever asking why.
>
> Perhaps we should look to our rip cords. Our lifelines, in December as always, are our inner quiet, the love we exchange, and our efforts to make the world whole. We can slow the descent. We can take in the view. And we can anticipate a gentle landing on the twenty-fifth.[4]

Spirituality can be of either the enlivening or quieting kind, and deciding what is needed is something that preachers have to develop skills for—whether it is during the week or on Sunday morning, finding the blend of encouragement and calm that tends the whole of a person's spirituality, or a congregation's.

The other author referred to that blend in a January sermon on *acedia,* or spiritual torpor, also known as the devil of the noonday sun:

To the indolent, I wish you energy and discipline; and to the driven, I wish you serenity and renewal.

And for the rest of us, insofar as the cause of our spiritual boredom and sense of drift is neither endemic laziness nor chronic hyperactivity, but just the season, just a tiredness that creeps upon us after annual inventory, or the last day of classes, or too many verses of "It Came Upon the Midnight Clear," know that the world is still tantalizing, as it was before and will be again.

Wait it out, keep breathing, be faithful in small ways. The juices will flow again. Hang in there and try to stay open to the newness as it awakens your spirit afresh: a new book, new interests, new loves, new caring, and yet again, the demon's demise, new energy, new joy.[5]

To be a caring, effective clergyperson is to be on the side of that awakening, to foster it in many of our pastoral interactions, and to raise the chances of its happening most times we preach.

Three points before the chapter ends: First, our success at inspiring parishioners in the long run depends in no small part on our own ability to maintain enough of an inner life to raise up our own sense of hope, our own sense of enthusiasm for life, our own feeling that things are okay and that there is a peace that can be ours, despite the agony on the way.

Second, as it is true for every one of the eight types of sermons in this section, emphasis can be placed on inspiration and spirituality too often and carried too far. This is especially true if one defines inspiration and spirituality too narrowly, to the neglect of social issues. Phillips Brooks knew the importance of inspiration. "The trouble in much of our pastoral work is [that] it tries to meet the misfortunes of life with comfort and not with inspiration,"[6] he wrote. But in the same collection, he also wrote, "The more sacred the preacher's office is, the more he [or she] is bound to care for all the interests of every child of God…When some clear question of right and wrong presents itself…then your sermon is a poor, untimely thing if it deals only with the abstractions of eternity, and has no word to help the men [and women] who are dizzied with the whirl."[7] Spirituality and inspiration are fraudulent when they operate in isolation from religion's other central concerns.

Finally, religion as it is defined from the pulpit is equally inadequate if the preacher is constrained from using evocative skills that lift the congregation's spirit. Reason, doctrine, social analysis, and institutional support can receive too much attention, important as these may be. Other truths live in other forms, in story and poetry, quiet and calm, enthusiasm and drama, comfort and dream.

As Gail Caldwell said about "works of recent fiction that mattered most," effective sermons have "what art should always share: Each book [or sermon, we would add], through its prose or vision or depth or aesthetic reach, offered a cohesive universe and left a trace of heart or wisdom across the sky."[8]

People in the pews hunger for heart and wisdom, for hope and courage, as much as they did two centuries ago when John Murray advised, "You may possess only a small light but uncover it, let it shine, use it in order to bring more light and understanding to the hearts and minds of men and women. Give them, not Hell, but hope and courage."[9]

SAMPLE SERMON

One memorable sermonic attempt to inspire congregations to appreciate life more fully has been delivered on a number of occasions, with an evolving set of quotations and stories, by the parish minister Scott Alexander, now minister of the River Road Church in Bethesda, Maryland. In person, the effect of his words is heightened for most congregants by his enthusiastic presentation. Indeed, those who have heard him preach will not be surprised that in his own manuscript, many more passages are rendered in text that is capitalized, italicized, and/or presented in boldface, with even freer use of exclamation points and robust language. His remarks are all the more powerful for his personal sharing, mid-sermon, of his own difficulty in hearing the lesson, his own involvement in a situation of painful loss, and the effect of that situation on his own acceptance of the sermon's message.

N.D.Y. [10]
SCOTT ALEXANDER

I am a fortunate, blessed man. Aside from AIDS and heart disease, I have no problems.

Arthur Ashe

I am a runner. I run religiously (some say compulsively!) every day, usually 12 to 14 miles, in all seasons, weather, and conditions. Running is my noontime joy, my zen discipline, my cheap psychiatrist, my blessed addiction. Over the years, I have seen many amazing things and learned many important spiritual lessons while jogging my way through my world.

Some years back I had a running partner named Stan who went out virtually every day with me, a curmudgeonly conservative who loved to complain about the state of almost everything. Over the years, Stan and I had a lot of significant interactions, but one autumnal run with him I shall never forget. It was a bright and crisp mid-November day. Everything was radiant, alive, stunning…The trees (gleefully dropping their cascading leaves) were ablaze in bright shades of red, yellow, purple…

We finally ran into one particularly beautiful neighborhood canopied by massive oak trees. As we turned one corner I was struck by the huge, block-long, three-foot-high pile of dry, inviting oak leaves the homeowners had neatly raked into the street. Stan (as usual) was droning on pompously about the evils of teenage welfare cheats (or some such nonsense), but I, by then, was paying no attention to his negative rantings. I was paying full attention to the reckless holiness of the autumnal day before me.

All of a sudden I was seized by an impulse of the heart I could not control. Without warning I dove headfirst into the luscious leaf pile, completely disappearing from sight. Stan jogged and droned on for several seconds before he noticed that I was gone. Finally, sensing my absence, he turned around and howled with delight as my leaf-strewn head popped up out of the pile.

I cleaned myself off of the aromatic leaves, caught up to Stan, and we resumed our run in silence. Then Stan begun chuckling. "All right, wise guy, what if there had been something awful just beneath the surface of that pile where you dove in?" I instantly laughed; it was after all pure Stan, negative and sarcastic. And he was right, of course, I would have *not* been a very happy existential camper if, in my impetuous moment of reckless abandon, I *had* encountered trash cans or abandoned tricycles or some big pile of ripening manure. I pondered all this for a moment as we ran on, and then turned to Stan in a moment of genuine spiritual insight and said, "But Stan…*there wasn't…there wasn't.*"

Off and on for the rest of that day, I pondered the spiritual implications of my reckless, joyful dive (juxtaposed by Stan's negative foreboding), and I came up with an affirmation that has remained with me. To the wise simpleton—to the innocent soul who takes life at face value and enjoys the simple gifts and pleasures it so recklessly offers up—leaf piles into which you dive seldom hold unpleasant surprises. But for those of you for whom there is always something awful lurking in leaf piles that you are about to dive headlong and headfirst into, life will not disappoint your negativity either. Put bluntly, if you are one who always assumes that something bad is about to happen, it will be there waiting for you!

Now, this is a dangerous idea for a rationally trained, nonsuperstitious minister! I surely cannot prove this scientifically, mind you, and please know that I categorically reject the idea that floats around some "New Age" circles that suggests we human beings "choose," "will," and "are responsible for" everything bad that happens to us. I once heard someone say to a woman struggling with cervical cancer, "Why did you choose to get cancer at this point in your life?" Dear God, protect us from such nonsense. Even the most clever and capable amongst us is *not* in control of the countless things, both good and bad, that happen to us during a lifetime.

But in the same spiritual breath I must say that I have come to believe that most often *what we lead with spiritually*—that is, the essential attitude of heart we bring to any moment or encounter—goes a long way in determining how satisfying (or unsatisfying) that experience will be for us. I believe that (generally speaking) if we lead with innocence, anticipation, and joy in daily life—if we *lean* into life with trust and gladness—we will be rewarded with innocent, joyful pleasures. But if, on the other hand, you lead with suspicion, negativity, and fear, your life will somehow, usually, curiously, "lower itself" to conform to your pessimism and negativity. Does this spiritual observation ring true to any of you?

Unfortunately, you and I live in a culture that increasingly relishes and systematically nurtures our "negativity" about life, that encourages us to whine and complain about the very substance and structure of the astounding existence we have been given, that supports those who chronically see themselves as victims of a cruel and capricious creation, that bemoans the fact that our world doesn't seem to singularly devote itself to our personal happiness…

I am reminded of a meditation written by my colleague Al Perry on Maine:

> In the fall we complain about the cold and all those leaves to rake…
> In the winter we complain about all the ice and snow…
> In the spring we complain about all the mud and rain…
> In the summer we complain about the mosquitoes and heat…
> But in what season do we rejoice and give thanks,
> that this earth seems to possess just the right climate
> to permit the existence of life…and us?

The words of Catholic mystic Thomas Merton come to mind:

> Life comes into being without any invitation of our own: we suddenly find ourselves in it. And as soon as we recognize ourselves as alive, we become aware that we tend toward inevitable death. If we do not gain some adequate understanding of our life and our death during the life-span that is ours, our life will become nothing but a querulous refusal, a series of complaints that it must end in death.

Then the fear of death becomes so powerful that it results in a flat refusal of life. Life itself becomes a negation, a neurosis, a frivolity.

If Thomas Merton is a little too esoteric for you, try Pogo. In one of my all-time favorite strips, Churchy La Femme is passing the day with Porky, in that leaky little boat down in that leaky little swamp that is their home, reading the newspaper, the headline of which proclaims, "Sun to burn out in 3 billion years, ending all life on earth." Churchy breaks into self-pitying tears, crying, "Woe is me. I'm too young to die," to which the ever-wise and sarcastic Porky retorts, "Aw shut up. You're lucky to be here in the first place."

Recently I walked into a flower shop near my home, stepping out of one of those cold, driving rains New England is so famous for. The saleswoman behind the counter was clearly *not* in a good spiritual mood. With a scowl etched both in her face and voice she greeted me with, "What a miserable day!"—to which I spontaneously responded with my characteristic cheerfulness, "Yea, but it sure beats being dead." Now, when I said it I had truly not expected my little "throw-away" line to be some sort of profound revelation for her—but it was! She looked at me like I had hit her in the face with a brick. "Sure beats being dead," she repeated thoughtfully, "Wow, I guess if you look at it that way it's not so miserable a day after all." She cheerfully wrapped my flowers, and as I left the shop I could still hear her muttering to herself, "Sure beats being dead. Sure beats being dead." When I was ready to leave she said, "Have a nice day!"

My message to you today, dear friends, is as spiritually simple as it is blunt. While I might prefer to say it a bit more elegantly, Porky had it right! We are lucky just to be here in the first place. When are we going to wake up to that holy simplicity? Our first, everyday spiritual principle ought to be to shut up, stop our incessant whining and complaining, and be grateful, truly grateful, for the gift of having the opportunity to hang around this rich and amazing world in the first place! As Jewish theologian Abraham Heschel put it, "Just to be is a blessing. Just to live is holy."

How easy it is, beneath the inevitable press and irritation of daily life, to lose sight of that towering and gracious truth. Only when we spiritually cut through all the distractions of daily living do we ever have a chance to remember this essential truth. Never mind, for the moment, the details, even our most cogent complaints against this often difficult, irritating, and capricious creation. For the moment, let us simply breathe deep of life and be struck dumb in common gratitude for this rich miracle of human being that has so generously been given us. Even with all the irritations, ironies, and idiocies, this gift of everyday being is a pretty stunning treasure. Even on a bad day, our hearts should drop to a simple, grateful knee, and give quiet thanks for the mere fact of having the chance to be around! It's like my colleague Dick Gilbert writes: "The gift of life is not a gift of great sweeps of years, but in the exhilaration of a single day—the day which we live now. Why can we not look at the gift of today and fall on our knees in gratitude?"

Like all ministers, I preach this sermon on spiritual gratitude first and foremost to myself this morning. As optimistic as I naturally am, I know all about finely cultivating my own spiritual ingratitude. Every time (for example) every time I get the flu (or some other virus that's going around) and feel awful, *every time* I say (to God or the "life force" or whatever), "Oh, if I could only feel as good as I do on an ordinary, uneventful, nonsick day, I will never, ever take that simple, pleasant normalcy for granted again." And (without fail) as soon as the virus runs its course and I feel better, I forget my spiritual promise to cultivate and keep a lively gratitude for the ordinary in my heart. Any of you do that?

In *The Riddle of the Ordinary,* author Cynthia Ozick points out what a pickle we have gotten ourselves into when it comes to appreciating the gift of ordinary life. She writes:

> By making itself so noticeable—it is around us all the time—the Ordinary has got itself in a bad fix with us: we hardly ever notice it. The Ordinary, simply by *being* so ordinary, tends to make us ignorant or neglectful; when something does not insist on being noticed, when we aren't grabbed by the collar or struck on the skull by a presence or an event, we take for granted the very things that most deserve our gratitude. And this is the...deepest point concerning the Ordinary: that it *does* deserve our gratitude. The Ordinary lets us live out our humanity; it doesn't scare us, it doesn't excite us...The Ordinary is above all *what is expected*. And what is expected is not often thought of as a gift.[11]

I am a forty-eight-year-old gay male. For more than a decade, the AIDS pandemic has swirled painfully around me, touching and transforming almost every aspect of my life (except, blessedly, my own personal health and that of my partner). This terrible disease has deepened my spirituality and ministry in ways I never could have imagined (nor, God knows, ever wanted). Like most gay men and lesbian women my age, I have lost so many wonderful friends in the prime of their lives: Charles, Mark, Sandy, Jeffrey, Ross, Bruno, Tony, Chuck, and (most recently) my dear colleague Deane.

I have lost count of the many acquaintances who have died of this disease. My own church, the Universalist Meetinghouse in Provincetown, Massachusetts, has been ravaged by this disease. Hundreds have died in that village over the last decade, and the layers of grief in that community are unbelievable. My heart will never, ever accept or integrate these losses. My dreams at night will always be haunted by the images of these sweet souls.

A part of my spiritual response to this epidemic as a Unitarian Universalist has been to *fight*—to resist and refuse to believe that this disease, and our society's inadequate and intolerant response, needs to happen. I am an AIDS activist on both the national and local level. I know the struggle with this disease—for compassion, for justice, and yes, for a cure—must go on…and I am committed to personally see the struggle through.

But what I really want to tell you is that something else has happened to me as a result of my painful encounter with this epidemic, something wondrous and healing that I could never have guessed could or would arise out of all the hell and havoc that is HIV/AIDS. Somehow my encounter with all the life negation of AIDS has quietly filled my heart with a saving sense of just how holy is the gift of my being alive. Somehow witnessing so many good and lovely people bravely struggling for life against death has filled me with a fierce appreciation for the holy blessing of life's ordinary moments.

This spiritual sense breaks into my life in little, mundane moments of everyday existence, when—for no particular reason—I suddenly see, with fresh and grateful eyes, the simple glory and goodness of this world.

It happened the other day when my partner Collins and I were running (somewhat distracted and disengaged from both nature and one another by a predictable variety of life's little irritations) when we suddenly came over a high Cape Cod dune to see the radiant winter sun gently sinking (in all its red-hot glory) into Massachusetts Bay—and the whole world suddenly felt holy.

It happened when I caught a glimpse (a few weeks back) of a gaggle of squealing little kids playing on a jungle gym with that unfettered innocence and glee that come so naturally to the young. How is it we lose that reckless appreciation for fun?

It even happened recently (believe it or not) on the 405 expressway in Los Angeles. There I was, stuck in traffic as can only be in Southern California, going nowhere fast. But I had recently read Jon Kabat-Zinn's wonderful book *Wherever You Go, There You Are,* and was somehow able to take a deep breath and see how much there was to appreciate in that moment. I put on the classical radio station, began smiling at the drivers around me (and they smiled back and did not pull weapons and begin shooting), and looked around me at the sun-kissed clouds billowing gently around the mountains off on the horizon. Even stuck on the 405, one can be blessed by life's simple beauty and wonders.

How wildly generous is the hand of life, how profligate its blessings! And each of you—no doubt—could recite your own lists of such grateful and glorious moments, but there would be no end to it. It will have to suffice for you to remember and relish these moments in your own hearts.

[*Pause*]

Very early in the AIDS epidemic, my good friend and colleague Mark DeWolfe contracted AIDS/HIV disease, one of the first ministers to become ill (and eventually die) from this disease. Mark was a blithe and indefatigable spirit—a kind and intelligent young man with an irrepressible joie de vivre. The last time I saw him was at a continental gathering of denominational delegates. Mark, who would tragically be dead in just a few months, was wearing a T-shirt, just like this one—I'll bet some of you wondered when I was going to get to it!—with three great big letters emblazoned across it. N...D...Y. Any guesses?

Not Dead Yet. The reason he had this T-shirt custom-made for himself was that so many people had not yet known someone with this disease and were very nervous about Mark and AIDS. They were unintentionally treating him as if he were already dead. So Mark, ever the extrovert with a dry sense of humor, moved around the assembly in this T-shirt, and someone would inevitably ask, "N.D.Y., what's that?" To which Mark would exclaim, "Not Dead Yet—I'm not dead yet!"

And do you know what? He wasn't dead yet! Mark, ever grateful for the gift of life, wasn't done living. He wasn't done working with the congregation he so loved; he wasn't done sharing the pleasures of everyday life with his partner, Jim; he wasn't done traveling (near and far) to see the interesting marvels of this planet; he wasn't done living, caring, fighting, sharing, and loving. And God bless him for showing me (and so many others) how to live—fully, bravely, passionately, and purposefully—to its end.

And that is the good news this simpleton from Boston brings you this morning, dear friends: You are not dead yet either! And so you can tell your spouse (who stayed home in bed this morning to read the Sunday paper) what you learned in church today. I'd like us to all say it together: "I am not dead yet!" [*Congregation repeats.*] Once more for spiritual emphasis: "I am not dead yet." [*Again.*]

That's right, you *are* not dead yet! No matter what your complaints, irritations, limitations, or sorrows are (and God knows we all have some), you have (before all that *mishagoss*) been blessed with being alive in a rich and miraculous creation. You have been given life, a world filled with beauty, holiness, and grace, and it is your spiritual duty not to squander or miss it.

In the gospel of Thomas, one of the "unofficial" books written about the life of Jesus, it is reported that Jesus was asked by his followers, "When will the Kingdom come?" And he responded, "It will not come by watching for it. It will not be said, 'Look, here it is,' or 'Look, there it is.' Rather the [Kingdom of God] is spread out upon the earth and people do not see it" (Gospel of Thomas 113:1–4). The Kingdom of God is spread out upon the earth, and people do not see it.

It's true isn't it? We are often blind to the beauty and blessing that is all around us. We sleepwalk through most of our days, missing most of the simple glory that sings around us. I pray you, dear friends, today and every day that follows, as you return to your ordinary routines, *see* it, *savor* it, *celebrate* it, *sing* it. Open your eyes and your heart to the holy miracle that is all around you. For you are not dead yet, and there is time to be quietly saved by love, by hope, and by the simple joy of being alive in this world. Amen.

19

SERMONS THAT EXPLAIN
A PARTICULAR RELIGIOUS IDENTITY

As religious leaders, we are Baptists or Catholics or Presbyterians or Jews. Clergy are ordained by members of the United Church of Christ, a Unitarian Universalist congregation, or the Disciples of Christ. We see ourselves as Methodists or Muslims. Our religious denominations and traditions inform our theologies and our practices of ministry.

Yet what surveys show much denominational interest on the part of the average parishioner? Do today's churchgoers say they come to church to hear about what it means to be an Episcopalian or a Nazarene? Not that we know of.

Nonetheless, identification as a member of a particular religious group offers stability, credibility, and a sense of community to our church members. After all, we ministers have inherited or adopted a specific religious history, wisdom, and language that contribute to our own identities as spiritual people. Whether our parishioners ask for it or not, clergy are the bearers of that heritage.

In their book *The Teaching Minister*, Clark Williamson and Ronald Allen proclaim that the *central* task of ministry is *teaching*.[1] "That is to say, it is not only wrong but decidedly unhelpful and has contributed greatly to the present decline of the mainline churches, when clergy understand themselves in and act in ways fundamentally different from this."[2] Any number of observers of contemporary society comment on the fact that modern Americans have little knowledge of religious teachings, symbolism, literature, ritual, or story.

158

Teaching the tradition need not be as deadening and irrelevant as it sounds. We are not promoting a stifling rendition of constricting custom and doctrine, nor are we suggesting that all things traditional merit promotion. Where our denominations have displayed bigoted behavior; emphasized what we now see as idiotic, or merely ignorant, theology; embarrassed us by proudly proclaiming the righteousness of what now seems to be the "wrong" side of an ethical issue; and so forth, we can acknowledge the history, put the episode in perspective, and move ahead. The point is that our religious heritages can be a rich and positive source of grounding for the people in the pews.

Appropriately enlivened, our traditions invite us to welcome our religions as part of our very identities as human beings. "When we pass on a tradition, which families do when they tell stories from the family history, we also incorporate people into a tradition. Not to be incorporated into a tradition is not to know who you are, to whom you are related, where you come from, or where you are going."[3] We can offer this gift to members of our congregations.

In describing "religious identity" to his congregation, Shelter Rock in New York, the Reverend Barry Andrews says that having a religious identity

> is not necessarily the same thing as knowing our history and heritage, although it includes them. Our heritage is made up of our values and ideals, our art, architecture, music and poetry, our summer camps and sacred sites, our traditions and folklore. Our history includes all the facts about us—people, places and events, not only "from long ago and many lands," but also here and now at Shelter Rock. Fundamentally, religious identity is a feeling that, "This is my church. People know me here. And I know them."[4]

During the course of the year, the preacher may focus specifically on a denominational biography—a historical figure, musician, theologian, or social activist. Or maybe a drama will tell a story of the congregation's response to the crisis of AIDS/HIV, or indigenous music from Germany will link a Lutheran congregation to its roots, or a pantomime involving the children will enact the antiwar movement once active in the church. Perhaps an anniversary provides an occasion for describing a vignette, or an article in a popular magazine demands a particular religious response.

Or it could simply be the cycle of the seasons that provides the opportunity to tell of a local historical event. For example, in Wayland, Massachusetts, at Christmas time, one congregation sings the same carol at the end of every service. The words were written by a former minister of theirs, and every few years they tell the story of the first singing of "It Came Upon the Midnight Clear" in 1849.

> During my girlhood in Wayland [wrote Catherine Jewett Coolidge Tatnall], the people of the town had a keen and devoted interest in the activities of the First Parish Church and the affairs of the church were common topics for conversation.
>
> I remember many precious traditions of this dignified old parish, but one in particular appealed to my girlish fancy as being very dramatic and picturesque, so that it has always been a memory.
>
> It was a story told by some older member of the church, when calling upon our family. It related to the first singing of Mr. Sears' Christmas carol (sometimes called "The Angels' Song"), beginning, "It came upon the midnight clear."
>
> At the time it was written, Mr. Sears was living in a house on Plain Road in what is now the Tower Hill district of Wayland. He sent word out among his parishioners that he had written a new Christmas hymn which he would like to have the people try out at his home on Christmas Eve. So, from here and there about the town they came over the snow in their sleighs to sing, for the first time, this glorious carol, which is now sung throughout the world!
>
> The only spinet in town was brought to Mr. Sears' house on a horse sled from Abel Glezen's home on Training Field Road.
>
> A choir was chosen from the assemblage and the beautiful words of the hymn sung to the quaint accompaniment of the spinet.[5]

To be sure, nobody comes to church specifically to learn how a minister who served the congregation before any of us were born debuted his Christmas hymn. As Harry Emerson Fosdick put it, "Nobody except the preacher comes to church desperately anxious to discover what happened to the Jebusites."[6] But the congregation does have an interest in knowing what is special about this particular church, this congregation as opposed to the others down the street.

Of course, not only do we have the sermon at hand as a method of teaching our ways as religious people on a Sunday morning, we have all that surrounds it: the welcoming greeting at the door, rituals such as communion, the lighting of the chalice, the sharing of joys and concerns, passing the peace, flower Sunday, the use of sacred texts, social action announcements, the architecture and art in the church itself, coffee hour, distinctive hymns found in a denominational hymn book, the participation of children, the offering. We can refer to and explain these practices in our sermons. And once the members of the congregation understand the significance of our practices, rituals, and symbolism, those aspects of our religious traditions themselves become avenues for teaching.

Moreover, members of the church want to know how our church sees the world. What is unique to our theological perspective? What values and teachings does our tradition promote? What for us is sacred? Why should I care as a member of the United Church of Canada or as a Christian Scientist? Being Greek Orthodox, how should I behave in the world? Ministers are uniquely trained and have been granted the authority to offer perspectives on these questions. As Langdon Gilkey said in the 1960s, "A misunderstanding of the priesthood of all believers leads to the silly conclusion that all members of the congregation are equally educated in the faith and equal in authority when speaking about it. In a church that does not engage in the theological education of its members, this means that the lay voice simply reflects the voice of the culture."[7] We need to teach the laity the tools for thinking theologically for themselves, and we need to share our traditions and religious expectations.

One minister tells this story:

> Once upon a time, forty-five years ago almost to the day, eighteen people met in Alabama in response to an ad in the *Birmingham News*. It was an unlikely ad, an ad about starting up a Unitarian church. Two years later, the group that had begun by responding to the newspaper ad had grown into a full-fledged Unitarian church. In four more years, the church members were ready to move into their beautiful new building.
>
> And you know what they did in the midst of the flurry of the move? They took a vote. In October of 1958, our church in Birmingham voted that the doors would always be open to all people.[8]
>
> Not a big deal? This was Birmingham, Alabama, in the '50s. Segregation. African Americans and whites did not worship together. Blacks and whites were forbidden by law to sit together.
>
> I like to believe that if we had been Unitarian Universalists in Birmingham in the '50s and '60s, we would have behaved with the same courage and long-term commitment. Of course we would have, indeed, some of you actually did participate full force in the civil rights movement. You made the trip, once upon a time. And many of you of the next generation have carried the work forward, and will carry it forward into the next century.
>
> We're still making the trip, by inches, maybe, but our commitment is firm. Because as the Reverend Lynn Ungar says,

"There is something out there that calls to us, something not quite definable that calls us out of ordinary existence, and asks us not only to do more, but to be more."[9]

This is not just any story, it is a story about the members of one religious denomination. The sermon tells the congregation what the church values, what the church is grateful for, and what they, as parishioners, can be proud of. It is their story, their heritage, their religion.

As clergy, each of us is a teacher of the tradition. It is ours to pass along with passion and commitment.

SAMPLE SERMON

One would never guess the topic or purpose of this sermon from the opening story. In the course of describing a hiking trip near Mount Ranier, the Reverend Rebecca Parker establishes an extended metaphor. As the sermon unfolds, we begin to understand that in the next three sections, she's going to teach us about the three cornerstones of liberal religion: tolerance, reason, and freedom. She discusses each principle and tells a substantial story to illustrate each one.

This sermon represents a relaxed preaching style that takes its time and was delivered entirely without notes. (What you read here is a transcription.) Parker, president of Starr King School for the Ministry in Berkeley, California, delivered this sermon as a guest preacher to a group of laypeople and clergy at a regional meeting in Ohio.

Something Far More Deeply Interfused[10]
REBECCA PARKER

I'm awfully glad to be here with all of you today, to feel the crisp, cool air of the fall, and the moisture, both of which we miss out on in the Bay Area, where we've been in a long-time drought, where the land is thirsty for the refreshment of a change of season. It's a pleasure to be here and see you at work, with all the practical, diligent efforts it takes to sustain our life together as religious people.

I grew up a long way from Ohio, in a small corner of southwest Washington in a town named Hoquiam, which is just at the southern edge of the Olympic National Park and the rainforest that goes along the coast of northern Washington. It's so rainy in Hoquiam where I grew up that when I was a child, I believed summer was a one-day-a-year holiday, like

Christmas! We had 160 inches of annual rain there, and the whole world was wrapped in mist and moisture and gray skies.

The family I grew up in was one that had a hard time keeping body and soul together. We were rich in things of the spirit, and poor in things of the flesh—which meant that when it came to summer vacations for that one-day holiday, we had to use all of our ingenuity to have as much fun as possible with scarce financial resources. So what became our family tradition was to spend our summer vacations hiking the high country of the Olympic Mountains and perhaps the Cascade Mountains. Some of you may have seen these high mountains of the Pacific rim.

This was before the days when hiking had become the high-tech sport that it is today. All of our gear was homemade, makeshift. I remember my very first backpack was something that my father had constructed out of two halves of an old broomstick and a Girl Scout cookie box—all strapped together into a contraption, and my goods were carried there. We had a lot of fun making do with very little.

When I got to be a teenager, my two brothers, Howard and Theodore, and I used to go hiking by ourselves on occasion; and one of our most memorable trips was one that we took up to the high country of the Cascades, up to a place where we'd never been, Spray Park Meadows. We decided to go exploring to this high, alpine meadow on the shoulders of Mount Ranier. We began our hike at Mowich Lake, under the protection of the tall forest. This hike began like almost every hike that we ever went on—it began in the rain. We had on our ponchos, and our gators—we knew how to deal with the wet.

We hiked through the quiet, soft, drizzling rain for the first three-quarters of the day; then, toward the late afternoon, we realized that we no longer were hiking through the rain—because we had walked right into the cloud. By the time we came through the alpine forest up to the upper edges of the alpine meadow, the cloud encompassed us so thickly that we could only see the muddy trail ahead of us by staring straight down at our feet. Nevertheless, we walked across the meadow to the upper reaches where the heather was blooming with its bright pink little flowers, and the Indian paintbrush was bending over, wet with dew.

We made a camp up against the edges of a high protective boulder. We cooked our chicken soup, spread out our sleeping bags, and stretched our tarp, and then when all was set up, my brother Howard got out the geological survey contour map, looked at it, and said, "Mount Ranier must be around here somewhere!"

And so we took the contour map and spread it out on top of the boulder, and Howard and Ted and I gathered 'round and stared at the compass.

We had one of those compasses that had the arrow that wavers as it points to the north, but even with that somewhat faulty compass, we could figure out where we were: Howard said, "Here's where we came, and here's where we must be right now, which means Mount Ranier must be right…THERE."

Now, this really happened. The instant Howard said, "Mount Ranier must be right…THERE," we all turned our heads and looked into the pea soup fog; and just as we turned, the fog went like this: it opened, like two opaque sliding glass doors, pulling away from each other at the center—and Mount Ranier was THERE. It filled up the entire sky; and it was just that moment of twilight when the sun was sinking over the Pacific Ocean, and the last long gleams of light were skimming across the top of the snow-crested peaks of the Olympics and splaying out across the sides of the glaciated mountains, so that the upper edges of the mountain were outlined with gleams of gold, and the crevasses and valleys were deepening from magenta into purple into midnight blue. Behind the mountain the sky was turning into that shade of evening blue that cannot be named. The first stars were blinking forth. I felt "a presence that disturbs me with the joy of elevated thoughts; a sense sublime of something far more deeply interfused, whose dwelling is the light of setting suns, and the round ocean, and the living air, and the blue sky, and in the mind of humanity—a motion and a spirit that impels all thinking things, all objects of all thought, and rolls through all things."[11]

The hair on the back of my neck literally stood up. We held perfectly still, transfixed by this stunning beauty. And then—this really happened—the fog went like this: it closed in on itself; the opaque sliding glass doors drew together again. We were wrapped once more in fine mist and couldn't see beyond our toes.

Our religious lives are like this. Most of the time we trudge throughout the lowland forest. We have makeshift packs on our backs. Our gear isn't quite what we need it to be. We've had to cut so many things from the budget. People look at what we're doing and say, "You're all wet!" Nevertheless, we keep on our path, continue going to meetings in our local fellowships, societies, congregations, both districtwide and nationwide. We do what we can to study, to learn, to pray, to worship, to gather together with others, to serve our communities, to make a difference. We stay with it. And there are moments when we come to the upper edges of the alpine meadow, and the fog parts, and we find ourselves standing in the presence of a glory that transfixes us with its stunning beauty; and we know that all along our labor and our work have been in relationship to this—this something far more deeply interfused. Always there, though rarely seen. And in those moments we are strengthened in our commitments. Then they pass away.

As religious liberals, the principles, purposes, and ideals to which we commit ourselves—those things that we try to put into practice—are not mere abstract ideas or lofty ideals, but are a conceptualization of the sacred land—a map, if you will, drawn by those who have, themselves, stood in the presence of glory. And they pass on to us the principles and ideals as clues for the path that we are also invited to follow. With that map there is a promise: if you travel to this country, you will see great beauty.

Take as example of one of those clues, the principle of *tolerance*, one of the fundamental principles of liberal religion. Most of us have reasons we believe in tolerance. We understand the principle. For one thing, many of us have seen religious intolerance, and we don't want to see any more of it. We recognize how much conflict in the world is a consequence of human beings' refusing to see the contributions of their neighboring religion as worthy of respect. In fact, we see religions relating to one another with an effort to conquer the other, and we know how much actual violence in our world is connected to religious intolerance.

We think of northern Ireland, the Middle East, the struggles that have gone on for centuries in India and in our own land, here, between the imperial forces of Christianity and the native traditions that were present in the pre-Columbian times. We agree with the Catholic radical theologian Hans Kung: there will be no peace in the world until there is peace among the world's religions.

Some of us uphold the principle of tolerance, furthermore, because we have been persuaded by the ancient teaching story of the East about the blind person and the elephant. The blind person and the elephant story is about a group of blind persons who were taken to encounter an elephant. Each one of the blind persons touches a different part of the elephant. One touches the side of the elephant and says, "I know what this is. This is a wall." And a second blind person touches the leg of the elephant and says, "I know what this is. This is a tree." And another touches the tail and says, "I know what this is. This is a rope." And one of them touches the trunk and says, "This is a snake."

The point of this story is that each one of the blind persons has had a real encounter with the elephant, but no one of them alone has encountered the whole of the elephant. The only way in which any one of them could know the whole truth would be if each one of them listened to what their neighbor knew. Part of our reason for believing in tolerance is not just that we put up with what our neighbor thinks; beyond that, we recognize that our neighbor may know something vitally important about the ultimate mysteries of life that we, in our experience, have not even begun to know. And so, beyond tolerance, there is an openness to the one next to us, recognition that that person next to us may have something to contribute to us. Furthermore, we recognize that an individual search for the truth is not sufficient; in fact, we must make a communal, collective—perhaps global—search for the ultimate values, mysteries, and meanings of life. And in that searching we are not heroes ourselves, trying to comprehend the whole, but each one of us is a member of an expedition team with a neighbor who has something to teach us.

Some of us believe in tolerance because we have been persuaded by the post-Newtonian paradigm shift. The post-Newtonian paradigm shift is one way of naming that shift in consciousness with the advances of physics beyond the Newtonian understanding of the universe. The advances have suggested to us that it is naive for us to think that there is any point in the universe from which one has a perspective—absolutely—on the whole. Every view of the truth is from a specific point on the space-time continuum. There is no perspective from above and beyond—only perspectives from within. And so, the whole looks different from every standpoint. We practice tolerance because of this marvelous diversity of how the truth is always connected to a standpoint and a context.

What I'd like to suggest to you is that for whatever reason each of us is persuaded of the importance of tolerance, in the practice of tolerance we have come to discover something deeper: We come to discover an experience of other human beings, one in which the fog that separates us from our neighbor begins to part, and the face of the other comes to shine forth more and more with its own authenticity. The reason this happens is that in the practice of tolerance, we begin to let go—of all of our preset opinions, our prejudices about the other. Instead of seeing the other through the veil of our preset opinions of who they are or what their value is, we let that fog part and become more and more open to the other as a real presence. And so we begin to see the uniqueness, the particularity, of each one next to us. We don't define who they are; we allow them to define to us who they are. A greater intimacy is experienced, a more vivid presence of others. There's a name for this: love. The practice of tolerance comes down to love.

I learned something about this quality of love, which allows the other to touch us, from a story that my father likes to tell, which was told to him by his friend Elton Bennet. Elton Bennet was one of the people who lived in Hoquiam, that town I told you about, and Bennet was the local artist in 1950. He had moved to Hoquiam in order to make silkscreen pictures of the fog covering the trees, the clamdiggers in their red shirts on the shiny sand, digging the clams, the half-turned tugboats when the tide is out. Bennet liked to tell this story of what happened to him when Dorothy Smith moved to Hoquiam.

Dorothy was the most interesting woman that the men in Hoquiam thought they had ever met. Dorothy came to Hoquiam after graduating from Radcliffe College back east, and the young men in Hoquiam had never met a person such as this. She was a social worker. She came to Hoquiam to start a program for children and youth, and to expand the social services in the community. She was erudite, charming, beautiful, and liked to hike. What more could anyone in Hoquiam want? Bennet decided to court Dorothy, but he wasn't the only one. So did Helgae Erikson.

Now, Helgae was different from Bennet. Helgae was not an artist, but was a logger. He was a very interesting man who not only logged the forest, but was committed to the natural environment. He helped found the Olympic Park as a national park, helped build many of the trails. He was also an inventor and experimenter. I can remember as a small child going out to Helgae's cabin in the woods where he was experimenting with generating electricity through the stream that went down by his house.

Well, both Helgae and Bennet carried out their courtship of Dorothy at the same time; in fact, they both carried out their courtship by taking Dorothy on long walks along Gray's Harbor River through the wet trees. And while they walked, Bennet sought to win Dorothy's heart by impressing her with his erudition; he talked to her about art and artists and poetry and politics and world events and put on a marvelous display of how interesting he was.

Meanwhile, Helgae walked on the other side of Dorothy, and all the while they traipsed through the forest paths, Helgae held Dorothy's hand. Dorothy married Helgae, which proves that all of the pretense of our communication is not as important as those gestures and actions by which we become really present to one another. Tolerance makes such real hand-to-hand presence possible.

Now, there's a second great principle of liberal religion. That's the principle of *reason*. Most of us have reasons why we believe in reason. The most important one, coming from our liberal heritage, is this: Our roots are in a religious protest against those forms of religion that include a despairing and negative view of the human being. The Universalists and the Unitarians of the previous centuries reacted against the Calvinist doctrine, for example, of total depravity, which thought the human being at birth so wounded and fraught with sin that the human being could not be trusted to do what was right, comprehend what was just, or discern what was true. The only hope for the human being was that he or she would become obedient to sources of truth and revelation outside of him- or herself, that were then imagined to possess a trustworthiness that the human being could not claim.

So, authoritarian religion is religion that views the human being negatively and establishes sources of authority beyond human experience—sacred texts, holy religious leaders, or canonized tradition and law. All those things have an authority that the individual human being cannot have. And to be a religious person is to submit in obedience to that authority.

Our heritage was displeased with that form of religion, and displeased with that view of the human being. Our forebears claimed instead a more positive view of what it is to be human. They said that at birth we have multiple capacities for good and evil, and we have the power of choice, and we have a whole array of gifts and abilities; that this humanness that we have at birth can be used in the service of all sorts of values, but the choice is in our hands. And so, because we affirmed the giftedness and the power of choice that every human being has, we rejected authoritarian structures of religion. And chief among the human gifts we celebrate is the human capacity to think and to reason. Our affirmation of reason is part and parcel of our whole affirmation of the essential goodness and worthiness of human life. We replaced those outside authorities with the inner authority of our own conscience and mind.

I learned about the importance of reason in religion from my grandmother Ernst, who was an old-fashioned, rationalist liberal Christian. Perhaps you've known such a person. My grandmother taught that you should never believe anything unless you can, with your own mind, reason that it's trustworthy. My grandmother has this ability to dismiss whole systems of thought with one word: "Nonsense." Her ultimate criterion in religious and theological and philosophical thinking was, "Does it make sense?" Sense and nonsense—that's the dividing line for my grandmother. She taught me about reason and religion the same way she taught me to hem a skirt.

My grandmother had a radical theory of hemming skirts: first of all, she believed you should use a double thread. Second, she believed you should take the stitches so securely that they could be seen from the outside. Now, the application of this is that you should never trust anything unless you, yourself, can see that it is stuck together well. And you should never give your trust to a system of thought unless you can understand its whole structure and whether that whole structure is one that is sturdy.

The deeper importance of reason I also learned from this grandmother. I learned it as she took me, summer after summer, on long walks from her summer cabin through the woods of the Puget Sound region. Every day in the summer when I stayed with her, we would go on the same three-quarter-mile trail, up and down, through the woods. On that pathway, we would stop, every few feet, as my grandmother endeavored to teach me what I could observe with my senses. She'd say, "Listen—do you hear that song? That's the meadowlark." And she'd say, "Look through the trees there. Do you see that tall slender tree with the branches that come out evenly like this, with smooth bark? That's a Cascara tree, and from its bark you can make medicine that will heal the heart." She taught me the names of all the trees, all the shrubs, and all the wayside flowers on that one little three-quarter-mile trek. And as we went up and down in different seasons, I learned in which seasons to look for the bloom of the skunk cabbage, and when the gingerroot would come into full leaf, and when the colt's foot would be at that stage when it was good to eat, and when the vine maple would turn orange, and when the big leaf maple's leaves would fall. Up and down that path, I learned that the practice of reason is essentially the practice of intimate attention to the world. And in that intimate attention, there is a fog that falls away, and the earth itself becomes more and more vivid as a real presence, full, if you will, of faces—each face with its own character and uniqueness. Through the practice of reason, the world becomes a realm buzzing with living presences, and the intrinsic value of things becomes known. The practice of reason comes down to an experience of the real presence of the earth. There's a name for this—love.

There's a final, or third, great principle of liberal religion—that is *freedom*. Freedom is a principle we believe in for good reasons. I think the most important one is this: We believe in freedom because we believe in the sacred worth of every individual human being. We, as religious liberals, do not want to see any single human being have the possibilities of the fullness of life be constrained by the lack of access to decision making (democracy), by the absence of fundamentals needed for survival (food, shelter, health care), or by the absence of those things that nurture the full growth of our spirits (freedom of religion, education). We work hard in countless ways to ensure and protect human freedom because we want to see the full development of the human being. We don't want to see the soul and spirit imprisoned or cut off. We rejoice when totalitarian systems fall and there are fresh opportunities. We celebrate what we see of the unquenchable human desire for growth, vitality, casting off of injustice and imposed burdens. I'm persuaded that in the practice of trying to protect and preserve freedom, many of us come to a place where we begin to discover that that which constrains the full development of human beings is not always out there. Sometimes that which constrains is within our own being. For some of us it is wounds so deep that we have been unable to heal. For some of us it is an internalized message that we have nothing to offer, that we should remain quiet, that our gifts or talents are worth nothing. For some of us the internal oppressor is sufficient to keep us, over a lifetime, from ever doing that which we are most capable of doing, or contributing that gift to the larger human family that we have to give. The internal oppressor can keep us from showing our own true face to the people we are closest to. It can keep us from naming our talent, offering our gifts. In the commitment to freedom, we eventually come up to the challenge of finding our own freedom.

Early in my ministry, as a very young minister, I got a glimpse of what we might call "spiritual freedom," and a glimpse of how much I lacked that freedom, simultaneously. I was one of those young people who went straight from college to seminary to the parish, and so when I was twenty-four years old, far too young, I found myself the minister of a small congregation—very small, fortunately. My first few years in the ministry were very difficult, as I think they are for most ministers, no matter what age they start as a parish minister. I was struggling constantly with my feeling that I could never meet everybody's expectations. Everybody had different things that they wanted me to be good at or wanted me to do, and I used to lie sleepless at night because I worried that I couldn't meet these expectations. It hadn't occurred to me that I didn't need to meet all the expectations. I was sure I was supposed to.

But more than my struggle with people's expectations, I was overwhelmed at my discovery of the depth of human suffering and the hiddenness of that suffering among the people in the religious community I was a part of. I found out that the people in my church had buried aspects of themselves and had sorrows and pains that they had not told one another, that they had only told the minister. I, coming from a very trustworthy and sheltered home, had not really ever known that some people were severely beaten throughout their childhood, that some people were sexually abused. I hadn't really known that men come home from war with haunting scars from being forced to participate in violence. I hadn't known that grown-ups sometimes lose their children to death. And I was overwhelmed at the realization that I had no resources for responding to the needs of the people around me. I thought, "I have nothing to give." Then I really couldn't sleep at night!

All of this difficulty came to a crisis one Friday afternoon when the church bulletin wasn't ready yet for Sunday morning because there had been so many calls all week. Just as I was frantically trying to finish choosing the readings for Sunday, a phone call came into the office from the husband of one of the young women in the church. He was calling from the hospital. He said, "Debbie has gone into labor." Bells went off for me because I knew that the child wasn't due for another six weeks. And he said, "And they've told us that...the child is dead. Will you come?"

I hung up the phone, and I said to my secretary, "Doris, you've been secretary of this church for forty years. Debbie is in labor, and the child is going to be stillborn. What shall I do? What can I do? I don't know what to say to her. How is she going to go through this whole pain of labor knowing that she's not laboring to give birth to life?" (I don't think I was quite that eloquent at that moment.) Doris looked at me and she said, "Do what the angels do."

Now, this was the kid who was raised by the grandmother who had said you shouldn't believe anything unless you could see how it was stitched together; so I wasn't too interested in whether there were angels, or if there were, what they were doing. But I was desperate. So I said, "What do the angels do?" And Doris said, "Just be there."

So I went to the hospital, and I remember crossing the threshold into the room where my friend Debbie was sweating and struggling in labor, and she turned and looked at me in her exhaustion, and she stretched out her hand. I walked over to the bedside, and I put my hand in hers, and she gripped very tightly. I didn't have any words to say; but I want you to know that in that moment, I felt like the mountain. I was there. It was enough. And that's when I learned, or glimpsed, that freedom is being present, being here, not performing, not saving or changing the world necessarily, but being here. In the moments we are doing that, we are free.

Friends, I commend to you the path of liberal religion. Liberal religion is not a head trip. Its values and principles are not something dreamed up by armchair philosophers who think these might be good things to believe. The principles of tolerance and reason and freedom are principles articulated by those who have touched life and been touched by life. To be committed to these principles is to follow a path that leads us into deep intimacy with those things of abiding beauty and power that are holy. And so I suggest to you that the purpose of all our religious life is to see the mountain; and when we can't see the mountain, it's to feel the mountain; and when we can't feel the mountain, it's to be the mountain; and if there are moments when you can neither see, nor feel, nor be the mountain…then read the map.

20

SERMONS THAT PROVIDE
INTELLECTUAL STIMULATION

Mind has mattered so much, and knowledge
Is bottomless as the golden bowl
In the myth, ceaseless as light, grave,
Unemptiable as the sea...
    To know, to understand
Has been my passion and addiction.

Barbara Howes[1]

A young, single parent is home with two toddlers all week. An elderly college professor lives in a retirement community where the only activities offered are bingo and stretching exercises. A department store manager who works sixty hours a week once majored in astronomy in college and loved it. A bright middle-aged accountant always wanted to learn more about poetry, and his partner, the potter, loves science but doesn't know much about it. All of them are eager to explore ideas, and all of them come to your church.

Indeed, who among us would not be intrigued by an innovative, creative, lively sermon that, among other things, stimulated our brain cells? Which of us doesn't appreciate, on occasion, the chance to mull, imagine, and follow an idea through?

As participants in "the learned ministry," we are often expected to be an intellectual resource, as when we chat about the new second-grade curriculum with the Religious Education Committee, when a member questions us about Isis at the supermarket or the town recycling center, or when we take to the pulpit.

While all aspects of the worship service and the life of the religious community are important on Sunday morning, it is during the sermon that most congregants, at some level, will try to locate an actual idea and track it. Even when a sermon is of another type essentially, even when its style is emotional or evocative, almost everybody is also listening in a thoughtful, reasoned way for what point is being made, how it follows from the one before, whether it makes sense, and what it implies. "The art of writing," claims Virginia Woolf, "has for backbone some fierce attachment to an idea."[2]

While the prospect may sound dry to some, many parishioners will be eager to hear a sermon on, say, sociobiology and evolutionary psychology:

> Now, of course nobody really thinks like an evolutionary biologist day to day. Nobody says, "Oh, if I hook up with that person over there, my genetic material will surely flourish." What we experience is sexual attraction, or romance, or it seems we've found a soulmate. We're more apt to feel all aflutter over potential partners' renditions of "Walk on the Wild Side," or the way they look in that Navy uniform, or the touching way they speak to children, or that thing they do with their eyes when they listen to our deepest thoughts. Surely it doesn't feel as if it's about reproduction—we can be eighty years old, or gay or lesbian, or phobic around children, or we've had quite enough babies thank you very much...
>
> As religious people, we have to ask ourselves how we want to act in the world. First, we need to try to determine more accurately what we, as human beings, are starting with—what our so-called natural state is. We have to know it and name it, whatever it is. And second, given our values, we have to decide what about ourselves and society we'd like to change and improve: Just because it may be natural doesn't mean it's how we want to behave.[3]

Some fair number of the congregation feels especially gratified when, in the cycle of the sermonic year, they have a turn to wrestle with a matter of meaning and importance that gives the mental muscles a good workout. According to Ronald Allen,

> Anyone who thinks that the teaching sermon is extinct, or ought to be, will want to reconsider...Baby boomers avoid institutional religion but are drawn to churches that...articulate a distinctive statement of transcendent reality, through which the church can

make sense of itself and of the world. While the teaching sermon may be out of favor in some quarters, it can meet this need and is often a component in churches experiencing growth.[4]

Inspiring as it may be week to week, a calendar that avoids that theological task over time defines religion in a way that is both narrow and inadequate to the individual parishioner in his or her search for sustaining faith.

As a minister, you may want to discipline yourself to preach every year, for example, specifically on the topic of a theologian, commit yourself to delivering at least one sermon a year about something scientific, treat yourself to a world religions topic, or research the background of a subject in the news. You will be gratified, we think, to see that every time you preach one from your "famous author" genre or offer your annual sermon on geology or astronomy or, in this case, the general topic of science itself, some parishioners simply will not want to miss it[5]:

> The scientist and author Carl Sagan knew that indulging too lax a standard of proof leads to all manner of evil, not just nonsense, but evil. Given regrettable but recurrent human inclinations, it can lead to a demon-haunted world, which was the one most people in the West since ancient times believed to be real.
>
> The belief in demons led to the witch-burnings of the late medieval period, and that began to end when brave people such as Thomas Ady challenged the evidence as unreasonable in 1656. These superstitions led to much suffering and death among the ill, and that began to end when the science of medicine began.
>
> In one of my favorite footnotes, Sagan tells this story: "At a dinner table recently, I asked the assembled guests—ranging in age, I guess, from thirties to sixties—how many of them would be alive today if not for antibiotics, cardiac pacemakers, and the rest of the panoply of modern medicine. Only one hand went up. It was not mine."[6] Nor would it have been mine.
>
> Thinking back to the candle that Ady lit in that darkness of unreason, Sagan worried that, "especially as the Millennium draws nearer, pseudo-science and superstition will seem year by year more tempting, the siren song of unreason more sonorous and attractive…Habits of thought familiar from the ages past reach for the controls.
>
> "The candle flame flutters. Its little pool of light trembles. Darkness gathers. The demons begin to stir."[7]

Our self-expectations when preaching an intellectual sermon are four: to be creditable (and on almost any subject there may be people there who would know if we were not); to make the subject understandable, accessible; to make it interesting enough to engage even the people who think they do not like such subjects; and to have real hope that speaking of it might count for something in the religious struggles of those who are there.

The sermon that aims to stimulate intellectually must be carefully prepared. "Most sermons show a superficiality in background; it is obvious that the preacher has not spent adequate time to research the topic," notes our colleague Peter Raible.

> I do not mean to suggest that all sermons must be intellectual, but if the "informational" side of the topic shows nothing beyond what newspapers, magazines, and conventional wisdom says on the topic, then I feel cheated. I expect any preacher to honor me, a hearer, with some sense that the literature has been read and the questions posed by the topic have been confronted. Once upon a time, we probably had too many preachers who were strictly cerebral and lectured rather than preached. Today, we have too many surface sermons, weak in content, and deficient in probing the issues posed.[8]

It occurs to Rev. Billings in the middle of point #2 that point #3 misses the point entirely.

© 1985 Dan Pegoda

We have all heard "intellectual sermons" denounced. They are deemed an antiquated, unwanted heritage of patriarchal modes of ministry. We beg to differ. No good intellectual sermon is intellectual at the expense of other crucial elements such as emotion, pizzazz, internal tension, personal relevance, religiosity, and the like. This combination is inherent in many of our religious traditions, including the old Puritan-based tradition that appealed to the intellect and the emotions together, that fed both the spirit and the mind. Preachers have long been expected to preach sermons that are simultaneously rich in content and affect, in ideas and imagery, in conviction and emotional impact. "The intellectual and the spiritual belong together."[9]

Intellectual sermons, done well, need no apology. "I know two things," says R. C. Sproul, "that God made us with minds, and that he made the mind as the chief organ of receiving information, analyzing that information, and responding to it. To accommodate our preaching to a temporary fad of mindlessness is to deny the very nature of divine creation."[10]

Rational discourse alone, however, is dangerous sermon fare. Done poorly, intellectual sermons are as deadly and unwelcome as their critics claim. Nobody likes a show-off, or preachers absorbed only in their own academic interests, or a sermon that merely moves from one intellectual point to the next. Finally, no members of the congregation arrive at church in hopes of hearing a know-it-all preacher. "Ill-written, pompously self-righteous, lamely jocular forays offend," as the writer Elizabeth Hardwick puts it, "because an air of immature certainty surrounds them."[11]

Sermons that stimulate intellectually present us with a special challenge, the challenge of melding thought with spirit and making all of it matter. Ministers who want to preach to the whole parishioner must meet the challenge.

Sample Sermon

The subject of this sermon is "the biological aspects of personality" and how we view them and live with them as religious people. The subject is dense, ethically complicated, and controversial, and its applications to daily life are not obvious. The danger of boring or overwhelming the congregation is high.

The Reverend Jane Rzepka delivered this sermon to a congregation in Madison, Wisconsin, a group accustomed to wrestling with academic concerns. Careful research, plain speaking, and the use of down-to-earth humor and examples were goals.

Two Kinds of People[12]
JANE RZEPKA

There are two kinds of people. There are people who can sit there and let the phone ring, and people who just *have* to answer it. There are people who want to lay out a vacation's precise itinerary, and people who'd rather drift. Cat people. Dog people. Two kinds of people: People who like to shop; people who hate to shop. People who wear hats. People who don't. Shower people; bath people. Two kinds of people. People who believe a cup needs a saucer; and those who never notice. People who always know what time it is; and others who lose track. Some people keep everything; some throw it away. Some read the manual, and some fiddle with the knobs. Some like sailboats; for others, it has to be a power boat. Two kinds of people. There are people who file every warranty, nice and neat. Others set them free. There are people who cross only at the crosswalk; and others who just…cross. Some people leave the dishes in the sink; others need to get them washed right away. We have morning people; night people. Some people jump into the pool; and the others like the slow, inch by inch approach. Two kinds of people. Two kinds of people.

The notion of "kinds of people" seems to be a natural one. We know it's never true, exactly, and that life is more complicated than that and the distinctions more subtle. We know how dangerous stereotyping is. But who hasn't heard children talk about teachers: "You have Mr. Garcia? Oh yeah— he's the boring kind. Mrs. Jackson? She's the yelling kind. Mrs. Hansen? She's the type that makes you sing a lot of songs and put on plays." They talk about parents, too; they'll say, "My stepmom is the kind who when she gets mad, just blows up real bad, and then ten minutes later she's fine, and my dad's the kind who stays a little mad for the whole day."

We have our little systems for categorizing. They make sense, they create order, they seem obvious, real, and true —until we're confronted with someone else's categories, for example, this entry in an ancient Chinese encyclopedia, which tells us how to divide animals into categories:

> Category (a) belonging to the Emperor, (b) embalmed, (c) tame, (d) fabulous, (e) stray dogs, (f) frenzied, (g) innumerable, (h) drawn with a very fine camel hair brush, (i) having just broken the water pitcher, and (j) that from a long way off look like flies.[13]

Once we hear a list of categories so distinct from the ones we ordinarily encounter, we are reminded that all categories in our lives are wholly artificial. Yet categorization does seem to be the way we approach the problem of understanding other people.

Ancient Western scholars divided human beings into types. Hippocrates, in the fifth century B.C.E., described four temperaments, which he believed were associated with bodily fluids, which he called "humors" (this was a very early biochemical approach, it seems to me): The sanguine temperament is optimistic and energetic; the melancholic is moody and withdrawn; the choleric is irritable and impulsive; and the phlegmatic is calm and slow.

And then we have Galen of Pergamon, seventeen hundred years ago, who believed that in large part we inherit our constitutions as either "melancholic" or "sanguine" individuals, that is to say, introverts or extroverts. In other words, for a couple of thousand years, the human family has thought that something called "personality traits" dictated, to some extent at least, the way a person interacted with the world. We believed in a kind of biological determinism.

What happened? We changed our collective minds. We stopped believing we're cast in concrete.

At about the turn of the last century, we abandoned the idea of inherited personality traits, and we began to favor the effects of early relationships and environmental circumstance as the creator of personality. Freud. Pavlov and his dog. B. F. Skinner. If you're an angry sort of fellow, we aren't inclined these days to say you inherited that anger by means of a gene passed along from Grandpa, that you were "born" to be the angry type. It's more likely that we'd hypothesize a mother who always hit you, or that the kids picked on you at school, or that the only time you could get anybody's attention was when you threw a tantrum.

The reasons for this shift from biology to environment as agents of personality formation were more than intellectual; they were demographic too. For one thing, this country was being flooded by new waves of immigrants. If we were to remain a democracy, where people could be viewed as having equal potential, we had to believe that every person, once situated in the same American environment, could indeed become a full-fledged American. We did not want to entertain the notion that some "types" of people—or nationalities—would never be able to measure up.

And then of course came the horrors of Nazi Germany, where ideas of biological determinism, of "types," led to nightmarish conclusions. What American scientists could study genetic typology in the post-war environment?

In the last decade or so, gingerly, cautiously, many more scientists and academics have felt able to pursue studies again about biological aspects of personality. This change is apparent in the variety of therapists we go to now: Some folks have therapists who recognize chemistry in the body that affects one's relationship to the world, and those therapists write prescriptions as their primary strategy, while talk is secondary. Others find therapists who credit the effects of life experience—sexual abuse, for example— and those therapists will help you bring those memories to the surface and process them, offering medication as a more peripheral possibility.

As a society, we are wiser now. We are wiser about the implications of research and where they might lead us. What does it mean if many girls test low in math ability, and many boys test low in verbal ability? What does it mean for American culture if more blue-eyed, thin people with narrow faces test as introverts, while sturdy, brown-eyed, full-faced people often turn out to be extroverts, as they do? What happens if at the age of two weeks, Asian babies have the biochemical characteristics of introverts, as they seem to? Because we remember World War II, we know that ethical considerations of studies of personality type are of paramount importance.

So now it seems that science is telling us what any of us walking around already know: There are two kinds of people. The most prominent example at the moment seems not to distinguish morning people from night owls, or cat people from dog people, or any of the other silly distinctions we can make. I'm talking about one of the basics: Biologically speaking, there are two kinds of people, and they are introverts and extroverts.

We know it's not nice and neat—the introvert, in a surprise move, might just agree to accompany a partner to the high school reunion, or the extrovert goes upstairs early on a Saturday night to read a book. No matter how thoroughgoing our hardwiring may be, our scripts are not written, our biochemistry and genetic material don't fully control us.

And even if we were neatly divided into categories of introversion and extroversion, other related factors enter in. You are extroverted, you do enjoy being around people, and you experience a renewed energy when you're out and about, but if you also happen to be generally fearful, you may not seem extroverted. You may be introverted, you are renewed by spending time alone, but you are a concert pianist, and you feel a sense of reward playing to a house of two thousand people. You are introverted, but your fans would never know it.

So how do you know if you're introverted or extroverted in the first place? I looked at several psychological instruments, and frankly, I didn't like any of them, so I made up my own completely untested questionnaire. Five forced-choice questions:

1. When you were a very young child and a clown approached you, did you say, "Whoopee!" or "Oh, no"?

2. When you get home and see the light blinking on your answering machine, are you glad somebody's called you? Yes or no.

3. It's your birthday, and everybody in the restaurant sings happy birthday. Does this make you happy?

4. After church, it will be time to socialize at coffee hour. Is this good news?

5. You take your young nephews to the circus. Front row seats. The ringmaster picks a volunteer to demonstrate the hokey-pokey and that person is you! Is this your lucky day?

There is no mystery to the scoring. You know who you are: If you had a "Whoopee" and lot of "yes's," you are an extrovert. You are probably more oriented toward the external world; you are energized by the people around you and can't imagine the appeal of extended stretches alone. If you tended toward "no's," you're inclined to find renewal in more solitary pursuits and feel worn out by lots of interpersonal interaction. Your primary resources are inside yourself.

I read in the newspaper once about a young fellow from St. Paul, Minnesota. It is a tragic story—I know that—but still it's a classic. It reads, "Upon walking into his apartment, the guest of honor at a surprise 30th birthday party thrown by his girlfriend, tried to chase everyone out, then stabbed a visitor to death Saturday."

Mercy. What a situation. I can imagine that the girlfriend planned this party for weeks as a true act of love. "Who wouldn't be thrilled by a surprise party?!" Well, an introvert. Presumably, the boyfriend walked into the privacy of his own home after a long day out in the world interacting with lots of people and faced an introvert's worst nightmare: a surprise party, where quite unexpectedly he found himself the center of attention in a large group of people. There are two kinds of people.

One of my father's greatest joys was to order an entree or dessert at a restaurant that arrived at the table more or less on fire. If there was a spectacle on the menu, my father would order what a recent Robotman comic strip calls "an extraverted meal." All eyes in the restaurant would turn to admire the grandeur of this flaming treat. My father would glow with happiness, and the other six of us would slouch in our seats, stare at our laps, and hope that the moment would pass quickly. There are two kinds of people.

This is where religion comes in, it seems to me. We have two kinds of people. Keeping in mind that the designations "introvert" and "extrovert" are artificial designations, just tools or framework to help us think about ourselves and one another, given that caveat, how can people live in one home, one workplace, one classroom, one church, one world, when we seem so fundamentally different?

Unitarian Universalists, along with most others, care about ethical behavior, about treating each other fairly and with love. But how can two people love each other when the extrovert wants to go over every detail of every day and the feelings that went with it and who said what to whom, while the introvert wants to watch the news? How can a parent and child co-exist when the introverted child wants to sit alone in front of the computer after school and the extroverted parent feels it's more normal for the child to play outside with the other kids? How can people work in the same office when the extrovert enjoys chatting throughout the day, and the introvert prefers a quiet work environment? How can a child and a teacher exist in the same classroom if the introverted child wants to sit and write a story, and the extroverted teacher is bent on helping the child to "overcome her shyness" and insists that she join in the "fun" of the class musical?

These are ethical and religious questions: How do we treat one another? And what's the knee-jerk religious answer to an ethical question involving the treatment of another person? What do we tell children? We "do unto others as we would have others do unto us." If *we* would like a surprise party, then we should throw one for our friend. All of a sudden the Golden Rule is not so Golden.

Religion requires not only good heartedness, but thought about the guidelines. When introverts and extroverts are dealing with each other, what is required is not the Golden Rule so much as a respect for one another wherever we fall on the introvert/extrovert continuum.

Oh, and it can be hard. When the introvert withdraws, it can feel to the other like rejection, or the lack of love or care, or that the person is depressed, or missing out, or woefully out of touch with the emotional side of life. When the extrovert wants to interact, it can feel to the introvert like incessant shallow chatter, or relentless prying, or superfluous conversational noise, or a lot of talk that rarely has a point, or some exhausting and incomprehensible interpersonal obligation that is difficult to meet.

Of course, introversion and extroversion have ramifications for life together in a church family too. For example, when we gather in our churches for committee meetings or social events, we need to understand that introverts may require a lingering break in the conversation before they feel able to enter in. They may appreciate being asked for their opinion, they may want time to think things through before they speak, or they may prefer to stay quiet. Extroverts, on the other hand, may be thinking out loud, processing their thoughts externally. Don't always expect ideas in final form—don't hold extroverts to the first position they take.

When we teach Sunday school or plan adult programs, we may want to try to remember that often the introverted child or grown-up does not find the group-building exercise fun, or the game of charades, or the song with the hand motions, or the chance to get up here in the front of the sanctuary. In our churches, we want to honor the person who writes the poems that move us to tears, just as much as we honor the "life of the party."

And so in our Unitarian Universalist churches, and in life in general, each of us adapts a little—we learn to live with the other species; the extrovert tries to tone it down, and the introvert cranks up enough to get through the New Year's Eve party with the lampshades and the karaoke. We face the fact that somewhat extroverted behavior is rewarded in twentieth-century American society. We grow toward wholeness, we compensate, we fool each other, we find safe places to be our true selves, and we try not to cause one another too much pain. But as religious people, fundamentally, we try to honor our own true selves and the natures of those around us.

There are two kinds of people—sort of, with a lot of qualifiers. And both groups are made up of people who can grow and change and adapt and understand and act with kindness.

And as religious people, in the words of the poet Marge Piercy, "we must sit down and reason together. Perhaps we should sit in the dark. In the dark we could utter our feelings. In the dark we could propose and describe and suggest. In the dark we could not see who speaks and only the words would say what they say. No one would speak more than twice. No one would speak less than once. Thus saying what we feel and what we want, what we fear for ourselves and each other into the dark, perhaps we could begin to listen. [Some] must learn to dare to speak, [some] must learn to bother to listen. [Some] must learn to say I think this is so. [Some] must learn to stop dancing solos on the ceiling."[14] We must sit down together.

21

SERMONS THAT STARTLE,
AWAKEN, OR AMUSE

Sunday morning's subject was the congregation's connection to its partner congregation in Romania, one of ethnic Hungarian heritage. The children of elementary school age usually attended the first part of the service; so that week, the preacher told a Hungarian folk tale. It was about a violin that played beautiful music for its owner, a peasant, music so beautiful that the nasty king appropriated the violin, only to have it produce nothing for his efforts but ugly squeaks. In time, the peasant recovered his violin, which again played beautiful music.

When he first said that the peasant could play beautifully on his violin, the preacher lifted an invisible instrument to his shoulder and drew an invisible bow across its strings—at which point lovely, live violin music was heard, thanks to the soloist hidden in the choir loft—who later produced an impressively unpleasant squeak when the preacher pretended to play as the king, and who later found her melodious ability restored when the violin itself was restored in the story to its rightful owner.

At every playing, the preacher conducting his imaginary performance, for better or worse, captivated the congregants of every age.[1]

There are sermons that intentionally seek to startle, amuse, or awaken. They use humor or surprise (and often both) to capture the congregation's attention, to help put a point across, and even to establish a subtle, ongoing sense of suspense, excitement, and impending delight.

183

Such an element of unpredictability can be an asset in the liturgical year. Weeks may go by when it is not employed, but the very possibility of the unexpected can help hold interest. Not uncommonly, parishioners praise their preachers as humorous and even just a little bit outrageous (in a way that they generally like) even if on most Sundays the message is successful in more customary ways.

Week in and week out, at least a touch of the funny or the unpredictable can be welcome and effective. And every now and then, there can be a whole sermon whose major design is discombobulation, one of those adventuresome forays when the preacher cashes in on his or her reserve of congregational respect and trust to speak an unusually distinctive message or invite to the pulpit a seldom-heard voice.

For instance, Sunday morning might feature a special performance by someone who portrays a historical character; a jazz service or other special music; a play reading; a dance performance; a dialogue sermon; a service involving laypeople; or a storyteller. Or the preacher might don a clown wig or a hand puppet, a walrus mask or a baseball glove (all of which one or the other of the authors has done, and more), with children there, too, or without.

Such goings-on can be important parts of the sermon itself. They seem to work especially well in sermons of a historic or educational sort, which threaten to be soporific. If the subject somehow concerns the seventeenth-century roots of a congregation, for example, why not have them reseat themselves with men on one side and women on the other, a practice of the time? If the preacher is discussing a figure like John Wesley, the congregation or the choir might sing verses during the sermon from hymns that Wesley wrote.

One of the authors, in speaking of homelessness, had a parishioner dressed as a street person deliver lines from Jane Wagner's play, "Search for Signs of Intelligent Life in the Universe," in the midst of the sermon; and on another Sunday, she had another parishioner, hidden from view (again in the choir loft), read passages from the writings of Martin Luther King, Jr., interspersed with her remarks about Dr. King.

Furthermore, as we have said before, we favor the occasional use of props or visual aids. It is one thing to remark how cultural bias is built into our views of life, but an effective way of drawing attention to the point is to show a large-enough map of the world with the southern hemisphere at the top, and the equator across the very middle (instead of its usual place, with more space given to the northern hemisphere).

We know preachers who have reconstructed on a smaller scale the three doors from the television program *Let's Make a Deal* to illustrate a complicated point about laws of probability; who have dressed themselves as Augustine or Origen or Margaret Fuller; who have concluded a sermon by flipping a baseball up into the air, to be caught in a glove that had just appeared, or by blowing bubbles and catching one intact, or bursting into song.

Why might one do such things? Well, in all the cases cited, there were real religious points being made. But the manner of their making also served in every case to provide relief from responsible, reasonable regularity, which can become boring in time; to present a predictable message in some notable new way; to show the preacher in a less staid or stern mode than usual; to provide a feeling of freedom and fun, so that the congregation knows that when it comes to life and worship, part of its religion involves openness and laughter; and, of course, to awaken parishioners to a point being made, "that even if a man [and woman] will not follow where one attempts to lead [them], one thing…is still possible to do for [them]—compel [them] to take notice."[2]

Of course, one needs to respect the grounds for reserve just as well. There are some people who don't like to be surprised or amused, or at least not this week, when they have come to the service especially seeking security and safety because their brother just died, their daughter just got fired, their therapist is off on vacation, or the bank has foreclosed on its loan. Or else on this as on every other week, they seek a predictable ritual, a continuity with tradition, a sense of grounding in a faith tradition that has been doing things in a welcome, familiar pattern as long as memory.

Few have expressed the concern for caution more urgently than Thomas Jackson. Among several examples, he cites:

> A person of considerable power was preaching one night to a large audience, but failed to arrest their attention. In the midst of his sermon three young men came into church, to whom he addressed himself as they were entering, "If I had known you were coming in with that dagger to arrest these men, I could have had the whole matter amicably adjusted, and avoided all this trouble."
>
> The people were so startled that many sprang to their feet, and he had to assure them that there was no danger, and that he had only adopted that plan to wake them up, before he could get them quiet. He succeeded in arresting attention, but "paid too dear…" His hearers felt that he had been trifling with them, and the reaction was very unfavorable.[3]

With a number of such incidents in mind, Jackson later concurs with a Mr. Taylor, who wrote that

The degree of excitement which you wish to produce by an illustration should be graduated by the character of the subject to be illustrated. The background of a picture may be so clearly drawn, and so highly coloured, as to weaken or destroy the effect of the principal figure. So the exciting character of a mere incident may be such as to carry the feelings of the hearer away from the subject, instead of carrying them to it.[4]

With careful acknowledgment of their concerns and of the valid expectations that parishioners may have of comfort and pattern, a preacher hopes to achieve a service and a sermon that allow for the startling; for an occasional, disruptive awakening; and all along religion's earnest way, for pleasure in the ironic, the silly, and the fun.

In that spirit, one of the authors (Jane, as will become apparent), speaking to a congregation of fellow ministers about to begin a new church year, recalled:

I was in Istanbul one recent summer. When I travel, I try to blend. I leave my camera at home. I don't buy any souvenirs. I eat local food where local people eat. I stay away from tourist haunts.

So I'm in Istanbul, in the marketplace—adrift in the covered bazaar to tell you the truth—and I'm blending. Blending there in the marketplace—I'm walking amidst the tables of figs, flip flops, saffron, carpets, apple tea, hookahs—there I am, now I'm walking past booth after booth of pistachios, evil eyes, satellite dishes, Islamic holy books, Bart Simpson T-shirts, brass trays—harem girl outfits. And the fellow in the harem outfit booth looks at me for a split second and says to me in perfect English: "It is your destiny."

This particular sales pitch did not work on me. At least to date I have not put my name on the harem girl sign-up sheet, regardless of my destiny. I laughed out loud is what I did, and there it was in the Turkish covered bazaar, a moment of perfect clarity: I choose ministry. I call myself a minister.

Some might ask how we do what we do [referring to a reading]. Well, we choose it. We call ourselves ministers. Every day, sometimes more, we choose ministry in its joy and surprise and skewerings and commitment to the good. Here in September and right on through the year I choose ministry, and you do too.

You do too. You're not a harem girl either (at least that's not your day job), you're not a lawyer or flight attendant or stay-at-home mom or whatever it is you might have been or used to be.

It's September now in New England, and Sunday is that first Sunday after Labor Day, and so chances are that on Sunday you will march yourself into a church and choose ministry all over again. You will call yourself a minister.[5]

SAMPLE SERMON

Like many other preachers, each of the authors employs startling or amusing techniques now and then, both for the congregation's enjoyment and to awaken them to the message of a sermon. One December, the preacher not only talked about Christmas spirit, but early on in his sermon he briefly donned a silly hat. At the morning's second service—since the gesture had been so well received at the first service—he kept the hat on throughout the sermon. This proved even more delightful to most, although unsettling to a few.

Have a Jolly Holiday, or The Minister's Festive Hat[6]
KEN SAWYER

I was given a wonderful hat by one of you not long ago, and I have his permission to tell you that the maker and giver of the hat was Brad Keyes. It arrived just before the Christmas season started its descent upon us. Not that it is really a Christmas hat, much less one for Hanukkah, solstice, or Kwanzaa. What it is, I think, is a jester's cap, a jolly hat reminiscent of the European middle ages or the Renaissance.

I put it on immediately, and have worn it often ever since, indoors and out. This has made a difference in my mood, and in the mood of some around me with whom I have shared the news of the lift that the hat has brought to my December.

The timing of the present may well have been coincidental—but it was fortuitous, coming just when I needed to be reminded of a certain spirit of the holidays, all too easily forgotten by those of us for whom the season comes laden with responsibilities and pressures. I would not burden you with this observation did I not know that that description fits a fair number of people in this room, who may not be worrying over the nativity tableau for Christmas Eve at First Parish, but who have their own long list of tasks at hand, meals to plan, presents to buy, cards to write, mail to send, trips to plan and take, visitors to accommodate, gatherings to anticipate, and all the rest.

Downstairs on the bulletin board I have posted a cartoon from the *New Yorker* magazine of a few years ago, showing an urban sidewalk crowded with people looking very harried and distressed. The caption reads, "It's Beginning To Look a Lot Like Christmas."

Well, my hat put me in a different mood, and one I decided I would associate with the season at hand. It wouldn't occur to me for a while that I might wear it this morning, but I knew immediately I would wear it for the Community Carol Sing this evening out front on the lawn, albeit probably not for Christmas Eve, what with my robe and all. But I really do think it expresses a very important element of Christmas, as of most religious holidays, their spirit of festivity and fun.

I know that festivity may not be quite the word that comes first to the minds of many at this stage of the preparations. And there may be memories of Christmases, Hanukkahs, solstices, and Kwanzaas past that were less than fun, maybe including the ones last year.

But shouldn't fun be one of the goals? You can amend that to gladness or glee, if you want, even happiness or joy, but I want to hold out a hope for the sillier sort in the mixture, too, for frivolous enjoyment, relaxation, chuckles, and delight. Yes, I say: for goofiness and jolliness and silliness and fun (assuming that we are not picturing anybody drinking too much, or poking fun at anyone, or otherwise ruining the simple holiday cheer).

Already, just answering the question of what I was going to preach on this Sunday, in telling of my happy hat I have helped some colleagues get in better touch with that part of the holiday spirit. In response, one minister plans to be in the pulpit this morning feeling better about the holidays, wearing deely-boppers on her head, little plastic doohickies on antenna-like springs.

Now I know that fun is only one of the goals. There are things that we do this month even if the promise of fun is pretty low. We volunteer time to serve the poor and needy. We spend time with relatives just to maintain the connections, or because we know it will mean something important to them. We do what seem to be the right things to do for their own sake, though hardly fun and sometimes barely bearable. And I honor the effort.

But is it not another big part of the season to learn to savor that which makes us truly, deeply carefree, giddy, giggly, or glad?

You may wonder if I am not being impious, urging simple silliness as mete response to the impending celebration of the anniversary of the birth of Jesus. But there is something altogether apropos in the connection between joy and Jesus, not to mention the connection between laughter and babies. (Just wait till you see Jesus at the 5:00 service on Christmas Eve. At least he always makes me laugh, about the same way one assumes the baby Jesus lit up the stable, and even more so the house back in Nazareth.)

The connection between Jesus and the comic spirit is not novel with me. For instance, the late actress Colleen Moore tells the following anecdote in her autobiography, *Silent Star*. In 1922, Charlie Chaplin invited some of the owners of First National Pictures to his studio. Moore went along.

> We were all sitting there chatting, waiting for lunch to be served, when Charlie stood up and, turning to Robert Leiber, the president of First National, said, "I hear you've bought Papini's *Life of Christ*."
>
> Mr. Lieber nodded.
>
> Charlie nodded, too. "I want to play the role of Jesus."
>
> If Charlie had bopped Mr. Lieber over the head with a baseball bat, he could not have received a more stunned reaction. Not just from Mr. Lieber. From all four of them. They sat there like figures in a waxworks. Even their faces had turned sort of waxy yellow.
>
> "I'm a logical choice," Charlie went on. "I look the part. I'm a Jew. And I'm a comedian."
>
> The bosses looked more stunned if possible than before.
>
> Charlie explained to them that good comedy was only a hairline away from good tragedy, which we all knew to be true. "And I'm an atheist," he added, "so I'd be able to look at the character objectively. Who else could do that?"
>
> They all had no answer for him…
>
> There was silence in the car going back until Richard Rowland said, "He's the greatest actor alive, and he'd give an historical performance, but who of you would have the nerve to put in lights on a movie marquee: Charlie Chaplin in *The Life of Christ*?"
>
> Mr. Lieber said wistfully, "It would be the greatest religious picture ever made, but I'd be run out of Indianapolis."[7]

More recently, the Baptist theologian Harvey Cox made the connection between Jesus and jollity even more extravagantly. He was writing in praise of Ebenezer Scrooge. Cox blamed Christians for

> mutilating Christianity and, in the process, reducing Christmas to humbug…in a number of ways. For one thing, they have tried to make the story of Jesus over into a legend about an eviscerated, bloodless ascetic and Christianity itself into a dreary life-denying philosophy of flesh-despising abstemiousness…This has been a little hard to manage, in view of the Biblical portrait of Jesus. On at

least two occasions, the Gospels report that his enemies rejected Jesus because he was "a glutton and a winebibber." He frequented parties, kept company with notoriously shady characters and supplied some booze when an embarrassed wedding-reception host found he was running low...

The churches have also helped destroy Christmas by turning Christianity into a petty-rule system and picturing Jesus as a finicky moralizer who spent his life telling people what *not* to do. Jesus himself spent his life breaking most of the taboos of his era— violating the Sabbath, [talking] with "impure" men and women, wandering around with no visible means of support, sharply ridiculing the righteous prudes of his day. When people did come to him with moral dilemmas, he invariably tossed the questions back at them at a deeper level...[But] most people don't like to assume the responsibility of making ethical choices for themselves. They long desperately for someone, anyone, to do it for them...Jesus refused...But the churches have gladly obliged. So instead of a feast of freedom, the churches have turned Christmas into one more doleful reminder of how grievously we have all wandered astray. Perhaps the most appropriate way to mark the birthday of Christ, in his spirit, would be to pick out a particularly offensive cultural taboo...and celebrate Christmas by trans-gressing it.[8]

I'm not sure my hat in the pulpit qualifies, but it may be the best I can do.

Well, Jesus as comedian, as party guy, or as jester or clown (a popular image when I was in seminary) may not be customary readings of the Bible, but they become less startling as contemporary scholars study the texts again and find a historical Jesus there who—if not at all a funny guy in obvious, joking ways—is a wit whose messages are often parables and word games that perplex and startle and amuse, and a prophet of unconcern about so much we let weigh us down.

And, of course, he is the guy that Cox reminds us hoisted cups with the hoi polloi and challenged rules that foolishly restricted freedom and feeling. Cox believes that it is because some of that celebratory spirit survives in Christmas that we celebrate it still, despite the stifling efforts of religious authorities. It survives because humans are incurable celebrators and dreamers, "and Christmas, for all its sham and fakery, grabs [us] at those two vital points." Cox goes on to point out:

In industrial societies, we tend to repress...festive and imagina-tive faculties...All our American religions are deeply infected with…moralistic and antifestive qualities…[But] the truth is that in religion, dance precedes dogma; saturnalia comes before sermon. [We are] *festive*. [We] thrive on parties, *fiestas*, holidays, breaks in [our] routine, times for toasting, singing the old songs, remembering and hoping. Animals play or gambol; [we] celebrate.

In the end, Cox toasts Scrooge again, but also, secretly, Christmas:

Not the humbug Christmas we Christians have foisted on the world…admittedly with a little help from our friends at Gimbels and Saks. No, I drink to Christmas as it may someday be: a *fiesta* when we celebrate earth and flesh and, in the midst of our hang-ups and tyrannies, remind ourselves that at least once one guy lived a reckless, ecstatic and fully free life *every* day—and that maybe someday we all can.[9]

I have two demurrers to demur to my own case this morning, though I will keep my hat on still. The first is to acknowledge that for many of us there is a richness to the memories, the beauty, and the meaning of the holidays that goes deep, and to a place less festive than reverent and contemplative. There is for many in this season, and for most of us at least a little, a sadness of the deepest sort, a remembrance of people with whom we shared holidays once but who have died or moved away or otherwise become estranged from us. And there is a gladness in some moments, as in my own heart when I look out on Christmas Eve at families regathered, knowing all that people have been through, that is more lovely and poignant than jolly.

And second, I want to stand up for the jollity of introverts, of people who may relish the silly as much as the clown with the funny hat or lampshade on, but in quieter, less attention-getting ways. I was recently asked to list the things I remembered most fondly about the Christmases of my childhood. They are much the same as now: along with the family rituals of giving and receiving and feasting, they are the red balls on the tree, the lights on houses we drive around to look at, and as a boy, the little houses that made up a village on white cloth, like snowy hills, under the tree at my grandparents.

Those are all pretty solitary activities, though they take place in company, and it occurred to me that an outsider, looking at the festive scene of my extended family gathered in that living room in Westfield, New Jersey, in 1954, might not as easily notice how happy the skinny blond kid with the glasses is, there lying beside the tree, rearranging the hillside community, as he would perceive the jollity of my cousin Paul, entertaining the household with his stories and high spirits.

That observer, you see, will not have been aided at the task by my remarks this morning. It is surely Paul, if anyone, who has on a jester's cap, and good for him for that, and for being the life of every party. But good as well for those whose chuckles and delight find less obvious expression.

For me, the point is to find whatever works for you, that brings to focus the season's cheer, that kindles the joy in your heart, including that precious, silliest sort. It's December, time to treat yourself to a jolly thing that brings a smile. And when it comes to that, why not one in January, too, and June and July? And why just one?

As writers keep reminding us, Christmas is like that: a chance to remember what we wish we would through the rest of the year—kindness, generosity, attention to the everyday miracles that ever abound, love, hope, joy, and peace, and a sense of the festive, the silly, the fun.

In closing, let me point out, in case it has not been obvious, that this is an effort that a person does not always have to do alone. This sermon is about my hat. I have been talking about the way I allowed it to remind me that the season is meant for delight. But somebody gave me that gift, gave me that chance, when he gave me this hat.

"A hat for happy," the brief note began. "A hat to make happy from sad. Enjoy!" And enjoy it I have, and will. I hope you find, make, recognize, and are given whatever it takes to help make happy for you, and happy from sad, that this December you, too, may enjoy!

SECTION THREE

ISSUES IN PREACHING

Preaching is a functional skill that requires particular knowledge and talent, to be sure. And successful sermons accomplish any number of tasks during the course of the worship service. Yet we all know that preaching is much more than the sum of skill and function: good preaching requires not just a preacher, but a true minister.

According to Rebecca Parker, the president of Starr King School for the Ministry, the Association of Theological Schools is changing its standards for the Master of Divinity degree from a functional approach to more fundamental criteria: the Association wants its candidates for ministry not just to have the ability to perform all the jobs that congregations require, it wants students to learn to speak and act *theologically*.[1]

At the heart of ministry is a person, and we believe that this fact raises a number of personal issues with regard to preaching. From where do we get our authority to preach—what gives us the right to step into the pulpit? What is it about us, regardless of outside criteria, that allows us to deem ourselves preachers? Why does anybody believe we know what we're talking about?

How much of ourselves as private people can we take along with us into the pulpit? What are the boundaries? What personal stories are appropriate to share? How authentic should we be? Is it okay to "perform"—at least a little? Must we "speak and act theologically" all the time?

Parish ministers are people who preach, people who bring personality and personal history to the work of ministry. That fact can be a blessing to all who are listening.

22

WORTHY NONETHELESS:
Ministerial Authority and Presence

What is the source of my authority in the pulpit? When I approach the spotlight on Sunday morning, that is the question that turns the tongue to dust.

At such a moment, a verbal facility and a polished style are weak companions—cosmetic devices that hide the quivering lip, but do nothing for the pounding heart. The faces in the pews are filled with hope and expectancy:

"Who am I?…Is there a God?…Can I trust the universe?… Where do I come from?…Where am I going?…How can I confront the finalities of suffering and death?…"

And I stand in the pulpit. Am I merely a bundle of pretension? Or do I speak from a position of authority? From what source is that authority derived?

David O. Rankin[1]

Why on earth does any preacher imagine she or he has anything— much less twenty minutes' worth of it—that anyone would want to listen to from the pulpit? What gives us the right to go shooting off our mouths like that? Where is the source of our authority to do so? As one veteran minister once put it succinctly, pondering the Sunday morning situation, "How dare we preach?" The answer she got at the time was, "How dare we not? We keep cashing their checks."

195

Though flippant, the response points to one large source of any preacher's authority: Sermons are what most congregations want and expect. As one minister, Roy Phillips, puts it, "They look to us expectantly, waiting for something from us, something creative, liberating, enlivening, something that will come to them through us and make a difference in their lives."[2]

But we may not feel up to their hope and expectancy. We are only human, know only so much, had only so much time to prepare our remarks, are only somewhat capable of speaking in the first place. The Bible has many examples of reluctance to presume to speak to the people (Moses, Jonah, Paul). A less traditional source occurred to one minister, Kimi Riegel, to describe the dilemma. "My authority as a minister is always in question from within," she writes. "In a rather stupid film called 'Wayne's World' the main characters bow to people and chant 'We are not worthy.' Those words sum up my general feeling."[3]

Harry Baker Adams writes, "We find the prospect of preaching to be terrifying because we don't have all the gifts that are needed. The demands of preaching weigh heavily on us because they seem to require more than we have to give."[4] Yet among the gifts that we do have is one not given by nature but by the congregations we address. The minister who felt no worthier than Wayne and his friends goes on to say, "My authority to minister comes from the congregation I serve...What I have to offer, what I have to say is worth listening to because it is grounded in the community. I may not be worthy, but the gift the community has given me, of choosing me as their minister, is worthy. I may not be worthy, but the relationships I serve are."[5]

The gift of our authority comes largely from the congregation, but not randomly or gratuitously. It is given because in a variety of ways we have earned that authorization, or at least are in the process of doing so. For ministers who serve in traditions with congregational polity (Baptist, UCC, UUA, Reform Judaism, etc.) that recognition is direct: Through a formal process, a local congregation decides who will preach, at least on regular occasions. In other traditions, the preacher may be assigned by a church hierarchy or other denominational body.

We leave to other books the problems that occur when a congregation is soured on its new preacher because of an ill experience with a predecessor, dissatisfaction with denominational process, or the like. We will assume instead the normal case, that a congregation has found a preacher by a process customary and acceptable to them. The person selected arrives with that authority, and in almost all cases, with good reason for its being granted.

After all, by the time we receive our first appointment or call, we are apt to have spent years at college and seminary. We may well have done an internship in a congregation where we had chances to lead worship and to receive advice from supervisors, parishioners, and perhaps an intern committee. We may possess a wealth of life experience and deep reflection on it, including such formal training as clinical pastoral education and equally instructive time spent watching preachers from the pews.

Our own deep commitment to ministry and to service in our own faith tradition has been demonstrated by our dedication and perseverance. And chances are good that representatives of that tradition have certified us as capable and prepared.

We ourselves may be more aware at times of our incapacities and unpreparedness. If the congregation thinks it's getting Aimee Semple McPherson, Harry Emerson Fosdick, Billy Graham, William Sloan Coffin, Dana McLean Greeley, or Barbara Harris (or any notable from our own faith tradition), we know better. But really, they know that too. In any but the oddest placements, they don't think they're getting anyone other than a dedicated, well-trained, reasonably able mortal. And that much, we are. They have reason to trust us.

Ultimately, it is upon that trust that our authority rests. Our dedication, our training, our certification, our personal history, our traits, and all the rest of what we bring to the congregation encourage them to invest that trust and its authority in us.

Anyone in the pulpit has a lot of authority before a word is said, which the congregation (for the most part) grants in expectation of basic professional competence, believing that the preacher has both a fair idea of what is expected and the capacity to handle the assignment. Even a good preacher may verbally stumble a time or two reading as familiar a text as the story of Jesus' birth in Luke, before a full house on Christmas Eve. But presumably no preacher will say that evening, "Actually, my throat feels a bit scratchy. I've decided to take this as a sick day. You're on your own," nor embarrass them by mispronouncing "Epiphany," nor announce that, "Instead of singing 'Joy to the World' this evening, let's sing 'Here Comes Peter Cottontail' just for fun."

They trust that we have the education, training, certification, denominational knowledge, talent, integrity, faith, hope, sincerity, and plain good sense to be given the authority to fill their pulpit, and to fill twenty minutes with words worth listening to. It is a trust we cannot hope to fulfill every week in every way. But it is a trust that comes, more than anything, from our very trying, from their awareness of the care we show for our craft, for the assignment, and most of all for them. That awareness and trust can be won in a single guest appearance, and over the course of a congregation's relationship with a settled religious leader they can grow powerful and deep.

If our authority as preachers comes in large part from the congregation, it also comes from our response to that offer of trust. The gift of authority must be accepted. And if we are to keep, even to enlarge upon, that authority, we need to use it well—not too much or too little, nor too seldom or too often, nor at the wrong time or in wrong ways.

Denominational traditions and individual congregations vary greatly in how much authority they expect their clergy to exercise in the pulpit (as well as elsewhere). But whatever the normal range, preachers can get themselves in trouble by varying from it too far. We need to find suitable places for ourselves in the middle ground between timidity and arrogance, obsequiousness and bossiness, offhandedness and pomposity.

"It was a little preachy."

These days, the nature of the preacher's authority is undergoing challenge in many traditions that once expected authoritative declarations of truth from the pulpit.

Ronald Allen claims that

> as contemporary philosophical skeptics continue to cast corrosive doubt on our traditional understandings of knowledge and truth, *authority* looks more and more like an endangered species. Actually, the concept has been in trouble for some time. As early as 1961, Hannah Arendt argued that the world was beginning to experience "a breakdown of all traditional authorities." The work of today's postmodern thinkers, however, has quickened this already rapid deterioration, bringing preaching to a crisis point.[6]

Allen credits Fred Craddock's 1971 book, *As One Without Authority*, for its observation that there is a "completely new relationship between the speaker and hearer."[7] As Allen puts it, "Listeners were no longer willing to absorb passively the theological conclusions reached by the preacher each week in his or her study. Instead, Craddock suggested, the listener was eager (in fact, naturally inclined) to play an active role in the making of meaning."[8]

For some of us in the more liberal religious traditions, this collaborative style that Craddock calls "inductive," where congregants determine for themselves the truths to be taken from the preacher's efforts, is nothing new, even if many liberal congregations originated in colonial New England, where

> for all intents and purposes, the sermon was the only regular voice of authority...By organizing New England towns around autonomous local churches, and by authorizing ministers—and only ministers—to speak on all occasions of public note, the founders established patterns of community that would ensure the sermon's place at the center of New England society...Sermons were authority incarnate.[9]

But times changed, and by 1887, the Reverend Christopher R. Eliot of the First Parish, Dorchester (Mass.), could note of Unitarian preaching that

> We differ somewhat from our friends of other churches, though the difference is becoming less and less marked as time goes on...The preaching of one church derives authority from the peculiar sanctity, or rather supposed peculiar sanctity, of its servants and priests, who speak with authority, as the representatives of God or Christ on earth. The preaching of another church derives authority from its supposed agreement with scripture, the Old and New Testaments; and as the sermon rests upon the text, it derives authority from that. In one way or another some external authority is sought. But with us, and more and more with many others, it is a different matter. Our preaching, whether uttered from the pulpit, the platform, or through the press, derives no weight of authority from the priestly office, nor from texts, but goes out to the world, to be received [or] to be rejected on its own intrinsic merits. For its authority, it rests upon the reasonableness of its arguments, the eternal fitness of its teaching, the strength of its conviction, and whatever truth it may contain.[10]

These days, over a century later, the word "true" is deemed dubious by some. John S. McClure noted that preachers "are all likely to have had [the experience of] finishing a...sermon and hearing a young university graduate exclaim, 'Thanks for sharing your opinions. They really help me to understand where you're coming from.'"[11] This is the most that some imagine a sermon can convey.

But Eliot's words already convey a sense of humility about the preacher's authority of a sort that is more and more common and a recognition that ultimately, a sermon only succeeds on its own merits, as judged by its reception or rejection. Few styles are more often declared dead (or less grieved over) than that of the heavy-handed preacher on high, telling the flock what they should believe. Preachers are not invited into pulpits much any more to hold forth authoritatively on any matter that may happen to strike their fancy or even to dictate doctrine. "The old-fashioned sonority of the pulpit six feet above reply is dead and buried beyond resurrection."[12]

People in the pews expect to have room left for the possibility of valid disagreement and freedom to decide matters for themselves. This expectation is in line with a growing understanding of "ministry" as something that the members of a congregation do together as a whole. The professional clergy are part of a much larger team, and play a much more subtle, more collaborative, and less directive role than formerly, in the pulpit or out.

And yet they do play a role, one that is still distinctive. It is a mistake in avoiding heavy-handedness to go to the other extreme, frustrating valid expectations. Some radical theories to the contrary notwithstanding, in practice most congregations still want heartfelt, thought out, artistic, articulate spiritual leadership from their preachers. They want their professional clergy to embody a strength of purpose, a prophetic vision, a set of opinions, a professional demeanor—a certain sense of authority.

What such authority will look like physically varies, just as do styles, personalities, goals, traditions, and circumstances. It is hard to describe in general or precisely. In some circles, authority is commonly referred to as ministerial presence; one imagines there might be a like appreciation for a person's rabbinic or priestly presence, in every case connoting some combination of personal and professional attributes that give cause for trust, respect, appreciation, comfort perhaps, or challenge.

The Reverend Ellen Brandenburg wrote of presence in describing a visit to a church where a colleague, the Reverend Betty Foster, was to be installed as the ministerial associate a few years after suffering a severely debilitating stroke.

Much might be said about this remarkable woman who, in spite of enormous physical obstacles, is determined to live her life to the fullest. But what I want to share with you has something to do with *ministerial presence,* because Betty has it. It has nothing to do with what she wears or how she stands or how she moves her body—because Betty gets around in a wheelchair and uses her arms and hands with great difficulty. It has nothing to do with her eloquence or presentation skills—because Betty must struggle to enunciate each sentence, each word. It has everything to do, I believe, with the faith she has in herself and her ministry, a deep knowing that she has something of worth to share. Perhaps she commands attention because she has something important to teach us from her own experience—that difficult as her life has become, it is still possible to live with hope, courage, love, and an abiding sense of purpose. Betty communicated this message to me very powerfully, and if this isn't ministerial presence, I don't know what is.[13]

We all have something of worth to share, something important to teach from our own experiences. The congregation believes it, expects it. We justify their faith in us by our own professional presence, by our own measure of hope, courage, love, and purpose, and by the proper, effective use of our authority.

23

"CAN I TELL THE STORY ABOUT THE TIME I...?":
The Question of Self-Revelation

What if I am preparing a sermon about loneliness?

I am not especially lonely tonight; in fact, the last ten months have been remarkably free of that empty, humiliating feeling. But oh, last summer was rough, the summer when my sister moved to Phoenix and my only "non-church friend" moved in with her partner.

The cats weren't enough, but they were about the only ones I knew who were free to watch a video on a Sunday night, my only night off. Sure, my old college roommate invited me down to New York for the weekend, but she never quite understood that on weekends I work. Parishioners, too, invited me out, and there I would be, out with a crowd of parishioners, the occasion feeling no different from a morning's stint at coffee hour. Nobody knew who I really was, and I felt desperately lonely.

The Fourth of July was the worst, a Saturday night, of course. A group of women from the gym—people I liked and would have loved to know better—invited me for a sail out past the harbor to the islands to watch the fireworks. We'd be home by Sunday dinner. I couldn't go, of course; there was no postponing church. They never asked again. I had no "Plan B."

For some reason that day really got to me, and I questioned everything from my ability to build and sustain relationships to my odd choice of career. By the time the fireworks went off, I felt abandoned by the human race.

Should the minister tell her story on Sunday morning? The congregation claims to want a minister who is "human," who can relate to them, one to another. Certainly this story fits that bill. On the other hand, church members also want a strong, confident spiritual leader, not a minister whose emotions get the best of her.

Long ago, Phillips Brooks noted that "there are some sermons in which the preacher does not appear at all; there are other sermons in which he is offensively and crudely prominent; there are still other sermons where he is hidden and yet felt, the force of his personal conviction and earnest love being poured through the arguments which he uses, and the promises which he holds out."[1] While variations exist beyond Brooks's three, today's ministers recognize the dilemma. In any given preaching week, the question arises: How much should I reveal about myself in the sermon?

Many preachers believe that the sermon's very essence arises out of personal experience. Lucy Atkinson Rose describes sermons as being "shaped by the stuff of our lives—the sounds in our hearts; our tears, hopes, fears, loves, desires, confessions; our glimpses, experiences, and interpretations of God. And I suspect that the passion of preaching is linked to how deeply preachers are speaking their own lives."[2]

Today, one finds a general consensus that lively preaching includes personal story. "Preaching is getting more personal, and the preacher has to be more open and more transparent," writes the evangelical preacher Warren Wiersbe. "The day is over when people simply accept the authority of the text; they also need to be more transparent. When I started my ministry over forty years ago, a preacher would not tell publicly about some dumb thing he [or she] did that week, but now many preachers do it."[3]

Success, of course, depends on controlling self-indulgence and focusing on the quality of the sermon. Ronald Allen suggests, "Pastors cannot refer, in detail, to their own experience very frequently. Personal experience can be very powerful when it is used selectively and for well-chosen occasions. But, ministers who, week after week, tell stories from their own kitchens, workshops, bathrooms, lawns, canoe trips, and basements soon leave the congregation bored."[4] "We need to be self-aware, but not self-preoccupied."[5]

Phillips Brooks also offers words of caution:

There are some preachers to whom one might listen for a year, and then he [or she] could write their biography, if it were worth the doing. Every truth they wish to teach is illustrated by some event in their own history. Every change of character which they wish to urge is set forth under the form in which that change took place in them. The story of how they were converted becomes as familiar to their congregation as the story of the conversion of St. Paul. It is the crudest attempt to blend personality and truth. They are not fused with one another, but only tied together.[6]

Then again, church members often complain that "the preacher isn't *in* the sermon." They want to know why the minister cares; they want to see the passion; they want to know the person who presumes to preach to them. They want to feel that the words ring true to the person who is proclaiming them.

But while some ministers delight in displaying their lives from the pulpit, others find it painful, inappropriate, or untoward. In Søren Kierkegaard's words, "There is something painful in being obliged to talk so much about oneself."[7] Preaching expert James Earl Massey points out that some are fearful, "lest they be viewed as calling undue attention to themselves."[8] Indeed, any number of ministers, when asked to share more of themselves from the pulpit, cannot quite imagine what the request even means!

In the medieval period, the question of self-revelation did not present a problem. Preachers neatly solved the quandary by including stories told at second- or thirdhand—never one of their own: "A Dominican preacher, Brother John of Chester, has not only heard tell of a lady's pet monkey that strayed into church, swallowed the Host, and was burned by its mistress but has seen with his own eyes that same Host which was rescued from the animal's stomach unchanged," or "Brother Hugh of Hereford remembers seeing in his earlier days as a layman the horrible sight of a toad which fastened itself to the face of an undutiful son for two whole years."[9]

Thankfully, those preachers who feel reticent about divulging personal anecdotes need not resort to such concoctions. Lee Barker, a minister in California, offers this advice:

> A sermon topic which seems to have no personal relevance may not be, upon further reflection, as dry as one might think. As I look over the sermons I have preached, it strikes me that there are some that demanded more from me than others. In writing and meeting those demands, I had to stretch and dig to find my private reflections. Such stretching has led to a variety of sermonic constructions. Bearing in mind that these did not all occur in the space of one year, I will tell you that I have preached on how my life would be different had William Ellery Channing not lived (an historical sermon), I have imagined that Ronald Reagan occupied

a front pew in our sanctuary (a social action sermon), I have preached as if I were a millionaire (a canvass Sunday sermon), and I have preached as if I had but one year left to live (an everything sermon). What I am saying is that if an idea does not suddenly appear to have a personal dimension, a deeper look may yield it. A new form of sermonic construction may give way to it. There may be a spot in the imagination where it truly does live within.[10]

When faced with a dilemma regarding self-revelation, you may find the following considerations helpful:

DO YOU WANT TO BE LABELED THAT WAY? To take this chapter's opening example, do you want the congregation to think of you as a person who may be touchy about relationships, who is prone to feeling pathetic and left out, who only pretends to enjoy coffee hour, someone to whom they can't safely describe what happened at a party—much less the Fourth of July picnic to which half the church was invited, but not the minister?

Parishioners often remember even the most trivial of your personal stories. The authors of this book have personally included anecdotes in sermons about everything from shoes to pinball, and forever onward we have been associated in the minds of many with shoes or pinball, although the truth is the pinball was just a phase from years ago, and the shoes were an example tossed into a sermon in desperation one Saturday night. When you use stories about yourself, remember that someone may be listening.

Then again, the minister's personal experience can provide a wonderful opportunity to evoke real recognition of a particular emotion or circumstance. Handled well, an incident—if moderated, clearly defined as past history, and resolved—could make the sermon ring true. The minister can address issues after the fact, at a time when he or she has achieved some emotional closure. He or she has weathered the storms and can always be counted on. By telling the story within the context of appropriate boundaries, ministers can demonstrate that while they have personal lives, they do not come so far out of the ministerial role that the congregation feels discombobulated.

When in a quandary about self-revelation, you might ask yourself, WHY AM I TELLING THIS STORY? Is it because everybody has been telling you their problems all month, and nobody ever listens to you, and you want some air time for a change? Do you feel the need, frankly, to brag a little, show off, or blow off steam? Or is it a healthier motivation, where you've been racking your brain for some reading, some anecdote, some...something to fit into your sermon, and *bingo*—the perfect story occurs to you, and the fact that it happens to be about you is incidental. You become your own sermon device, a device the congregation engages with not especially because it's about you, but because somehow it's about everyone.

HOW WILL THE CONGREGATION RESPOND? Will they come through the receiving line and say, "I'm so sorry to hear that you were lonely last summer; John and I feel terrible that we didn't have you over," or will they respond as though they've been to a worship service that touched them religiously? Where will they focus their attention after hearing the story?

There is also the matter of CONFIDENTIALITY. When you tell your story, who else are you talking about? With regard to our example, how would the women from the gym feel about your telling two hundred people about their boat outing, not to mention that they never invited you again? They might feel fine about it; they might not. How would your best friend and your sister feel about your announcing to your congregation that they ruined your summer by leaving you alone?

The author Calvin Trillin says, "My theory has always been that it's perfectly OK to embarrass or wound people in your family by what you write if you have reason to believe you're Dostoevsky. But if Dostoevsky doesn't come to mind when people read your stuff, then it's probably not a good idea."[11]

If the story involves any other people, we believe that explicit permission is needed to tell it, and that includes family, friends, neighbors, parishioners—whether they are named or not. Nobody wants to think that what they say to us from their hospital beds, in a chance encounter at the mall, or during counseling sessions might show up as a story sometime without their knowledge, even years from now, in another church on down the road. We personally do not believe that hospital chaplaincy stories or stories about former parishioners and the like are fair sermon fodder unless we have permission and say so in the sermon.

Ronald Allen agrees: "An incident from another congregation ten years ago may bring an aspect of the sermon to life. But, hearing such a story, the present congregation may wonder, 'Are we going to be in the pastor's sermons ten years from now when the pastor is serving another congregation?' Such questions can distract the congregation and even erode trust in the pastor."[12]

YOUR PARISHIONERS MAY JUST LOVE IT WHEN YOU TALK ABOUT YOURSELF, BUT THAT DOESN'T MEAN IT'S GOOD PREACHING. Maybe it is, maybe it isn't.

Let's face it. People are curious about their ministers. The ethicist Ralph Potter reminds us that, "Ministry is a public role...Public figures relate to their publics as performers do to audiences. Their lot, most often, is unsympathetic scrutiny, envy, rivalry, and gossip, obscured by the illusory glamour of being recognized."[13] While we suspect that most ministers would describe their relationships with parishioners in broader and more complex terms than does Potter, surely there is an element of truth in what he says. As Phillips Brooks says, "You cannot help listening to the garrulous unfolding of [the preacher's personal] history...It feeds that curiosity about each other's ways of living out of which all our gossip grows."[14]

YOU HAVE A LIFE TO LIVE. Beyond your ministry, in spite of your ministry, in addition to your ministry, you have your one life to live. As we said earlier in this book, reflections on your day-to-day experience are often helpful when writing a sermon.

Then again, living life may have a number of purposes, but none of them is exclusively to provide sermon illustrations!

Once again, Ronald Allen puts it plainly:

> It is important to remember that the preacher's life is the preacher's life and not a series of sermon resources. We make the best "use" of our experience when we live as fully and deeply as we can. When we too quickly glom onto the preaching possibilities of a particular moment, we may violate the integrity of the moment. The event is no longer an event in its own right, but merely a sermon resource. Such a preacher is a cannibal.[15]

Each of us must learn to find an appropriate professional balance between saying too much about ourselves and saying too little. Instincts vary. Congregational customs, tastes, and senses of propriety vary too. The point of the sermon and everything in it is ministry. Not you, not me, but ministry.

24

"AM I A PERFORMER OR AM I ME?":
The Question of Authenticity

It was mid-afternoon on December 24, the day of the biggest service of the year at my church, the celebration of Christmas Eve. And I knew two things above all others: first, that in a few hours the sanctuary would be packed, standing room only, pew after pew stuffed full of families reunited for the holidays, gathered in church if only for this one time all year to participate in the pageantry, the nostalgia, the beauty, and the joy of the season.

That I knew, because I had been minister of the church for seven years, and that was how it always was at Christmas. Even though it was a pretty nontraditional congregation in most ways, it was one that loved the warm feeling of the extended church community regathered—the candles, the old songs, and the familiar story of the wonder of new life.

So one thing I knew was that I could expect to see them there in great number. The other thing I knew was that emotionally, I felt worse than I ever had before.

Which was saying something, because it had always been a strain for me to get into the appropriate mood, finding a way of feeling excited about a holiday that in a very fundamental way was a celebration of the birth not just of a child but of the child Jesus, whose name could easily go unspoken for months on end in our church.

But there they would be, packed to overflowing, twice as many as had heard my remarks on subjects that mattered to me, there to watch me look excited and moved about Christmas. It was a task I think I had done well in previous years, focusing my attention on the miracle of birth itself, with the nativity tale as an emblem of all such stories.

The year I am recalling, though, was the year—indeed, the very month—that my partner and I gave up on the effort to repeat that same story ourselves. It was the month that our fifth pregnancy ended unsuccessfully. Each had begun only with much cost and effort, and a week before Christmas, we agreed to stop trying.

It was a hard decision, and one that we did not make easily or particularly well. For once, my having to be at work on Christmas Eve was the source of no complaints. I thought of calling home, but paused, not knowing what I would say; and during that pause, I heard the first of the Christmas Eve worshipers arriving.

The story has been made up, but it could be true. How authentic will that minister be? It is Christmas Eve, and he feels sad, depressed, disappointed, at odds with the universe—a total lack of congruity with the obligatory message.

Yet there he is, dressed in his red and green tie. Before you know it, the choir is warming up with "Joy to the World"; children are bouncing off the walls with glee; and parishioners duck into his office aglow, bearing little wrapped gifts of food they would like him to eat and books they would like him to read.

Authenticity, honesty, "life passed through the fire of thought"[1] is a mainstay of the preaching ministry. So how authentic will he be, how publicly expressive of the state of his mind and heart at the moment?

The homily is coming up. And he can decide to "perform," the way he always has before: the baby, the star, the wonder, the happiness. After all, the congregation trusts him by now to enhance the deeper joys of their holiday. Who knows? If he does it well enough, maybe he'll be persuaded himself.

But he could decide to go with authenticity, to scrap the homily he has prepared and launch forth from the gut. He's not the only unhappy person during the holidays; isn't it high time that somebody acknowledged the pain of Christmas Eve? What about the loneliness, the dreadful family experiences, the agony of infertility?

He could give voice to so much pain, pain he is feeling himself. And maybe in the long run, the congregation would be the better for it.

"Very good, Benson. That's what I want to see."

For some, the answer is obviously to go with Christmas Eve as planned. And for others, the answer is obviously to go with the truth of the immediate experience.

When facing such a question of authenticity, it is important to remember four things:

First, THE CONGREGATION IS PAYING YOU TO DO A JOB, AND THAT JOB IS NOT ABOUT YOU. You and the congregation work together every day. You know them. You preach about the issues that arise either from within their midst or on issues from outside that seem imperative. It is not about you.

Second, YOU ARE CALLED TO BE AUTHENTIC, BUT AUTHENTIC IN A WAY THAT SERVES THE PEOPLE WELL. As the Right Reverend Paul Moore puts it, "I think you should communicate as much as possible with your whole being. It's more like acting."[2] Although a number of clergy are upset to imagine

Garfield   by Jim Davis

that theater might contribute to what they hope to be their authentic preaching style, Richard Ward has tried to redeem the term *performance* as it relates to preaching. Ward "notes that the word comes from an old French expression that means to 'carry through to completion' and also meant 'form coming through.' What great images for preaching!"[3]

The preaching event is unnatural, an art form in present practice: Having prepared, preachers stand up, talk in a loud voice, speaking distinctly, to a lot of people at once. Congregants sit down, listen, doze, participate as laypeople, mutter under their breath, agree and disagree, engage in all kinds of psychological projection, daydream, or whatever.

Ministers bring a wide range of experience, mood, enthusiasm, expertise, and quirks of personality into the pulpit every Sunday. Much authentic information and emotion commands their attention as the church service approaches. Imagine that the preacher is you and all that you might have in your heart and mind: Your last child is going off to college, you won the lottery, you had to wait in the hall for forty-five minutes while the board discussed your salary, your test results were positive, your true interest at the moment is with the homeless shelter, you spilled oatmeal down your front this morning and you wonder if it shows, and darned if you can remember the name of the tall guy sitting right there in the front pew, but you're pretty sure it starts with "G"…or "W."

On a given Sunday morning it is not always going to be the glory of the every-member canvass that is most on your mind, or the horrors of hunger in the world, or the joy of birth at Christmas time just because that is what you put in the newsletter a week ago Thursday as a sermon topic.

The advice Phileman Robbins gave Jonathan Edwards, Jr., during his installation sermon in 1769 still applies: Ministers should "preach carefully, plainly and intelligibly. They are not to indulge themselves."[4] We do care about our congregations, and some part of us does indeed care about the topic at hand. It is one we cared enough about to have picked it for that occasion. We muster that caring and step into the pulpit.

Garfield **by Jim Davis**

Third, keep in mind that INAUTHENTICITY IS UNHEALTHY. Not that church work ever made a particularly good "clergy wellness program." To stand up and share what one is going through; to process one's feelings; to talk about one's hopes, fears, anxieties, and dreams is a healthy thing to do. The thing is, the way our world really works is that we pay people to listen to us; they don't pay us.

When you do decide you are going to have to be inauthentic in the pulpit, know what you're doing. Be clear with yourself. Know that you are in no mood for Christmas Eve, if that is the way it is, and know that you have decided to do it anyway.

Finally, BE AUTHENTIC SOMEPLACE. If there is a stretch when it seems inappropriate to take your authenticity into the pulpit, get out your journal. Go dancing. Complain to a colleague. Talk to a therapist. Chop wood. Find a friend. Be authentic someplace other than the pulpit.

You may know the Wendell Berry poem "A Warning to My Readers":

Do not think me gentle
because I speak in praise
of gentleness, or elegant
because I honor the grace
that keeps this world. I am
a man crude as any,
gross of speech, intolerant,
stubborn, angry, full
of fits and furies. That I
may have spoken well
at times, is not natural.
A wonder is what it is. [5]

It may not be natural or authentic to rise to the occasion at hand and offer forgiveness, acceptance, encouragement, and hope when those are not your own most present personal feelings. But the triumph and wonder is that every week, preachers can and do. They get behind the topic, whatever it is, however they may feel; they muster a mood appropriate to the worship service at hand, knowing the feelings of those who will be there; and they offer up as much impassioned authenticity as they can.

The congregation is waiting expectantly.

CONCLUSION

The point is: Preaching matters.

Our parishioners arrive at church out of habit, curiosity, desperate need, or mild interest, because they feel unsettled, or merely because someone signed them up to usher, bring the flowers, or chauffeur the children. Maybe they are engaged in a private theological struggle or an ethical one. Or they are feeling sad, overjoyed, overwhelmed, or scared. Perhaps the weekly worship service is a regular source of deep inspiration and satisfaction. In any case—in every case—the responsibility is ours to offer ministry to them by means of the sermon.

Whatever the theology of the preacher and congregation, the job of the sermon is ministry, pure and simple. In our experience, the members of a congregation are eager to live satisfying lives according to their values. Sermons can address that. People want to do some good in the world. Ministers preach about that. Parishioners want us to remind them of the glory of life. Worship services can accomplish that. And they want to feel grounded and connected. Preachers speak to those needs.

We hope this book helps.

NOTES

Introduction

[1]David O. Rankin, *So Great a Cloud of Witnesses* (San Francisco: Strawberry Hill Press, 1978), 176.

[2]John T. Stewart, *The Deacon Wore Spats: Profiles from America's Changing Religious Scene* (New York: Holt, Rinehart and Winston, 1965), 180.

[3]Fred B. Craddock, an ordained minister in the Christian Church (Disciples of Christ), was "one of the most creative and influential voices in the latter third of the twentieth century," wrote Charles L. Campbell in William H. Willimon and Richard Lischer's *The Concise Encyclopedia of Preaching* (Louisville, Ky.: Westminster John Knox Press, 1995). In 1993, Craddock retired as the Bandy Professor of Preaching and New Testament at the Candler School of Theology at Emory University.

[4]Fred B. Craddock, "A Preaching Interview with Fred Craddock," ed. J. Albert Mohler, Jr., *Preaching* (March/April 1988): 3.

[5]Bernard Lang, *Sacred Games: A History of Christian Worship* (New Haven: Yale University Press, 1997), 139.

[6]Willimon and Lischer, 36.

[7]Lang, 164.

[8]Richard Jackson, "A Preaching Interview with Richard Jackson," ed. J. Albert Mohler, Jr., *Preaching* (July/August 1989): 25.

[9]R. T. Kendall, "A Preaching Interview with R. T. Kendall," ed. J. Albert Mohler, Jr., *Preaching* (September/October 1988): 16.

[10]Karl Barth, *Homiletics* (Louisville, Ky.: Westminster/John Knox Press, 1991), 49.

SECTION ONE—The Art and Craft of Preaching

[1]Jack Mendelsohn, "On Preaching," *The Newsletter of the Unitarian Universalist Ministers' Association* (Winter 1989): 2.

1   What Matters in a Sermon?

[1]Harry Baker Adams, *Preaching: The Burden and the Joy* (St. Louis: Chalice Press, 1996), 53.

[2]Joseph Friend and David Guralnik, *Webster's New World Dictionary of the American Language* (New York: World Publishing, 1960), 1147, 1331.

[3]Francis de Sales, *On the Preacher and Preaching,* trans. John K. Ryan (Chicago: Henry Regnery, 1964), 12.

[4]Phillips Brooks, *Lectures on Preaching Delivered Before the Divinity School of Yale College* (New York: E. P. Dutton, 1882), 5.

[5]Ibid., 179.

[6]Kenneth Velo, "Didn't He Show Us the Way?" *Harvard Divinity Bulletin* 26 no. 2/3 (1997): 8.

[7]Carol Shields, "Unmask, Embrace, Sympathize, Love…Behold: The Writer," *The Boston Sunday Globe,* 21 May 1995, 80.

[8]Lucy Atkinson Rose, *Sharing the Word: Preaching in the Roundtable Church* (Louisville, Ky.: Westminster John Knox Press, 1997), 60.

2   Preaching to Real People

[1]Fred B. Craddock, "Preface," in Lucy Atkinson Rose, *Sharing the Word: Preaching in the Roundtable Church* (Louisville, Ky.: Westminster John Knox Press, 1997), ix.

[2]Milton Crum, *Manual on Preaching* (Valley Forge, Pa.: Judson Press, 1977), 24.

[3]Leonora Tubbs Tisdale, *Preaching as Local Theology and Folk Art* (Minneapolis: Fortress Press, 1997), 11.

[4]Ibid., 19.

[5]Gillian Evans, "Alan of Lille," in *The Concise Encyclopedia of Preaching,* ed. William H. Willimon and Richard Lischer (Louisville, Ky.: Westminster John Knox Press, 1995), 9.

[6]J. Alfred Smith, *Preach On!* (Nashville: Broadman, 1984), 51.

[7]Tisdale.

[8]Francois la Rochefoucauld, *Maxims,* trans. Louis Kronenberger (New York: Random House, 1959), 550.

[9]Søren Kierkegaard, *The Point of View,* trans. Walter Lowrie (London: Oxford University Press, 1939), 29.

[10]Karl Barth, *Word of God and Word of Man,* trans. Douglas Horton (Gloucester, Mass.: Peter Smith, 1978), 108.

[11]Leith Anderson, "Preaching to Churches Dying for Change," in *Communicate with Power: Insights From America's Top Communicators,* ed. Michael Duduit (Grand Rapids, Mich.: Baker Books, 1996), 11.

[12]William L. Self, "Preaching to Joe Secular," in *Communicate with Power: Insights from America's Top Communicators,* 175.

[13]Ronald J. Allen, *Theology for Preaching: Authority, Truth, and Knowledge of God in a Postmodern Ethos* (Nashville: Abingdon Press, 1997), 44.

[14]Lucy Atkinson Rose, *Sharing the Word: Preaching in the Roundtable Church* (Louisville, Ky.: Westminster John Knox Press, 1997), 111.

[15]Theodore Parker, *Theodore Parker: An Anthology,* ed. Henry Steele Commager (Boston: Beacon Press, 1960), 332–33.

[16]Eldred Johnston, "Preachers: Here's What I Want From Your Sermon," *Church Management: The Clergy Journal* (January 1985): 31.

[17]Charles L. Campbell, "Fred B. Craddock," in *The Concise Encyclopedia of Preaching,* 94.

[18]Rose, 3.

[19]Judith Meyer, "Foreword," in *The Relational Pulpit: Closing the Gap between Preacher and Pew,* ed. Scott Alexander (Boston: Skinner House Books, 1993), x.

[20]Cited in Rose, 95.

[21]Dietrich Bonhoeffer, *Worldly Preaching: Lectures on Homiletics,* trans. Clyde E. Fant (New York: Crossroad, 1991), 99.

[22]Margaret Beard and Roger W. Comstock, *All Are Chosen: Stories of Lay Ministry and Leadership* (Boston: Skinner House Books, 1998).

3   Whence Ideas? Topics and Materials "at Everybody's Hand"

[1]J. Alfred Smith, *Preach On!* (Nashville: Broadman, 1984), 50.

[2]Søren Kierkegaard, *The Point of View,* trans. Walter Lowrie (London: Oxford University Press, 1939), 70.

[3]Gardner C. Taylor, "Preaching and the Power of Words," in *Communicate with Power: Insights from America's Top Communicators,* ed. Michael Duduit (Grand Rapids, Mich.: Baker Books, 1996), 209.

[4]Chuck Swindoll, "Preaching and the Holy Spirit," in *Communicate with Power: Insights from America's Top Communicators,* 199.

[5]Taylor, 209.

[6]Ibid.

[7]Phillips Brooks, *Lectures on Preaching Delivered Before the Divinity School of Yale College* (New York: E. P. Dutton, 1882), 152.

[8]Quoted in Henry Grady Davis, *Design for Preaching* (Philadelphia: Muhlenberg Press, 1958), ix.

[9]Michael Kinsley, "Mamas, Don't Let Your Babies Grow Up To Be Pundits," *The New Yorker* (26 October 1992): 53.

[10]For more discussion of biblically based preaching, see such standard textbooks as Fred B. Craddock's *Preaching,* David Buttrick's *Homiletic: Moves and Structures,* and Ronald Allen's *Interpreting the Gospel: An Introduction to Preaching.*

[11]Brooks, 146–47.

[12]Fred B. Craddock, "A Preaching Interview with Fred Craddock," ed. J. Albert Mohler, Jr., *Preaching* (March/April 1988): 6.

[13]Frank Harrington, "A Preaching Interview with Frank Harrington," ed. J. Albert Mohler, Jr., *Preaching* (July/August 1992): 10.

[14]Allen, *Interpreting the Gospel,* 250.

[15]Craddock, "Interview," 4–5.

[16]Quoted in Denise Levertov, *The Poet in the World* (New York: New Directions, 1973), 111.

[17]Kurt Vonnegut, *Timequake* (New York: Berkley Publishing Group, 1997), 222.

[18]Quoted in Michael Holroyd, *Playbill: Arms and the Man* (Boston: Huntington Theater Company, June 20–21, 1993).

4   Finally Choosing This Week's Theme

[1]David Usher, *First Days Record* (April 1994): 47.
[2]Phillips Brooks, *Lectures on Preaching Delivered Before the Divinity School of Yale College* (New York: E. P. Dutton, 1882), 91.
[3]John A. Huffman, Jr., "A Preaching Interview with John A. Huffman, Jr.," ed. J. Albert Mohler, Jr., *Preaching* (July/August 1990): 19.
[4]R. T. Kendall, "A Preaching Interview with R. T. Kendall," ed. J. Albert Mohler, Jr., *Preaching* (September/October 1988): 17.
[5]Warren Wiersbe, "A Preaching Interview with Warren Wiersbe," ed. Michael Duduit, *Preaching* (May/June 1992): 40.
[6]Mary Louise Schmalz, *The Gleam* (Wakefield, Mass.: First Universalist Society, 1992): 1.
[7]Judith Walker-Riggs, "Intentional Preaching Plans," class handout, Meadville/Lombard Theological School, Chicago, Ill., 14 November 1979.
[8]Patrick O'Neill, "O'Neill's Theory of Sermonic Temperature," *First Days Record* (December 1986): 55, 56.
[9]John Gibbons, *First Days Record* (March 1990): 19.
[10]David Remnick, "Exile on Main Street: Don DeLillo's Undisclosed Underworld," *The New Yorker* (15 September 1997): 47.
[11]Barbara Kingsolver, "Intimate Relations," The *New York Times Book Review,* 2 September 1990, 2.
[12]Bruce Marshall, *First Days Record* (March 1990): 36.
[13]Mario Mazza, quoted in John Koch, "An Interview: Mario Mazza," *The Boston Globe,* 18 December 1996, 16.
[14]Bill Hybels, "A Preaching Interview with Bill Hybels," ed. J. Alfred Mohler, Jr., *Preaching* (January/February 1992): 4.
[15]Donald M. Murray, "Over 60, The Freedom to Be Who You Are," *The Boston Globe,* 21 April 1992, 26.
[16]Frank Harrington, "A Preaching Interview with Frank Harrington," ed. J. Albert Mohler, Jr., *Preaching* (July/August 1992): 13.

5   Trusting Instant Inspiraμtion, Words on Paper, or What?

[1]Quoted in Ernest Cassara, ed., *Universalism in America: A Documentary History* (Boston: Beacon Press, 1971), 115–17.
[2]James Freeman Clarke, *James Freeman Clarke: Autobiography, Diary and Correspondence,* ed. Edward Everett Hale (Boston: Houghton Mifflin, 1891), 69–70.
[3]Taylor Branch, *Parting the Waters: America in the King Years, 1954–63* (New York: Simon and Schuster, 1988).
[4]Quoted in Charles Smyth, *The Art of Preaching* (London: Society for Promoting Christian Knowledge, 1940), 178.
[5]Phillips Brooks, *Lectures on Preaching Delivered Before the Divinity School of Yale College* (New York: E. P. Dutton, 1882), 171.
[6]Ibid., 174.
[7]R. C. Sproul, "Theology and Preaching Today," in *Communicate With Power: Insights from America's Top Communicators,* ed. Michael Duduit (Grand Rapids, Mich.: Baker Books, 1996), 184.
[8]Brooks, 170.
[9]Ibid., 174–75.
[10]William Hethcock, "Phillips Brooks," in *The Concise Encyclopedia of Preaching,* ed. William H. Willimon and Richard Lischer (Louisville, Ky.: Westminster John Knox Press, 1995), 47.
[11]Brooks, 170.
[12]Ibid., 171.
[13]J. Alfred Smith, *Preach On!* (Nashville: Broadman Press, 1984), 45.
[14]Alvin Rueter, *Making Good Preaching Better* (Collegeville, Minn.: Liturgical Press, 1997), 189.

6   Getting Started: Those First Words on Paper

[1]Peter Raible, "The Art of the Sermon (Part II)," *First Days Record* (February 1993): 33.
[2]Dietrich Bonhoeffer, *Worldly Preaching: Lectures on Homiletics,* ed. Clyde E. Fant (New York: Crossroad, 1991), 120–21.

[3]Phillips Brooks, *Lectures on Preaching Delivered Before the Divinity School of Yale College* (New York: E. P. Dutton, 1882), 100–101.

[4]Francis de Sales, *On the Preacher and Preaching,* trans. John K. Ryan (Chicago: Henry Regnery, 1964), 64, 66.

[5]Quoted in Susan Bickelhaupt, "Names & Faces," *The Boston Globe,* 17 October 1997, C2.

[6]Quoted in Peter Raible, "The Art of the Sermon (Part I)," *First Days Record* (January 1993): 31.

[7]Fred B. Craddock, "A Preaching Interview with Fred Craddock," ed. Albert Mohler, Jr., *Preaching* (March/April, 1998): 6.

[8]Anne Lamott, *Bird By Bird* (New York: Pantheon Books, 1994), 18, 19.

[9]Mark Belletini, *First Days Record* (February 1989): 13.

7   Preparing a Sermon: Some Suggestions

[1]Ernest Fremont Tittle, *The Foolishness of Preaching* (New York: Henry Holt, 1930), 8.

[2]Peter Raible, "The Art of the Sermon (Part II)," *First Days Record* (February 1993): 32.

[3]Fred B. Craddock, "Do a Little Every Day," in Michael Duduit, ed., *Communicate with Power: Insights from America's Top Communicators* (Grand Rapids, Mich.: Baker Books, 1996), 38.

[4]Francis de Sales, *On the Preacher and Preaching,* trans. John K. Ryan (Chicago: Henry Regnery, 1964), 66.

[5]Charles Smyth, *The Art of Preaching 747–1939* (London: Society for Promoting Christian Knowledge, 1940), 177.

[6]Phillips Brooks, *Lectures on Preaching Delivered Before the Divinity School of Yale College* (New York: E. P. Dutton, 1882), 108.

[7]Stephanie Brush, "Stephanie Brush: Talented Humor Columnist and Renowned Jeopardy Champion," *Funny Times* (July 1991): 14.

[8]de Sales, 66, 67.

[9]Smyth, 177.

[10]William H. Willimon and Richard Lischer, eds., *Concise Encyclopedia of Preaching* (Louisville, Ky.: Westminster John Knox Press, 1995), 98.

[11]de Sales, 65.

8   Feelings That Get in the Way

[1]Philips Brooks, *Lectures on Preaching Delivered Before the Divinity School of Yale College* (New York: E. P. Dutton, 1882), 64–65.

[2]Paul Theroux, "The Writing Life," *Playbill* (1992–93).

[3]Anne Lamott, *Bird By Bird* (New York: Pantheon Books, 1994), 16–17.

[4]Christopher Lehmann-Haupt, "Edmund White's Tale of a Gay Youth," *The New York Times* (17 March 1988), C29.

[5]Harry Baker Adams, *Preaching: The Burden and the Joy* (St. Louis: Chalice Press, 1996), 160.

[6]Brooks, 87.

[7]Mark A. Kishlansky, "Serendipity and Skepticism: The Craft of Writing History, from Scholarship to Potboilers," *Harvard Magazine* (January/February 1996): 34–35.

[8]John H. Finley, personal communication, 1997.

[9]Quoted in David Rankin, "Saving the Lifeguard," sermon delivered at Fountain Street Church, Grand Rapids, Mich., 1986.

[10]John Gregory Dunne, "On Writing a Novel," in *Best American Essays 1987,* ed. Gay Talese (New York: Ticknor and Fields, 1987), 52.

[11]Kishlansky, 34.

[12]Steve Brown, "Preaching to Pagans," *Preaching* (November/December 1992).

[13]Quoted in Adams, 159.

[14]Annie Dillard, *The Writing Life* (New York: Harper & Row, 1989), 10–11.

[15]Lamott, 236.

[16]Brooks, 54.

9   Shaping a Sermon

[1]Francis de Sales, *On the Preacher and Preaching,* trans. John K. Ryan (Chicago: Henry Regnery, 1964).

[2]Fred B. Craddock, *Preaching* (Nashville: Abingdon Press, 1958), 171ff.

[3]Ibid., 172, 173.

[4]Ibid., 173.

[5]Ibid., 173–74.

[6]Rebecca Parker, classroom presentation, Harvard Divinity School, Oct. 7, 1998.

[7]Halford Luccock, *In the Minister's Workshop* (New York: Abingdon Press, 1944), 141.

[8]Ibid., 141.

[9]Ibid., 142.

[10]W. E. Sangster, *The Craft of Sermon Construction* (Philadelphia: The Westminster Press, 1951), 67ff.

[11]Henry Grady Davis, *Design for Preaching* (Philadelphia: Muhlenberg Press, 1958).

[12]John Killinger, *Fundamentals of Preaching* (Philadelphia: Fortress Press, 1985).

[13]Davis, 15 (see also 139, 143).

[14]Andrew Watterson Blackwood, *The Fine Art of Preaching* (Grand Rapids, Mich.: Baker Book House, 1976).

[15]Roy Phillips, "Preaching as a Sacramental Act," in *Transforming Words: Six Essays on Preaching,* ed. William Schulz (Boston: Skinner House Books, 1996), 17–20.

[16]Craddock, 177.

[17]Luccock, 142.

[18]Ibid.

[19]Ibid., 134.

[20]Ibid., 140.

[21]Ibid., 146.

[22]Ibid., 142.

[23]Ibid., 143, 144.

[24]Blackwood, 43, 44 (adapted).

[25]Scott Alexander, *The Relational Pulpit: Closing the Gap Between Preacher and Pew* (Boston: Skinner House Books, 1993).

[26]Ken Sawyer, "A Morphology of the Sermon," lecture delivered at Meadville/Lombard Theological School, Chicago, Ill., Aug. 20, 1986.

10   More Than a Message: The Use of Story, Examples, and Evocative Illustrations

[1]Robert C. Worley, *Preaching and Teaching in the Earliest Church* (Philadelphia: Westminster Press, 1967), 60.

[2]Charles Smyth, *The Art of Preaching 747–1939* (London: Society for Promoting Christian Knowledge, 1940), 106.

[3]Ibid., 15.

[4]Ibid., 122.

[5]Harry S. Stout, *The New England Soul: Preaching and Religious Culture in Colonial New England* (New York: Oxford University Press, 1986), 3.

[6]John Haynes Holmes, *I Speak for Myself* (New York: Harper & Brothers, 1959), 235.

[7]Henry H. Mitchell, *Black Preaching* (Philadelphia: Lippincott, 1970).

[8]Gayle White, "Amen! Preaching Has Been Born Again," *The Atlanta Journal,* 30 May 1993, D1.

[9]Lucy Atkinson Rose, *Sharing the Word: Preaching in the Roundtable Church* (Louisville, Ky.: Westminster John Knox Press, 1997), 69.

[10]Ibid., 81.

[11]Yngve Brilioth, *Landmarks in the History of Preaching* (Cowley, England: Church Army Press, 1950), 5.

[12]Smyth, 134.

[13]Ibid., 135.

[14]Ibid., 103.

[15]Ibid., 87.

[16]Francis de Sales, *On the Preacher and Preaching,* trans. John K. Ryan (Chicago: Henry Regnery, 1964), 13.

[17]Phillips Brooks, *Lectures on Preaching Delivered Before the Divinity School of Yale College* (New York: E. P. Dutton, 1882), 110–11.

[18]Bernhard Lang, *Sacred Games: A History of Christian Worship* (New Haven: Yale University Press, 1997), 188.

[19]Gerald L. Davis, *I Got the Word in Me and I Can Sing It You Know: A Study of the Performed African-American Sermon* (Philadelphia: University of Pennsylvania Press, 1985), 82.

[20]John Dufresne, "With Stories of the Everyday, Fiction Turns Gossip to Sacrament," *The Boston Globe,* 11 January 1998, F2.

[21]Garry Trudeau, "Anatomy of a Joke," *The New York Times* (August 1, 1993): 15.

[22]Ibid.

[23]Quoted in Kurt Vonnegut, *Timequake* (New York: Berkley Publishing Group, 1997), 141.

[24]Fred B. Craddock, *As One Without Authority* (Enid, Okla.: Philips University Press, 1974), 95.

[25]Alethea Hayter, *Opium and the Romantic Imagination* (Berkeley: University of California Press, 1968), 84.

[26]Brilioth, 12.

[27]Smyth, 60.

[28]Burton D. Carley, "The Reverend Benjamin Franklin?" *First Days Record* (October 1990): 11.

[29]Stout, 43.

[30]Geoffrey Stokes, "Good Writing, Fine Writing and Unwelcome Stop Signs," *The Boston Globe* (20 Aug. 1991): A16.

[31]Quoted in J. Alfred Smith, *Preach On!* (Nashville: Broadman, 1984), iii.

[32]Brooks, 56.

[33]John Dufresne, F2.

11   "The Hour Draws Nigh": Immediately before You Preach

[1]Dietrich Bonhoeffer, "The Pastor and the Worship Experience," *Worldly Preaching: Lectures on Homiletics,* trans. Clyde E. Font (New York: Crossroads, 1991), 123.

[2]Patty Ann T. Earle, "Anxiety in the Pulpit," in *The Concise Encyclopedia of Preaching,* ed. William H. Willimon and Richard Lischer (Louisville, Ky.: Westminster John Knox Press, 1995), 13–14.

[3]Ibid., 14.

[4]Quoted in D. C. Denison, "Nora Dunn," *Boston Globe Magazine* (23 Aug. 1989): 34.

[5]Earle, 13.

[6]"Mr. Blackwell Evaluates the High and the Mighty," *The Boston Globe,* 27 November 1993, 26.

[7]Paula Deitz, "Playing with Style," *The New Yorker* (4 November 1996): 91.

[8]Judith Martin, "When Hair Becomes Hostile," The *Boston Globe,* 1 July 1998, F9.

[9]Alex Ross, "Comfortable Shoes and Other Tricks of a Baritone," *The New York Times,* 29 September 1992, C1.

[10]John Updike, "Shirley Temple Regina," *The New Yorker* (22 April 1996): 81.

[11]*The Merriam-Webster Dictionary* (New York: Pocket Books, 1974), 48.

12   Sermon Delivery

[1]Fred B. Craddock, *Preaching* (Nashville: Abingdon Press, 1985), 218.

[2]Dietrich Bonhoeffer, *Worldly Preaching: Lectures on Homiletics,* trans. Clyde E. Fant (New York: Crossroad, 1991), 121.

[3]Ralph Waldo Emerson, "An Address Delivered before the Senior Class in Divinity College, Cambridge, Sunday Evening, July 15, 1838" in *Nature, Addresses and Lectures* (Boston: Houghton Mifflin Company, 1876), 137, 138.

[4]Pamela Gore, personal correspondence.

[5]Craddock, 220.

[6]Ed Young, "Preaching in a Changing Culture," in *Communicate with Power: Insights from America's Top Communicators,* ed. Michael Duduit (Grand Rapids, Mich.: Baker Books, 1996), 240.

[7]Francis de Sales, *On the Preacher and Preaching,* trans. John K. Ryan (Chicago: Henry Regnery, 1964), 64.

[8]Quoted in Harry Farra, *The Sermon Doctor: Prescriptions for Successful Preaching* (Grand Rapids, Mich.: Baker Book House, 1989), 138.

[9]Ibid., 139.

[10]Peggy Noonan, "Behind Enemy Lines," *Newsweek* (27 July 1992): 32.

[11]William Hethcock, "Phillips Brooks," in *The Concise Encyclopedia of Preaching,* ed. William H. Willimon and Richard Lischer (Louisville, Ky.: Westminster John Knox Press, 1995), 47.

[12]Pamela Gore.

[13]David Kaufman, "A Funny Thing Happened," review of *Laughing Matters* by Larry Gelbart, *New York Times Book Review,* 22 March 1998, 11.

14Craddock, 220.

15Jana Childers, *Performing the Word: Preaching as Theater* (Nashville: Abingdon Press, 1998), 18.

13   Preaching When Children Are Present

1Norma Veridan, letter to the authors, 6 May 1999.

2Ibid. Veridan goes on to note that "songs and hymns can be practiced, affirmations or chalice lighting words learned with other children before they join the adults in worship, to say nothing of learning when to be quiet, how to read the words to the hymns if they don't yet read music, etc."

3Sandra Gutridge Harris, *Getting Started in Storytelling* (Indianapolis: Stone Work Press, 1990), 18–19.

4Sandy Hoyt, letter to the authors, spring 1999.

5Bruno Bettelheim, *The Uses of Enchantment: The Meaning and Importance of Fairy Tales* (New York: Alfred A. Knopf, 1977), supported by Arthur N. Appleby, *The Child's Concept of Story: Ages Two to Seventeen* (Chicago: University of Chicago Press, 1978); Charles W. Faulkner, "The Fantastic Power of Fantasy," *Free Inquiry* (Summer 1995): 37; Ruth Griffiths, *A Study of Imagination in Early Childhood and Its Function in Mental Development* (London: Kegan Paul, Trench, Trubner & Co., 1935); Kenneth Marsalek, "Humanism, Science Fiction, and Fairy Tales," *Free Inquiry* (Summer 1995): 39–42; Molleen Matsumura, "To Dream Is Human," *Free Inquiry* (Summer 1995): 35–37; Michael O. Tunnell, "The Double-Edged Sword: Fantasy and Censorship," *Language Arts* (December 1994): 606–11; and others.

6Judith A. Boss, "Is Santa Claus Corrupting Our Children's Morals?" *Free Inquiry* (Fall 1991): 25.

7Marilyn Stasio, "What's a Good Scare?" *Parade Magazine* (26 July 1998): 4.

8Marsalek, citing Bettelheim, 41.

9Norma J. Livo and Sandra A. Rietz, *Storytelling: Process and Practice* (Littleton, Colo.: Libraries Unlimited, 1986), 12.

10Makanah Morriss, letter to the authors, 30 April 1998.

SECTION TWO—Preaching as Ministry

14   Sermons That Help the Healing

1Phillips Brooks, *Lectures on Preaching Delivered Before the Divinity School of Yale College* (New York: E. P. Dutton, 1882), 76.

2Harry E. Fosdick, *The Living of These Days: An Autobiography* (New York: Harper, 1956), 94.

3Wallace Fiske, personal conversation, 20 May 1998.

4Ken Sawyer, "Pain and Religion," sermon delivered at Wayland, Mass., 21 April 1996.

5Jane Rzepka, memorial service of Karen Zalubas, Reading, Mass., 30 May 1986.

6Fosdick, 94.

7William H. Willimon and Richard Lischer, eds., *The Concise Encyclopedia of Preaching* (Louisville, Ky.: Westminster John Knox Press, 1995), 363.

8Quoted in John T. Stewart, *The Deacon Wore Spats: Profiles from America's Changing Religious Scene* (New York: Holt, Rinehart and Winston, 1965), 136.

9Frank Harrington, "A Preaching Interview with Frank Harrington—A Vision for Preaching," J. Albert Mohler, Jr., ed. *Preaching* (July/August 1992): 8.

10Quoted in Willimon and Lischer, 363.

11Quoted by Chuck Swindoll, "Preaching and the Holy Spirit," in Michael Duduit, ed., *Communicate with Power: Insights from America's Top Communicators* (Grand Rapids, Mich.: Baker Books, 1996), 200.

12Patrick T. O'Neill, "The Hardest Act of Love," sermon delivered in Wilmington, Del., 11 May 1997.

13Jacqui Bishop and Mary Grunte, *How to Forgive When You Don't Know How* (Barrytown, N. Y.: Station Hill Press, 1993), 50.

15   Sermons That Tend the Institution

1Jane Rzepka, "Where Have We Come From and Why Keep It Going?" sermon delivered in Reading, Mass., 28 October 1990.

[2]Rzepka, pulpit editorial: "A Word in Response to the Bryant Gumbel Show," Reading, Mass., 12 October 1997.

[3]Rzepka, "Those Singular Rooms," sermon delivered in Milwaukee, Wis., 24 June 1990.

[4]Kenneth L. Patton, "To Be With One Another," *Hymns of Humanity* (Ridgewood, N.J.: Meeting House Press, 1980), 4.

[5]Parker Palmer, *The Company of Strangers: Christians and the Renewal of America's Public Life* (New York: Crossroad, 1983), 130.

[6]Ralph Waldo Emerson, "Society and Solitude," in *The Portable Emerson,* ed. Carl Bode (New York: Viking, 1981), 394.

[7]Emerson, "Experience," in *The Portable Emerson,* 276.

16 Sermons That Engage with the Larger World

[1]Bill Schulz, "Too Swift to Stop, Too Sweet to Lose," sermon delivered in Phoenix, Ariz., 22 June 1997.

[2]David Buttrick, *A Captive Voice: The Liberation of Preaching* (Louisville, Ky.: Westminster/John Knox Press, 1994), 9, 10.

[3]Harry Baker Adams, *Preaching: The Burden and the Joy* (St. Louis: Chalice Press, 1996), 132

[4]Elizabeth Ellis, "It Is Never Too Late," homily delivered in Boston, Mass., 18 March 1999.

[5]Rosemary Bray McNatt, "Birthing a New World," sermon delivered in Montclair, N. J., 10 May 1998.

17 Sermons That Build the Loving Community

[1]Kathleen Norris, *The Cloister Walk* (New York: Riverhead Books, 1996), 346.

[2]Israel Zangwill (adapted), *Singing the Living Tradition,* ed. Hymnbook Resources Commission (Boston: Beacon Press, 1993), no. 418.

[3]James Vila Blake, *Singing the Living Tradition,* no. 473.

[4]Ronald Allen, *Theology for Preaching: Authority, Truth, and Knowledge of God in a Postmodern Ethos* (Nashville: Abingdon Press, 1997), 148.

[5]This echoes William Blake's line in "Auguries of Innocence" that "Joy & Woe are woven fine…"

[6]Parker Palmer, *Christian Century* (22–29 March 1995).

[7]E. Annie Proulx, *The Shipping News* (New York: Simon and Schuster, 1994), 169.

[8]Ken Sawyer, "A Joinery of Lives," sermon delivered in Wayland, Mass., 24 September 1995.

[9]Jane Rzepka, "Room for Us All," sermon delivered at Unitarian Universalist Church of Reading, Massachusetts, September 10, 1995.

[10]E-mail message.

[11]"You're Over 40 If.....," *Explore!: Yellowstone County Edition,* Bozeman, Montana, June 1999.

[12]Thandeka, "Counting Our Blessings," sermon delivered in Salt Lake City, June 25, 1999.

[13]Robert D. Richardson, Jr., *Emerson: The Mind on Fire* (Berkeley: University of California Press, 1995), 461.

18 Sermons That Inspire

[1]Richard Wright, *12 Million Voices: A Folk History of the Negro in the United States* (New York: Viking Press, 1941), 131.

[2]Quoted in Beverly June Kramer, letter, *The New York Times,* 18 July 1999, 4.

[3]Harry Emerson Fosdick, *Hymns for the Celebration of Life,* ed. Unitarian Universalist Hymnbook Commission (Boston: Beacon Press, 1964), no. 410.

[4]Jane Rzepka, "Important Notice," in *A Small Heaven: A Meditation Manual* (Boston: Skinner House Books, 1989), 35.

[5]Ken Sawyer, "The Devil of the Noonday Sun," sermon delivered in Wayland, Mass., 9 January 1983.

[6]Phillips Brooks, *Lectures on Preaching Delivered Before the Divinity School of Yale College* (New York: E. P. Dutton, 1882), 79.

[7]Ibid., 141.

[8]Gail Caldwell, "Critic's Choice: Best Fiction, from Pigs to Pygmalion, from Great Jests to the Great War," *The Boston Globe,* 10 December 1995, B43.

[9]Henry H. Cheetham, *Unitarianism and Universalism: An Illustrated History* (Boston: Beacon Press, 1962), 80.

[10]Scott Alexander, "N.D.Y.," sermon delivered in Rochester, N. Y., June 1998.

[11]Cynthia Ozick, "The Riddle of the Ordinary," in *Art and Ardor* (New York: Alfred A. Knopf, 1983), 201.

19   Sermons That Explain a Particular Religious Identity

[1]Clark Williamson and Ronald Allen, *The Teaching Minister* (Louisville, Ky.: Westminster/John Knox Press, 1991), 7.

[2]Ibid., 8.

[3]Ibid., 73.

[4]Barry Andrews, "The Soul Only Avails," sermon delivered in Manhasset, N. Y., Nov. 2, 1997.

[5]Catherine Tatnall, "Archives," The First Parish in Wayland, Massachusetts.

[6]Quoted in Thomas Long, "Foreword," in *The Sermon as Symphony: Preaching the Literary Forms of the New Testament*, Mike Graves (Valley Forge, Pa.: Judson Press, 1997).

[7]Quoted in Williamson and Allen, 23.

[8]Alice Syltie, "Birmingham Unitarian Universalists in the Struggle for Justice," sermon delivered in Chicago, 23 January 1996.

[9]Jane Rzepka,"Birmingham and the Mandate of Faith," sermon delivered in Reading, Mass., 19 January 1997.

[10]Rebecca Parker, "Something Far More Deeply Interfused," sermon delivered in Columbus, Ohio, 19 October 1991.

[11]William Wordsworth, "Lines Written a Few Miles Above Tintern Abbey," in *Lyrical Ballads,* ed. W. J. B. Owen, 2d ed. (Oxford: Oxford University Press, 1969), 115.

20   Sermons That Provide Intellectual Stimulation

[1]Barbara Howes, "Carpe Diem," in *Collected Poems 1945–1990* (Fayetteville: University of Arkansas Press, 1995), 17.

[2]Quoted in Robert Atwan, "Foreword," in *The Best American Essays,* ed. Elizabeth Hardwick (New York: Ticknor & Fields, 1986), x.

[3]Jane Rzepka, "Why We Are the Way We Are," sermon delivered in Reading, Mass., 8 October 1995.

[4]Quoted in Paul Scott Wilson, "Review: Preaching," *Homiletic* xxii. 1 (1997): 16.

[5]Ken Sawyer, "Science and Religion, Carl Sagan and Us," sermon delivered in Wayland, Mass., 21 September 1997.

[6]Carl Sagan, *The Demon-Haunted World: Science as a Candle in the Dark* (New York: Ballantine Books, 1996), 11.

[7]Ibid., 26f.

[8]Peter Raible, "The Art of the Sermon (Part I)," *First Days Record* (January 1993): 32.

[9]Philips Brooks, *Lectures on Preaching Delivered Before the Divinity School of Yale College* (New York: E. P. Dutton, 1882), 92.

[10]R.C. Sproul, "Theology and Preaching Today," in *Communicate with Power: Insights from America's Top Communicators* ed. Michael Duduit (Grand Rapids, Mich.: Baker Books, 1996), 181.

[11]Elizabeth Hardwick, ed., *Best American Essays 1986* (New York: Ticknor & Fields, 1986), xvii.

[12]Jane Rzepka, "Two Kinds of People," sermon delivered in Madison, Wis. 21 January, 1996.

[13]Jorge Luis Borges, *Selected Non-Fictions,* ed. Eliot Weinberger, trans. Esther Allen, Suzanne Jill Levine, and Eliot Weinberger (New York: Viking, 1999), 231.

[14]Marge Piercy, "Councils," Responsive Reading no. 585, adapted, in *Singing the Living Tradition*, ed. Hymnbook Resources Commission (Boston: Beacon Press, 1993).

21   Sermons That Startle, Awaken, or Amuse

[1]Ken Sawyer, personal remembrance.

[2]Søren Kierkegaard, *The Point of View,* trans. Walter Lowrie (London: Oxford University Press, 1939), 34.

[3]Thomas Jackson, *Reminiscences and Anecdotes of Celebrated Preachers or Curiosities of Pulpit Literature* (London: Virtue, Spaulding, & Co., 1877), 229.

[4]Ibid., 233.

[5]Jane Rzepka, chapel service, Massachusetts Bay Chapter of the Unitarian Universalist Ministers Association, Winchester, Massachusetts, September 3, 1997.

⁶Ken Sawyer, "Have a Happy Holiday, or The Minister's Festive Hat," sermon delivered in Wayland, Mass., 10 December 1995.
⁷Colleen Moore, *Silent Star* (Garden City, New York: Doubleday and Company, 1968), 96–97.
⁸Harvey Cox, "For Christ's Sake," *Playboy* (Jan. 1970), 197ff.
⁹Ibid.

SECTION THREE—Issues in Preaching

¹Pamela Lund, "Interview With Starr King President Rebecca Parker," *The Aspire Journal* (Winter 1996–97): 10.

22 Worthy Nonetheless: Ministerial Authority and Presence

¹David O. Rankin, "The Peril of the Pulpit," sermon delivered at Fountain Street Church, Grand Rapids, Mich., 12 September 1982.
²Roy D. Phillips, "Preaching As a Sacramental Act," in *Transforming Words: Six Essays on Preaching,* ed. William F. Schulz (Boston: Skinner House Books, 1984), 34.
³Kimi Riegel, personal correspondence.
⁴Harry Baker Adams, *Preaching: The Burden and the Joy* (St. Louis: Chalice Press, 1996), 160–61.
⁵Riegel, personal correspondence.
⁶Ronald J. Allen, *Theology for Preaching: Authority, Truth, and Knowledge of God in a Post-Modern Ethos* (Nashville: Abingdon Press, 1997), 51.
⁷Ibid.
⁸Ibid.
⁹Harry S. Stout, *The New England Soul: Preaching and Religious Culture in Colonial New England* (New York: Oxford University Press, 1986), 4, 13, 23.
¹⁰Christopher R. Eliot, *Unitarian Preaching* (Dorchester, Mass.: Women's Auxiliary Conference of the First Parish, 1887), 10, 11.
¹¹John S. McClure, *Homiletic* (Winter 1996): 51.
¹²John T. Stewart, *The Deacon Wore Spats:Profiles from America's Changing Religious Scene* (New York: Holt, Rinehart and Winston, 1965), 26.
¹³Ellen Brandenburg, "Student News," in *The Ministry Packet of the Unitarian Universalist Association* (Spring 1998): 1.

23 "Can I Tell the Story about the Time I…?": The Question of Self-Revelation

¹Phillips Brooks, *Lectures on Preaching Delivered Before the Divinity School of Yale College* (New York: E. P. Dutton, 1882), 116.
²Lucy Atkinson Rose, *Sharing the Word: Preaching in the Roundtable Church* (Louisville, Ky.: Westminster John Knox Press, 1997), 126.
³Warren Wiersbe, "Preaching Is Not Just Story, It's Image," in Michael Duduit, ed., *Communicate with Power: Insights from America's Top Communicators* (Grand Rapids, Mich.: Baker Books, 1996), 222.
⁴Ronald J. Allen, *Interpreting the Gospel: An Introduction to Preaching* (St. Louis: Chalice Press, 1998), 217.
⁵Ibid., 54.
⁶Brooks, 116–17.
⁷Søren Kierkegaard, *The Point of View,* trans. Walter Lowrie (London: Oxford University Press, 1939), 64.
⁸James Earl Massey, *The Burdensome Joy of Preaching* (Nashville: Abingdon Press, 1998), 59.
⁹Charles Smyth, *The Art of Preaching 747–1939* (London: The Society for Promoting Christian Knowledge, 1940), 61.
¹⁰Lee Barker, "The Ego in the Pulpit," UUA Preaching Seminar, Chicago, Ill., 1986.
¹¹Quoted in Dwight Gamer, "Waxing Poetic," in *The Boston Globe,* 10 April 1994, 33.
¹²Allen, 58.
¹³Ralph Potter, "Convocation Address," *Harvard Divinity School Bulletin* 27, no.1 (1997): 6.
¹⁴Brooks, 117.
¹⁵Allen, 58.

24 "Am I a Performer or Am I Me?":
The Question of Authenticity

[1]"The true preacher can be known by this, that he deals out to people his life—life passed through the fire of thought." Ralph Waldo Emerson, "The Divinity School Address," *Selections from Ralph Waldo Emerson,* ed. Stephen E. Whicher (Boston: Houghton Mifflin Company, 1957), 109.

[2]Quoted in Elisabeth Bumiller, "Preacher Takes Thunder to a 'Tiny Chapel,'" *The New York Times,* 14 January 1998, A15.

[3]Quoted in Mike Graves, *The Sermon as Symphony: Preaching the Literary Forms of the New Testament* (Valley Forge, Pa.: Judson Press, 1997), 11.

[4]Donald Weber, *Rhetoric and History in Revolutionary New England* (New York: Oxford University Press, 1988), 50.

[5]Wendell Berry, "A Warning to My Readers," in *Collected Poems* (San Francisco: North Point Press, 1985), 213.

BIBLIOGRAPHY

Achtemeier, Elizabeth R. *Creative Preaching: Finding the Right Words.* Nashville: Abingdon Press, 1980.

Adams, Harry Baker. *Preaching: The Burden and the Joy.* St. Louis: Chalice Press, 1996.

Alexander, Scott. *The Relational Pulpit: Closing the Gap Between Preacher and Pew.* Boston: Skinner House Books, 1993.

Allen, Ronald. *Interpreting the Gospel: An Introduction to Preaching.* St. Louis: Chalice Press, 1998.

Blackwood, Andrew Watterson. *The Fine Art of Preaching.* Grand Rapids: Baker Book House, 1976.

Bonhoeffer, Dietrich. *Worldly Preaching: Lectures on Homiletics.* Translated by Clyde E. Fant. New York: Crossroad Publishing Company, 1991.

Broadus, John A. *On the Preparation and Delivery of Sermons.* San Francisco: Harper & Row, 1979.

Brooks, Phillips. *Lectures on Preaching Delivered Before the Divinity School of Yale College.* New York: E. P. Dutton, 1882.

Buttrick, David. *A Captive Voice: The Liberation of Preaching.* Louisville: Westminster/John Knox Press, 1994.

———. *Homiletic: Moves and Structures.* Philadelphia: Fortress Press, 1987.

Childers, Jana L. *Performing the Word.* Nashville: Abingdon Press, 1998.

Costen, Melva Wilson. *African American Christian Worship.* Nashville: Abingdon Press, 1993.

Craddock, Fred B. *As One Without Authority.* St. Louis: Chalice Press, 2001.

———. *Preaching.* Nashville: Abingdon Press, 1985.

Davis, Henry Grady. *Design For Preaching.* Philadelphia: Muhlenberg Press, 1958.

Duduit, Michael. *Communicate with Power: Insights from America's Top Communicators.* Grand Rapids, Mich.: Baker Books, 1996.

———, ed. *Handbook of Contemporary Preaching.* Nashville: Broadman Press, 1992.

Elbow, Peter. *Writing with Power.* New York: Oxford University Press, 1998.

Eslinger, Richard. *Narrative & Imagination: Preaching the Worlds That Shape Us.* Minneapolis: Fortress Press, 1995.

Farra, Harry. *The Sermon Doctor: Prescriptions for Successful Preaching.* Grand Rapids, Mich.: Baker Book House, 1989.

Francis de Sales. *On the Preacher and Preaching.* Translated by John K. Ryan. Chicago: Henry Regnery Company, 1964.

Harris, Sandra Gutridge. *Getting Started in Storytelling*. Indianapolis: Stone Work Press, 1990.

Jackson, Thomas. *Reminiscences and Anecdotes of Celebrated Preachers or Curiosities of Pulpit Literature*. London: Virtue, Spalding & Co., 1877.

Killinger, John. *Fundamentals of Preaching*. Minneapolis: Fortress Press, 1996.

Lamott, Anne. *Bird By Bird*. New York: Pantheon, 1994.

Livo, Norma J., and Sandra A. Rietz. *Storytelling: Process and Practice*. Littleton, Colo.: Libraries Unlimited, Inc., 1986.

Long, Thomas. *The Homiletical Plot: The Sermon as Narrative Form*. Atlanta: John Knox Press, 1980.

Lowry, Eugene L. *The Sermon: Dancing the Edge of Mystery*. Nashville: Abingdon Press, 1997.

Luccock, Halford E. *In the Minister's Workshop*. New York: Abingdon Press, 1944.

McClure, John S., ed. *Best Advice for Preaching*. Minneapolis: Fortress Press, 1998.

McGee, Lee. *Wrestling with the Patriarchs: Retrieving Women's Voices in Preaching*. Nashville: Abingdon Press, 1996.

Massey, James Earl. *The Burdensome Joy of Preaching*. Nashville: Abingdon Press, 1998.

———. *Designing the Sermon*. Nashville: Abingdon Press, 1980.

Mitchell, Henry H. *Black Preaching*. Philadelphia: Lippincott, 1970.

———. *Celebration and Experience in Preaching*. Nashville: Abingdon Press, 1990.

Parker, Joseph. *Ad Clerum: Advices to a Young Preacher*. Boston: Roberts Brothers, 1871.

Rose, Lucy Atkinson. *Sharing the Word: Preaching in the Roundtable Church*. Louisville: Westminster John Knox Press, 1997.

Sangster, W. E. *The Craft of Sermon Construction*. Philadelphia: The Westminster Press, 1951.

Schulz, William, ed. *Transforming Words: Six Essays on Preaching*. Boston: Skinner House Books, 1996.

Simmons, Martha J,. ed. *Preaching on the Brink: The Future of Homiletics*. Nashville: Abingdon Press, 1996.

Skinner, Clarence. *Worship and the Well Ordered Life*. Boston: Meeting House Press, 1955.

Smith, Christine. *Weaving the Sermon: Preaching in a Feminist Perspective*. Philadelphia: Westminster, 1989.

Smith, J. Alfred. *No Other Help I Know.* Valley Forge, Pa.: Judson Press, 1996.

————. *Preach On!* Nashville: Broadman, 1984.

Smyth, Charles. *The Art of Preaching 747-1939.* London: The Society for Promoting Christian Knowledge, 1940.

Taylor, Barbara Brown. *The Preaching Life.* Boston: Cowley Publications, 1993.

Thomas, Frank A. *They Like to Never Quit Praisin' God: The Role of Celebration in Preaching.* Cleveland: United Church Press, 1997.

Tisdale, Leonora Tubbs. *Preaching as Local Theology and Folk Art.* Minneapolis: Fortress Press, 1997.

Troeger, Thomas H. *Imagining a Sermon.* Nashville: Abingdon Press, 1990.

Vogt, Von Ogden. *Art and Religion.* New Haven, Conn.: Yale University Press, 1921.

————. *The Primacy of Worship.* Boston: Starr King Press, 1958.

Ware, Henry, Jr. *Hints on Extemporaneous Preaching.* Boston: Cummings, Hilliard & Co., 1824.

Webb, Joseph M. *Preaching and the Challenge of Pluralism.* St. Louis: Chalice Press, 1998.

Willimon, William H., and Richard Lischer. *The Concise Encyclopedia of Preaching.* Louisville: Westminster John Knox Press, 1995.

Wilson, Paul Scott. *A Concise History of Preaching.* Nashville: Abingdon Press, 1992.

————. *The Practice of Preaching.* Nashville: Abingdon Press, 1995.

Worley, Robert C. *Preaching and Teaching in the Earliest Church.* Philadelphia: Westminster Press, 1967.

INDEX